18.90
BT

- D ou find yourself unable to say
  " to your parents' requests for
  ti and attention—no matter hov
  of they visit or how busy you ai
- Do ur relationship with your
  par nterfere with your marria
  or fr ashine?
- Do your pa
  grow up, t

and develop a new, empathetic relationship of equals. Drawing on Dr. Atkins's twenty-five years of experience as a relationship expert, the book is a comprehensive, articulate guide for everyone who is desperate to break free of fruitless, frustrating interactions and build a life that they and their parents can live with—forever.

DALE ATKINS is a licensed psychologist, lecturer, and media commentator who appears regularly on the *Today* show. The author of five books, she has been a frequent contributor to the *Ladies' Home Journal*, *Cosmopolitan*, and *Parents*. She lives in Connecticut and has a practice in New York City.

I'm OK, You're My Parents

I'm OK, You're My Parents

HOW TO OVERCOME GUILT,
LET GO OF ANGER, AND CREATE
A RELATIONSHIP THAT WORKS

DALE ATKINS, Ph.D.

HENRY HOLT AND COMPANY   NEW YORK

Henry Holt and Company, LLC
Publishers since 1866
115 West 18th Street
New York, New York 10011

Library of Congress Cataloging-in-Publication Data

Atkins, Dale V.
    I'm OK, you're my parents : how to overcome guilt, let go of anger,
and create a relationship that works / Dale Atkins.—1st ed.
        p. cm.
    ISBN 0-8050-7353-1
    1. Parent and adult child. 2. Adult children—Psychology. I. Title.

HQ755.86.A85 2004
306.874—dc22   2003057032

Henry Holt books are available for special
promotions and premiums.
For details contact:
Director, Special Markets.

First Edition 2004

Designed by Paula Russell Szafranski

Illustration credits: Page xii: © The New Yorker Collection 2001 David Sipress from
cartoonbank.com. All rights reserved. Page 12: © The New Yorker Collection 1998 Victoria
Roberts from cartoonbank.com. All rights reserved. Page 36: © The New Yorker Collection
2002 Roz Chast from cartoonbank.com. All rights reserved. Page 43: © The New Yorker Col-
lection 2003 Robert Weber from cartoonbank.com. All rights reserved. Page 67: © The New
Yorker Collection 2002 Roz Chast from cartoonbank.com. All rights reserved. Page 89:
© The New Yorker Collection 1997 Tom Cheney from cartoonbank.com. All rights reserved.
Page 114: © 2003 Bruce Kaplan from cartoonbank.com. All rights reserved. Page 158: © The
New Yorker Collection 1998 Edward Frascino from cartoonbank.com. All rights reserved.
Page 189: © The New Yorker Collection 2001 Roz Chast from cartoonbank.com. All rights
reserved. Page 247: © The New Yorker Collection 2000 Eric Lewis from cartoonbank
.com. All rights reserved. Page 257: © The New Yorker Collection 1999 Pat Byrnes from
cartoonbank.com. All rights reserved. Page 283: © The New Yorker Collection 2001 David
Sipress from cartoonbank.com. All rights reserved.

Printed in the United States of America

1   3   5   7   9   10   8   6   4   2

To Sylvia and, in memory, Jerry,
and to Nettie,
all parents who seemed to
know these lessons
without being taught

CONTENTS

Contents

I'm OK,
You're My
Parents

"Seventy-seven. How about yours?"

Introduction: Sit Down Before You Read This

Here are a few remarkable statistics about how long your parents may be around. If you are thirty years old and your parents are in their fifties, scientists say at least one of them will almost certainly live well into their eighties. There is even a 35 percent chance at least one of them will live past age eighty-five. If you are in your forties, and your parents have made it past the heart attack–cancer watermark of sixty-five, they now have a 55 percent chance of the living past eighty-five. There's even a 30 percent chance they will hit ninety.

There's more: those statistics don't even take into account medical advances likely to emerge in the next few years. Longevity experts at the Centers for Disease Control believe that by 2020, average life expectancy may hit one hundred, which means that your relationship with your parents may well be the most enduring tie you will ever have.

If that isn't eye-opening enough, try this one on for size: 75 percent of us will wind up with significant caretaking responsibilities for at least one parent over the course of our life. The average length of time we will wind up taking care of that parent is twenty years—longer than we will take care of our children.

If these facts put an ear-to-ear grin on your face, send a warm rush through your extremities, and make you want to run out and drop a Hallmark card in the mail to your folks, you're very lucky. You are among the fortunate few who have stress-free relationships with their parents.

But if these statistics worry you, if they twist your stomach into a knot the size of softball, usher in a throbbing headache, or simply make you feel a bit lightheaded, read on. If the thought of having to deal with your mother or father (or both!) for another fifteen or twenty years—the guilt-laced, late-night telephone calls, the strained holiday meals, the constant requests from one or both of them that never seem to end—makes you want to pack your bags and flee to Micronesia under an assumed name (or just crawl up under the covers), this is the book for you.

If you cannot imagine, with good reason, how you will psychologically handle taking care of your parents as they age when you have enough problems dealing with them now, read on.

But first: remember, you are not alone. You're in good company and lots of it. If you doubt that, try this little experiment: mention to a handful of acquaintances or colleagues the longevity statistics I've just conveyed. You may be surprised at how many of them turn a bit pale, make a weary stab at black humor, or simply change the subject.

Parental relationships are hard for almost everyone. They are, by definition, challenging, and not just because they are weighted with baggage from when you were young, but because they continue to evolve, to become even more complicated as you gain experience, marry, have children (or not), grow older yourself. The intricacies and "thickly woven threads," as Thomas Moore called them in his book *Care of the Soul,* inevitably get denser and harder to sort out.

A generation ago, aging parents (think of your grandparents) tended to be humble folk who had come from little or nothing and later lived quietly on a fixed income. Now our parents are likely to have lives as complex as our own—more divorces, more money, more confidence, louder voices—a reality that can create as many problems as it solves.

But even though there is no simple relationship with a parent, that doesn't mean that relationship can't be simplified.

In my nearly twenty-five years as a therapist and during my long career as a television commentator and seminar lecturer, I've dealt over and over with grown men and women who are still struggling daily with their feelings toward their parents, still trapped in a cycle of fear and frustration, still psychologically embroiled with the people who brought them into the world. Scatch the surface of most of your peers, and I bet you'll find they're just like you—scared and discouraged to face how long their parents will likely be around because one of the defining aspects of their lives is how tightly they are entangled with them and how reliant they are on their approval, their advice, their money, despite the unhappiness and confusion that sometimes brings.

Even those who come to me for therapy or attend my seminars for other reasons—they are conflicted about their marriages, frustrated by their inability to find love, or confounded by their foundering careers—often eventually trace those negative patterns back to as-yet-unresolved parental issues.

Let's be clear here: I'm not talking just about people who come from severely pathological families with a legacy of incest, emotional destruction, or physical violence. I'm not referring merely to those with so-called toxic parents who mount campaigns of terror that leave their victims virtually unable to function. Those are the extreme cases that have gotten so much attention on television and in self-help literature, but they are not the norm.

I'm talking about the rest of us. Our relationships with our parents are not that black-and-white. Our childhood was more nuanced than a reign of terror. It may not have been "toxic," but it probably wasn't exactly a health food buffet either. It's more likely that we grew up with some love and caring, but also a level of manipulation and discomfort that continues to this day. We may honestly be able to say we love our parents and want their lives to be happy, but are stymied by a nagging question: Can our own lives be happy at the same time? It's the hangover of those conflicts that is disrupting our lives now, as adults.

Your interactions with your parents may sometimes seem to have you on a treadmill going nowhere but the House of Pain, but in reality it's not a treadmill at all—it's a complex dance. You and your parents, locked in a painful tango, each of you saying things and doing things over and over that only make matters worse.

Unfortunately, as we get older, that dance can become a stranglehold. Personality traits tend to get exaggerated with age, and your parents are probably no exception. (Guess what? Neither are you.) The particular problems run the gamut, reflecting our individual stories, but the same themes echo: guilt, remorse, anger, and frustration. The supreme unifier is a feeling of powerlessness, the ultimate curse of childhood itself. You may feel there is no decent answer and little hope of things improving—that anything you do will only make things worse or have no effect at all.

You may find yourself driven crazy by parents who insert themselves into every aspect of your life. Even though you know their heart is in the right place, you choke back the sensation of being smothered. You may deal with your overwhelming feelings by keeping your parents at bay, even moving across the country, but you may suffer for the pained distance. You may really love your folks, but, well, just can't stand being around them for more than an hour or two. Or the mere mention of your father or mother may cause your throat to seize up, your heart to race, your palms to grow instantly clammy.

Maybe you can't hold a telephone conversation with your parents without your blood pressure rising, yet feel wracked with guilt if you don't pick up the phone regularly. You may resent your father for unceremoniously dumping your mother and find it impossible to tolerate his new wife, or you may cringe at your mother's neediness as she goes it alone. You may think your parents still don't accept that you've grown up, or you may feel that you have been the parent all along, taking care of your mother or father throughout your life, regardless of the toll it takes on you.

Or you may feel your parents don't care enough about you, that they don't seem to understand how hard life is for you in this era of high career pressure and relationship havoc. You may seethe with quiet anger watching them live it up in retirement as you struggle with day-to-day existence, barely making ends meet.

Wherever your frustrations stem from, the unifying theme is that you believe your relationship with your parents is beyond your control, that even the simple interactions escalate out of proportion, despite your best intentions.

These problems may not be as dire as the cases we heard about for years on *Oprah* and other talk shows, the ones in which tortured adults "recover" memories of incest or ritual abuse, but they can be important and painful nonetheless. Even if you consider your relationship with your parents passable most of the time, even pleasurable, there are those junctures when you simply cannot seem to make them understand why their behavior is driving you mad. Just because your own family situation is not dramatic enough to be "toxic" doesn't mean things can't be better. Even in a bearable situation the pain and discomfort chip away at your self-respect and inner strength. Why should you be sentenced to that for the rest of your life?

"Treadmill" interactions with your parents may be hurting you in more profound ways as well. Struggling with your feelings toward your mother and father may be getting in the way of you getting what you want out of the rest of your life. You may feel so crushed by the weight of your parents' disapproval—"You had so much potential, and now you're just doing nothing with your life"—that it seems impossible for you to form lasting love relationships or build a career because you feel unworthy. Maybe you fall in love over and over with hypercritical people who just reinforce your parents' opinion of you, or you stay in a dead-end job because you think you're just no good. Or perhaps the opposite happens: you find your-self being as critical about others—boyfriends, bosses, friends—as your parents are about you.

You may even be one of those people—I meet a lot of them in my practice—who are *too* close, too attached to their parents well into middle age. That makes it hard to break away and form other con-nections. Are you always looking for—and never finding—someone as forgiving as your mother or father? Do you talk to your parents once, twice, three times a day, consulting them on even the most minor decisions? Did you move back in with them after college and now, years later, can't figure out a good reason to move out? Are your parents still sending you checks and picking up tabs, way beyond the occassional dinner, even after you have your own fam-ily, though that entails paybacks that you know, deep in your heart, ultimately harm you?

Staying locked in unsatisfying, frustrating, unresolved parental relationships can hurt more than just you and them. It can poison the people you care about the most.

Maybe you're in love with someone who has real trouble dealing with his parents. Your own relationship with your parents may be fine, but his is a disaster. You may be angry that he puts his mother's needs ahead of yours, that he becomes an eight-year-old boy in her presence. Or you may worry—with good reason—that her anger toward her father will scar your own children, carrying on the legacy of pain. That's enough to keep you up at night, permanently.

Over the years I've talked with thousands of people who fall into one or more of these categories, each struggling with complex parental relationships. But I speak from more than just my own experience. In a study conducted by the social scientists Grace Baruch and Rosalind Barnett, approximately 25 percent of women said they had "low rapport" with at least one parent, and another 25 percent rated their parental relationships as "only somewhat rewarding." In a survey conducted by a leading women's maga-zine in 2001, more than a quarter of the respondents said their relationship with at least one parent was "worse than I wish it were." Nearly half of those also conceded that "unresolved" issues with parents "significantly interrupted" their functioning in social, romantic, child-rearing, and professional situations. So you see, you are not alone. Far from it.

But you are also not alone in wanting things to be better. During the "inner child" era of the 1980s and 1990s when it was fashionable to hold your parents responsible for everything that had gone wrong in your life, some therapists encouraged patients to endlessly relive, even "recover," their childhood traumas. There were reams of books encouraging people to categorize their parents as "abusive"; these books made little distinction between true major trauma like incest, violence, nonstop emotional abuse, and less extreme forms of conflict. Many clients who came to me felt left out in the cold; either you had to see your parents as perpetrators, or you had to see them as perfect. "What about me?" many of my clients asked. "I have problems with my parents, but I don't feel they abused me. Where do I fit in?"

Worse, when those books came to the part about repairing things in the present, they lost steam. Sure, they had plenty to say about how your parents' inadequacies sentenced you to a life of unhappiness, but the advice for the future came as a skimpy afterthought. And their prescription for reclaiming the relationship with your parents? Confront the abusers with your litany of allegations and then, when they protest, as they inevitably will, cut off all contact with them. Move. Change your phone number. Tell the kids they have no grandparents. Give anyone who asks about them the evil eye.

But now people are waking up to the reality that it's unproductive to merely blame your parents for everything that has gone wrong in your life and wash your hands of them. To begin with, it keeps you in a powerless, childlike state that lets you off the hook for your own failings—aspects of your life that you could take into your own hands and turn into successes. Most important, it's a lose-lose strategy based in the past, not directed toward the future.

Besides, it's simply impractical to pretend to be an orphan, especially if you have children yourself.

(As for those who think the answer is simply to pretend your parents are dead until they indeed die, in my experience, you are making a terrible mistake. Many of my patients who have done so discover that their feelings grow more conflicted and disruptive after their parents' death.)

In all but the most extreme cases, cutting off contact completely is, in my view, just another admission of defeat. You may tell yourself that you have no choice, but on another level you may also be looking for yet another way to dole out punishment to your parents. Unlike figuring out how to make a difficult relationship work to your satisfaction, "divorcing" your parents doesn't make you stronger or give you a sense of accomplishment.

If you feel ambivalent about taking such drastic action, it's likely that you'll just wind up miserably in the middle, always threatening to cut them off but never feeling strong enough to do it or to live with the consequences. That will make you feel weak and bitter, like Michael Corleone in *Godfather III,* making excuses for reverting back to old, destructive patterns: "Every time I try to get out, they pull me back!"

This brings us back to the survey in which so many people admitted they had bad relationships with their parents. Half of them said they would "devote significant resources in money, time, and energy" if they felt they could improve the way they interact with their parents. Like you, they are searching for answers to make the future better.

Their search—and yours—is what led me to write this book. Despite the frustration you are feeling at this point, this is not the time to give up or give in. It's the time to try something radically new.

OK, I'll admit there's bad news and there's good news. The bad news is that it won't be easy. (By this point in your life, you've probably noticed that nothing important ever is.) This will not be a quick fix involving a few peppy "affirmations" that you say to yourself in the mirror in the morning, or some neat "empowerment" lists or "Life Laws" that you can go over in your head to make you feel better for a minute or two. This is not that kind of program.

It's a program about honest analysis that translates into action, about accepting the pain of change, altering your perceptions of yourself in relation to your parents, and transforming the way you deal with them on a day-to-day basis. Every day for the rest of your life.

A little more bad news: I am not going to impart to you some magic secret that will change your parents overnight, make them understand you at last and treat you the way you want to be treated. No one can do that; in fact, no one can magically change anyone's behavior. Instead, I'm going to teach you to alter your own behavior in order to trigger positive changes in your parents.

What I am suggesting will require you to take stock of your life by questioning old assumptions, never a painless task. It will require a deeper understanding of what makes your parents tick deep down, which is likely to ruin all those pat condemnations of them that you've fed on for years. And—most important—it will require you to exercise strength and courage—and humor—in using that information to change forever the way you interact with them.

In other words, the hard reality of this program is that you can't change your relationship with your parents until you change your own behavior.

Now the good news: if you do change your behavior in a permanent and consistent way, your parents' behavior is virtually guaranteed to change in response. Consider the metaphor of losing weight. Remember when people believed in the grapefruit diet or other wacky eating regimes? Now we know that the equation is simple: take in fewer calories than you burn, and you will lose weight. The same goes for dealing with your parents: change your behavior, consistently and permanently, and their behavior will change in response. (No one can guarentee that even if you follow this program, they will change precisely the way you wish they would or at the velocity you would wish, but that's not the point. The point is to shake things up and create new behavior patterns.)

For those of you who insist that no matter what you do, your parents will never change, I say this: it is still worth undertaking the challenge. Even if your parents' behavior does not change a whit—which I doubt with all my heart—the transformation of your behavior will be its own reward. You will be healthier, more honest, and, well, more adult. You will find enormous freedom in shaking loose from your parents' expectations and demands. Other relationships will crystallize for you once you have broken free. You will find incomparable satifisfaction in having had the courage to change your own destructive patterns. You will, I guarantee, be happier.

More good news: if you have the right tools and the right plan, changing your own behavior isn't as hard as you think. In the following chapters, I'm going to lay out those tools very clearly and give you an arsenal of behaviors as well as the means to design a plan that suits the individual dynamic of you and your parents.

Still more good news: this plan gets easier as it progresses. The hardest steps come at the beginning. The more you get into it and get past the big hurdles, the simpler and more obvious it becomes.

Best of all, the rewards are amazing. You will no longer feel like the victim of a relationship you can't control. Those moments when you find yourself suddenly hurled back into the worst traumas of your childhood will disappear. The anger you thought you could never control will dissipate. And you'll dump that load of guilt that threatens to break your back and your spirit at every turn. You may even wind up with a relationship that, over the years to come, transforms into something truly worthwhile and satifying—for both you and your parents.

PART I

PAST, TENSE

Victoria Roberts R.

"*You're born, you deconstruct your childhood, and then you die.*"

• Chapter 1 •

Making Sure
Your Past Doesn't Last

Maybe it won't be so bad, Zach* thought. Maybe I can stick him in my office for the week and do my writing in the bedroom. When he starts driving me crazy I can just go for a long walk. Or pop a Xanax. . . .

Damn. It will be bad. Maybe I should stay with Ben for the week. His place is small, but I could put an air mattress in his dining area. Or Kara. She's got a spare room. No, that's crazy—she's still mad at me. . . . Oh, geez, I forgot about dinner Friday night with Leona and Karl! What if he wants to come along, like he always does? God, why does he do this to me?

Hey, what am I talking about? Geez, I'm such a lousy son. My dad really doesn't ask for very much. Why can't I just hold my nose and smile when he comes to stay with me?

"You go through this every time," Kara said with an exasperated tone when Zach, a thirty-four-year-old writer, called her for advice on how to handle the chilling news that his divorced father was planning yet another trip to town and wanted to stay with Zach in his small apartment. "Why don't you just tell him to get a hotel room?" Kara said. "Would you let anyone else push you around like that?"

---

*I've changed Zach's name, and those of my other clients, to protect their privacy.

Ben wasn't particularly sympathetic either. "Just suck it up, pal. Let him bunk in your office, 'yes' him to death, and tune him out. It'll be over in a week. What's the big deal?"

Both alternatives put Zach in a cold sweat. His father, Ed, had always been a sweet, depressed, needy guy, which had bugged Zach throughout his childhood and made him feel more like the parent than the kid. But things got out of hand after Zach's frosty, get-up-and-go mother got up and left Ed for a wealthy entrepreneur a couple of years ago. Now his father wanted to pal around with Zach all the time—and without fail, he'd get drunk and weepy, telling Zach that his broken heart would never mend.

Every time his father stayed with him, Zach flashed back to when he was twelve and realized that his mother was cheating on his dad. He still cringes at the memory of his father weeping on the basement steps, and even today, twenty-two years later, anger toward his mother swells up. That's probably why Zach just can't bring himself to tell his dad to back off. On the other hand, Zach thinks, why should he have to tell his father to back off? Can't the old man see that his son is having problems, too, struggling to make it as a writer, struggling to maintain a decent romantic relationship himself?

"Why is it so hard to say no to him?" Zach asked me the day before his father arrived. (Zach had decided, with trepidation, to give his dad the bedroom and sleep on an air mattress in his cramped office.) Why couldn't he be more like Kara, who had simply cut her demanding mother out of her life, or like Ben, who didn't seem to give a second thought to his folks, a nice, wealthy couple who sent him monthly checks and demanded only a visit at Christmas?

"Is it because I had a crazy childhood?" Zach said. "Kara says I'm so conflicted because my parents abused me. Is that why I can't say no, and yet when I say yes I wind up wanting to punch him? Am I feeling this way because I'm burying what happened when I was a kid—or because I'm dwelling on it too much?"

.　　.　　.

It's a question I hear over and over: How important is the past? Should I blame? Forgive? Repress? Scream and yell? Just get over it?

Compounding the confusion are all the conflicting messages out there: an endless loop of afternoon talk shows with victims of family trauma regaling viewers with horror stories, religious leaders preaching forgiveness, therapists urging us to dredge up long-buried pain, motivational speakers hectoring us to stop whining and "start winning."

Our relationship with our parents is the "original" relationship of our lives, the template for all other connections. It plays itself out in our romances, in our friendships, and in the way we deal with our own children. It's the cradle in which our concept of intimacy was born—the need for approval, the nagging sense that we're being either smothered or rejected, the fear that we are, at some basic level, not really loved . . . or clutched too tightly to breathe. No wonder it's so hard to figure out how much weight to give the past when we're trying to figure out how to deal with our parents today.

We interact with our parents vividly (sometimes too vividly) in the present, but every moment we spend with them—every weird phone call, every tense holiday, every blood-boiling argument—bears whispers and shadows from the past. Like Jacob Marley, chains rattling as he walks through the chilly rooms of *A Christmas Carol,* we can't escape them.

My stand on the how to view your past can best be summed up in a quote from Alfred North Whitehead, the Harvard mathematician and philosopher: "The only use of a knowledge of the past is to equip us for the present. The present contains all that there is. It is holy ground; for it is the past, and it is the future."

I don't underestimate the power of the past. Remembering and understanding your childhood can be important on many levels, from making sense of the problems in your love life to gaining insight into why you are having conflicts on the job. Using a therapist to question long-held beliefs, investigate memories, and search for patterns can be a mind-expanding experience, and intense investigation of the past may be imperative if you are unable to function because of childhood trauma—physical, sexual, or psychological abuse.

But what about the rest of us, those of us who are unhappy with our relationship with our parents and want to change it *now*? Are we all, as some experts suggest, "victims" of childhood parental "abuse" and therefore required to embark on a lengthy course of psychotherapy to ruminate endlessly about it? Is all the tension we feel regarding our parents the result of a childhood robbed of love and unconditional support, as we've been led to believe? Must we delve deep into our psyches, strip bare our soul, before we can even contemplate change?

Absolutely not. The radical notion underlying this book is that *you can change your relationship with your parents now, WHILE you are learning to understand your past.*

I am not saying that there is no connection between your childhood and why you now feel guilty, angry, or powerless when dealing with your parents. There probably is. In fact, in later sections of this book we will discuss some patterns you and your parents may have established in your childhood and how these have an impact on your relationship with your parents today.

What I am saying is this: if you want change, all you need is a basic grasp of how your childhood may have laid the groundwork for the bad patterns you are stuck in with your parents today. You already possess the inner resources to change your behavior, and theirs.

The best way to make real progress is to carefully evaluate your childhood with an eye to discovering solutions for dealing with your parents today. That's how you avoid the trap, which many people fall into, of feeling used, abused, and wounded by their childhood memories. Note that both reflection *and* action are required. The more you learn about the past—provided you do it in a way that is forward-looking and solution-oriented—the easier it will be for you to make changes.

I compare the process to losing those fifteen pounds you know are endangering your health. Understanding the childhood dynamics that contributed to your overeating (never feeling like you could measure up to your supersvelte mom, inheriting your dad's chubby physique, being raised in a family where lasagna substituted for love) can be helpful, but it's not necessary to understand them before you start losing weight, before you start changing your relationship to food.

ALL PAIN HURTS, BUT NOT ALL PAIN IS ABUSE

The simple fact is that most of us did not have a pathologically dangerous childhood, weren't sexually or physically abused by our parents. You may have endured heavy emotional blackmail or selfish or immature parenting—I am not underestimating the pain that stems from that—but despite how it may seem from reading magazines or watching made-for-TV movies, the percentage of people who are victims of true parental terror is fairly small.

It's important to make this distinction because it is not healthy to see yourself as a *victim.* That term is wildly overused. Frankly, I'm not too crazy about how often *dysfuctional* is tossed around either, nor the profligate use of *abuse.* Or *codependent* or *survivor* or any of those jargony labels. In this book, I'm going to avoid labels, even the ones used by well-meaning therapists who have written about dealing with parents by putting them in categories like *smotherers, martyrs,* or *controllers.*

Victim terminology came into common usage in the 1980s, when therapists and self-help gurus—unduly swayed by new, taboo-busting press reports of incest and sexual predation of children by some adults—adapted the highly charged language of these crimes to help clients cope with parental issues. These therapists were convinced that the depression, anxiety, and guilt of their clients stemmed from the repression of childhood "abuse" of all kinds. Such labels seemed to make their clients feel more comfortable and less isolated—like instant heroes with a ready-made support group. The labels spread like wildfire.

I believe strongly that these terms have been too loosely applied, to the point where they now encompass almost every sort of bad parenting. Victim terminology is dangerous because:

- It defines us as "damaged" and imposes a feeling of help-lessness that is hard to shake.
- It devalues the experience of people who have been the victims of serious parental abuse, which I define as relent-less, systematic harm of a psychological, sexual, or physi-cally violent nature.

Don't be so eager to cast yourself in the victim's role. In deciding to wrestle with your relationship with your parents, you are embarking on a program that will require an enormous amount of courage, self-confidence, and optimism. Dwelling on the image of yourself as a victim will only make it harder for you to muster the tools you'll need to change your behavior toward them, and their behavior toward you. Viewing yourself as a victim may comfort you in the short term, but it will trap you in a powerless and childlike state that will rob you of a much-needed sense of strength. And at those moments when you feel like quitting—and believe me, it will happen along the way—you will find it too easy to slip into "blame" and "victim" mode.

The True Horror: Realizing That Your Parents Are Human

Seeing yourself as a victim can stop you from seeing your parents as fully realized human beings, a crucial step in improving your relationship with them. You must accept the fact that your parents are entangled in their own internal struggles and that those struggles may have been acted out on you in the form of manipulation, suppression and control, and even, at times, loving behavior. Once you understand this point, you can no longer simply define your parents in terms of what they "did" to you. That is, ironically, much more difficult than dismissing them as fireballs of destruction. But it is a step you must take.

HOW MUCH TALKING IS TOO MUCH?

Therapy has been called "the talking cure," and it is a valuable tool for self-awareness. But in recent years, more and more therapists have realized that endlessly rehashing childhood wounds can be counterproductive. Sigmund Freud believed that the "magic bullet" was uncovering repressed early childhood trauma, but in many cases that's not enough to effect real change. Repressing the past is not healthy—but neither is dwelling on it. Concentrating on action is the best way to jump-start real change. Making even small strides in the way you deal with your parents will give you the strength and sense of accomplishment necessary to confront the past on your own terms, on your own schedule. And that, in turn, will make you even more comfortable about confronting the challenges that will arise as your long life with your folks plays out.

SO, WHAT REALLY MATTERS ABOUT YOUR CHILDHOOD?

You don't need to have a full-blown, connect-the-dots understanding of your childhood dynamic to start changing your approach to your parents. But it is necessary to have a basic understanding of the "narrative" of your early life. With all our exposure to television, therapy, and self-help literature, most of us have some inkling of what made our family and parental interactions unique, but you may not have a mapped-out "narrative." Or you may have one that is too cluttered with psychobabble and victim labels. So start fresh with the lists at the end of this chapter.

In therapy, recollections of your childhood are explored at length to sort out reality from fantasy, and to illuminate entreched patterns of behavior—but it's not what we're doing here. Instead, we're simply trying to arm you with a concise, nondramatic synopsis of the most pivotal experiences of your childhood. We're doing this not as an exercise in catharsis or a way for you to "get in touch with your feelings," but as a diagnostic tool to help you identify which issues will likely crop up when you are trying to fix your relationship with your parents (Do keep in mind, however, that not all problems vis-à-vis your folks are "old" problems; some, like issues stemming from their aging or their hostility toward your spouse, may be relatively new.)

WE ARE FAMILY

If you're having trouble dealing with your parents, your childhood story likely involves sadness or anger. But be aware that the story may involve your entire family, not just you and your parents. You didn't grow up in a vacuum. Your parents' relationship to each other might have set the tone for your childhood, and you may have had siblings who further complicated the situation. This is the focus of what's called "Family Systems," an approach to therapy created by Dr. Murray Bowen. "Getting beyond blame," Dr. Bowen and his collaborator Dr. Michael Kerr once wrote, "does not mean exonerating people from the part they play or played in the creation of a problem. It means seeing the total picture, acquiring a balanced view—not feeling compelled to either approve or disapprove of the nature of one's own family."

Your past was also shaped by outside events: deaths, bankruptcies, job losses, accidents. Don't forget to weigh those events when you reflect on your past, because they can permanently disfigure families and deeply affect the way your parents relate to you.

The following exercises should help you understand how issues from your childhood are affecting your life today. When you are finished with them, you will need to keep this information handy—perhaps not emblazoned on your chest, but in your metaphoric back pocket—so that you will recognize your "hot buttons" when they are pushed.

1) TAKE INVENTORY OF CHILDHOOD ISSUES AND THEIR EFFECT ON YOU

Write down the three most traumatic family-related events of your childhood. A few examples: divorce, substance abuse (of any family member—including yourself), a grandparent living with you, or frequent moves.

1)

2)

3)

Now write down the top three things you still feel quilty about from your childhood—regardless of whether you think they were your fault. Omit this step if there's nothing you feel guilty about.

1)

2)

3)

Finally, list the top three things that still get you angry at your parents when you reflect back.

1)

2)

3)

2) WRITE YOUR STORY

Write a concise paragraph or two in the least judgmental language possible to convey the flavor of your childhood, your family, and your relationship with your parents. It may help to write in the voice of an alien who—unbeknown to you or your parents—lived invisibly in your childhood home and now must report back to the high commander. Remember to consider your family dynamic as a whole as well as putting the spotlight on the relationship between you and your parents. Be descriptive and honest, including the good and the bad.

3) DECIDE WHICH CHILDHOOD EXPERIENCE IS DOING THE MOST DAMAGE TODAY

Jot down which of these nine things from your childhood (refer back to "1) Take Inventory of Childhood Issues and Their Effect on You") you think cause the biggest problems in your relationship with your parents today. (I am not asking you to play shrink here, but your instincts are probably pretty sound.)

What Happened in the Past

_____

_____

_____

_____

What That Means to Me Now

_____

_____

_____

_____

4) HOW YOUR PARENTS SEE YOUR CHILDHOOD (OR HOW YOU THINK THEY DO)

Channel your parents. In their voices—each of them—write down how they would describe your childhood, and what you were like as a kid. (If one or both of your parents are dead, write it as of the time right before they died.) Pretend to be writing a letter, in their voice, to God or whomever they are most likely to be honest with.

This is an important part of the process because our reactions to our parents are often based on what we think they think of us. We get angry because we perceive judgment behind their words and their actions. We aren't always right about their opinions of us (later on, you'll find tips to ferret out what they're really thinking), and their opinions are often off base as well, but that's not the point here. Rather, it is to identify your "hot buttons" by leveling with yourself about how much you project onto your parents. So really put yourself into their head and write what you truly think they would tell someone they trusted about what kind of child you were . . . and what kind of parents they were.

CARY'S QUESTIONNAIRE

(age forty-two, a software programmer)

Top Three Traumatic Events
1. Moving every three years (my dad was in the military).
2. My mother had a Valium addiction when I was a young teenager.
3. My brother and I both had learning disabilities.

Top Three Things I Feel Guilty About
1. Sometimes I feel like my mom did pills because we kids were hard to handle.
2. My dad died when I was getting in trouble a lot in my twenties, and I feel guilty that he never got to see me straighten my life out.
3. I've never made enough money to buy my mom a better house.

Top Three Things I Still Get Angry about When I Think of Them
1. My dad never told me he loved me.
2. My mom wasn't really there for us a lot of the time.
3. My parents never acknowledged that moving around so much was hard on us kids.

LIANA'S STORY

(age thirty, an actor)

I was an only child, born when my parents were almost forty. I was everything to them. They made some bad financial decisions early on, and as I grew up, our positions reversed—I wound up taking care of them. They are really sweet and I adore them, but they need a lot of help and I've always felt responsible for them. We've always been a closed unit, very protective of one another and kind of isolated.

What Happened in the Past
I became the parent, and they became the kids.

What That Means to Me Now
They lean on me too much, and I don't know how to say no to them. Sometimes that makes me really mad, and then I feel guilty. I don't know how to get them to take better care of themselves.

BOB'S STORY

(age twenty-seven, a student)

My brothers are both superstars. They went to Ivy League schools—the older one is a lawyer; the other one is a scientist. I was the baby, and I felt very intimidated by them, as though I was a disappointment to my parents. I'm still struggling with how much of that is me and how much of it came from them. I had some bad drug years in my late teens and early twenties, and I always felt my parents were ashamed of me. I really hated them.

What Happened in the Past
I was kind of a screw-up, and my parents didn't deal with that very well.

What That Means to Me Now

I'm doing better now, back in school, and we're rebuilding our relationship. They're subsidizing me financially, which doesn't feel so hot, because I'm still trying to win their respect and I often wind up feeling like a kid, which I hate.

CAROL'S STORY

(age forty-three, an Internet executive)

My mother and father had a horrible marriage. I have a half-sister, but she's much older, so I was pretty much alone with my mother and father when I was young, which was awful. My dad left when I was six—he was a college professor, and he ran off with one of his grad students. My mom's drinking got pretty bad for a while, and I always resented having to take care of her, especially when I was in my teens.

What Happened in the Past

I pretty much got trampled by my parents' conflict. I felt abandoned by my father and leaned on by my mother. No one seemed to worry much about what was happening to me.

What That Means to Me Now

As it happened, I turned out fine, but I give myself most of the credit for that. I reconciled with my dad years ago—we get along great now—but I still have a really hard time with my mother. She's very demanding, always sick, always critical of me. I can't ignore her, and I can't seem to do anything that makes her happy.

MY IDEA OF WHAT MY PARENTS THOUGHT OF ME AS A CHILD

(Lisette, age forty-nine, a graphic artist)

My mother's voice: "We were so close. I knew everything Lisette was thinking. She never made a move without me. Her father died when she was five, so we relied on each other. We were more like sisters than mother and daughter."

MY IDEA OF WHAT MY PARENTS THOUGHT OF ME AS A CHILD

(Gavin, age thirty-three, a real estate broker)

My father's voice: "I thought the kid was going to be an NFL quarterback. When he was six, he could throw a football thirty yards. But he sort of lost interest when he was twelve. It always rankled me. That kid could really have been great. I think he just stopped trying to bug me."

My mother's voice: "I never really understood Gavin. He was very quiet, and no matter how much I tried to help him, he just pushed me away."

Chapter 2

Leaving It All Behind: A Word about Becoming an Adult

People whose childhood was abusive and bereft of love often are left so defenseless that they find it impossible to function like adults in the presence of their parents. They regress to childhood, cowering in the corner, becoming paralyzed or screaming like a banshee. Other elements of their lives go awry as well. They often need intensive therapy just to function.

You are not in this category. Yes, as the questionnaire you just filled out made you aware, you have some important childhood issues to keep in my mind as an "early warning system," but you are strong enough not to be disabled by them. You're among those who are capable of moving on and creating a working relationship with your parents.

But to do that, you must grow up for good, now and forever.

This is not always easy. As we will discuss in chapters 7 and 8, our parents sometimes act like children, which triggers our impulse to respond to them as children ourselves. There are many reasons why we and our parents revert back to immature postures. We'll discuss some of them when we tackle the subjects of guilt and separation, but for now, just keep in mind that in undertaking a new way of reacting to parents, you must resist the impulse to revert to child-like behavior, especially at the red-hot moment of conflict.

No matter how much prodding or goading your parents do, and no matter how angry or hurt you get, you must accept that—now and forever, even if they steadfastly refuse to engage you on an adult level— you will always be an adult.

GETTING AWAY FROM IT ALL: LEAVING YOUR INNER BABY BEHIND

The worst thing about childhood is that it is, by definition, a time of unavoidable dependence and helplessness. Even people who had, on balance, a good childhood may remember it as frustrating; as a child, you're told what to eat, what to wear, where to go, and how to get there. Being a child can be terribly stressful. Not being able to make decisions for yourself is excruciating.

Adulthood, despite its pressures, at least affords us the possibility of self-determination. It's a liberation; no longer do your parents hold sway over you. Life may be more complicated, more chaotic, and more expensive, but at least we have choices and the potential for freedom.

Unfortunately, many of the people I counsel seem to have forgotten the joys associated with this condition. They are still trapped in their past, still victims of their own sense of powerlessness. Some, luckily, get along fine in most areas of their lives—they are strong on the job and in their relationships—but fall apart as soon as their mother or father enters the picture. Others let this sense of powerlessness define their career and their love life as well, casting a long shadow on every aspect of their life.

In either case, until you have traversed the bridge to adulthood, a bridge that allows for traffic to flow in only one direction, you will not have the strength or vision to create a satisfying relationship with your parents. To place yourself squarely in the grown-up camp is to permanently sever your identification with the controlled, helpless child of your past.

DISTANCE ISN'T A PHYSICAL STATE

A defining aspect of adulthood is perspective. Children react to scary situations instantly and often inappropriately because they're unable to evaluate the danger from a distance. Adults can see and judge the threat, determine how grave it is, and anticipate ways to avert it. You may jump out of your chair while watching a rerun of a Freddy Kruger movie, but within an instant you know he's not *really* going to get you in your dreams. You know you are an adult, sitting on your couch, munching Doritos. You remember, with amusement, how terrified you were when you saw the movie as a kid. You remember how real and immediate that terror was. Now, however, you are an adult, and you know that Freddy Kruger can't hurt you.

Achieving this sort of distance from your childhood—on all levels, not just in terms of your parents—is crucial to cementing your own concept of yourself as a grown-up. Consciously viewing the chasm between your helpless child-self and your rational, powerful adult-self is not only comforting; it's invaluable.

Exercise: Regarding Your Childhood Self from Afar
Sit in a darkened room and recall at least three moments in your childhood when you felt the most powerless. For now, avoid examples that involved your parents. Perhaps you were always the last person picked for basketball teams or were constantly made fun of by the kids for wearing braces. Maybe a teacher regularly singled you out for ridicule, or your best friend dropped you cold.

With the lights still down, reconstruct each episode painstakingly, complete with the feelings of helplessness it engendered. One by one, let your mind go through them, splicing a reel together in your head like a home movie. Let yourself identify entirely with the frustration and loneliness you felt as a child; remember the sound of the taunts, the nasty glares. After doing this for a while, you will likely feel very agitated. Maybe you will also feel angry and vengeful. Probably you will feel very small and helpless. Those feelings are natural because you are allowing yourself—for the sake of this exercise only—to briefly reinhabit your childhood. Let the feelings flow through you for two or three minutes.

Now release those feelings. Lie on the floor on cushions, or recline on the couch. Close your eyes. Breathe slowly and rhythmically. Imagine yourself weightless, bodiless—perhaps floating in a warm pool, or anywhere you feel safe and calm. Within about five minutes, the negative feelings will pass. Keep breathing slowly until your muscles relax and your head clears.

Slowly begin to indulge in physical "take-charge" imagery. If you work out, imagine pushing through a set of biceps curls or running a seven-minute mile; if you mow your lawn, imagine looking back on a smooth field of green you've just cut down to size; if you write software, imagine you have written code for a new video game. Anything you associate with getting accomplished will work. Give yourself three to five minutes to enjoy these feelings (endorphins coursing through your veins, the smell of fresh-cut grass, the beep-beep of the computer confirming your genius). Keep breathing deeply and steadily.

Now you are ready for the next step. Begin the childhood "reel" again, but this time, with the adult you have been for the past five minutes transported into your childhood body (think Tom Hanks in *Big*). Imagine yourself at your most powerful, at the moment when you tend to feel most in control. Perhaps that is the you who runs a household with a steady hand, or the one who runs the departmental meeting. You are going back to the blackest moment of your childhood, but you now have the sense of proportion about the incident, and the intelligence, maturity, and courage to handle it.

- Last one chosen for basketball? You turn on your heels with a laugh, knowing that the team captain winds up in jail for embezzling.

- Teased for wearing braces? This time, instead of turning red, you stare with amazement at your tormentor's horrible case of acne. Maybe you call him Pizza Face, which sends all the kids into hysterics—or maybe you take the high road and say nothing, knowing that you will one day marry a guy who thinks your smile is sexy.
- Sixth-grade teacher calls you stupid? Looking at the woman from your new perspective, you realize she was a lousy teacher and a miserable human being to boot. Not the sort of person you'd let ruin your life.
- Your best friend dumps you suddenly? You now see that he wasn't much of a friend anyway, talking about you behind your back and always shopping around for a cooler hang-out partner. Plus he was uptight that you got better grades. Poor sap—no wonder he bailed.

What this exercise is designed to bring home is how huge the gap is between your confused, hamstrung, emotionally overwrought child-self and the adult you have become. After you've reflected on this for a couple of days, try the same exercise, now using examples that involve your parents. Is there a moment you replay over and over in your head, a time when they violated your privacy or independence? Embarrassed you publicly? Failed to be there when you needed them? Ignored you to pursue their own selfish desires? Made it painfully clear they didn't have any idea who you were, deep inside, and couldn't care less?

Using this exercise will help you to see those awful moments from across the river with a mixture of sadness, incredulity, and relief. It will also help you see how far the child you *were* has receded. As Thomas Wolfe said, you can't go home again, and thank goodness for that!

• Chapter 3 •

What Have You Done for Me Lately?: A Word about Guilt

Guilt is a rope that wears thin.—Ayn Rand

Pilar's stomach starts to hurt even before she reaches the airport. By the time the flight leaves, taking her and her ten-year-old daughter, Lucy, to Florida, where both her mother, Rita, and her mother-in-law live, she is consumed with dread. She goes three times a year, and it's the same ordeal every time. Rita makes each visit a guilt-fest. She is jealous of the "other" grandmother and lets Pilar know it, constantly. "I make sure to spend more of my time with my mother, but that doesn't help. She resents *any* time we spend with my mother-in-law," Pilar says. "She believes that we should spend *all* our time in Florida with her."

Worse, Rita isn't happy unless she's with Pilar and Lucy twenty-four hours a day. "On the second day I was there, while she and my daughter were modeling clay, I went into the bedroom and closed the door so that I could call a friend. She became livid and then sulked and told me, 'You can speak with *her* any old time. This is *our* time.' She even insists on sitting with me while I am in the bath, thinking this is a great time for a private chat."

When Pilar balks at such nonstop intimacy, Rita reminds her that she and her mother, who died just after Pilar was born, used to do *everything* together, and that the greatest loss of her life was when her mother died. "She knows that talk consumes me with guilt." If that tactic doesn't work, she reminds Pilar about several years in Pilar's late adolescence when Pilar had some trouble with drugs. Rita once had to bail Pilar out of jail and never lets Pilar forget it.

Rita also manages to slip in plenty of comments about those "so-called career women who think they can have careers and be good mothers." Pilar, who is struggling to get established as a costume designer, feels instant pangs of guilt about this issue as well. She knows her mother, who everyone in the family always says had a lot of performing arts talent, never pursued her goals, putting all her energy into raising her family. To Rita, there is one job and one job only that suits a woman, and it is to be the best mom you can be. "My mother has never given me any sign that she thinks I'm a good mother," says Pilar. "When we're in Florida and I want to go out for a walk alone, she acts as though I am abandoning my daughter."

Guilt is perhaps the most potent weapon in our parents' arsenal. Those fireballs they lob into every conversation ("Lorraine's daughter is so great to her . . . not that I'm comparing you two . . .") and even the mournful tone of the messages they leave on our answering machines ("I know you're really busy with the new job, but I haven't heard from you in a while . . .") stab us in the heart.

The roots of such guilt are deep. If you feel guilty now as an adult when your parents put you through your paces, chances are those patterns were established many years ago, in your childhood. Because this book is oriented toward forward-looking strategies, we aren't going to trace those twisted vines, but I do encourage you to think about when those feelings first arose, what things you were made to feel guilty about in your childhood. It will be much easier for you to handle the guilt your parents lob at you as an adult if you have a clear picture of when and how it all started. A therapist can definitely help, but you can begin the process by doing some of the work on your own.

Making a list of the things you remember feeling guilty about as a young child vis-à-vis your parents is a good place to start. Seeing it in black and white will help you realize that you have internalized many things that were not your fault. Those things can include your parents' divorce, their disappointed career dreams, their conflict-ridden marriage, their drug or alcohol problems, their own friction with their own parents.

In the bibliography, I recommend several good books that can help you begin to unravel the origin of your strong sense of guilt. While many of them likely refer to parents whose behavior was severe enough to classify them as mentally ill (suffering from clinical narcissism, for example, or alcoholism), you may be able to apply some of the observations these therapists make to your own situation, albeit in a modified, less dramatic fashion.

In the meanwhile, keep this rule of thumb in mind: for a variety of reasons, some of which you may discover when you delve a bit more deeply into your parents' background, some parents feel a lack of control when confronted with their children's growth and independence. It is deeply threatening to them. They try to maintain control by making us feel responsible for their own pain and unhappiness. It's an attempt, however wrongheaded, to keep us close.

As children, we tried desperately to make our parents happy; as adults, we tend to fall into the same pattern. Even though consciously we know we can't make our parents "better," we keep hoping that we will somehow find a way.

Society gives us one-size-fits-all advice on how to battle these feelings of guilt and responsibility. The conventional wisdom is all too glib: we "shouldn't let it get to us," and "they can't make you feel guilty, unless you choose to feel guilty." The underlying assumption is that the only course for survival is to just—poof!—stop feeling guilty.

Well, frankly, that's unrealistic bunk. The fact is that our parents often do their damnedest to get to us, either unconsciously or on purpose. They often come up with a tailor-made way to exploit our weaknesses. They, more than any boss or lover, know exactly what will get to us. And why not? They were, after all, probably there when our first sense of guilt set in; it's even likely they planted those early seeds. Those early patterns of manipulation and guilt are still effective to this day. They often don't have a conscious clue they're doing it, but they know one thing: it's a really good way to get what they want.

Sure, it's unfair. You wish they would put your needs ahead of theirs for once, but face it, that's not going to happen—at least not without some concerted behavior modification on your part.

Denying guilt isn't much of a strategy. Saying you "refuse to feel guilty about X, Y, Z" doesn't work for most of us. And believing that that is the only way to deal with guilt is a setup for disaster. When we try this approach and fail (which is almost inevitable), we surrender, and do what our parents want, barely hiding our resentment.

What you need to do is change your relationship to guilt. You can't "kill" it, so you might as well learn to live with it. Too many of us seem to believe that feeling guilty automatically precludes us from sticking to our guns, sticking to the program we have committed to, the program for readjusting our relationship with our parents. At the slightest hint of guilt, we collapse. We think feeling guilt means we aren't "free" after all, that we've failed. So we go back to our old, unhappy ways. We blame ourselves and feel defeated. And guilty for feeling that way.

There is another way to cope, however. You can acknowledge that you feel guilty but stand your ground anyway. Just because your parents are masters at dealing out the guilt doesn't mean you have to fold your hand and go home. When they throw that artillery at you, you can spring into action instead of slinking off in defeat.

Trying to rid yourself of all guilty feelings in your relationship with your parents is a noble long-term goal, but all is not lost if you can't do that. Even if you can't shake off guilt lightly, you can learn to manage it. Once you realize that it won't kill you, you can acknowledge that you are feeling it and yet not become paralyzed by it. Once you do that, you will defuse it. Soon it will lose its power over you.

A good trick here is to desensitize yourself to guilt. One of the best desensitization exercises was created by Dr. Harold Bloomfield in *Making Peace with Your Parents*. I've refined it, but the idea remains basically the same. It will work in any scenario that involves people trying to make you feel inappropriately guilty—your kids, your spouse, your boss—but it's especially effective with parents, whose voices are very loud in your head. The goal of this exercise is to remain calm even when you are being lit up by guilt pyrotechnics.

1) MAKE A LIST OF AT LEAST FIVE TYPICAL GUILT-INDUCING
STATEMENTS EACH OF YOUR PARENTS COMMONLY USES

Make sure you refine these statements to really reflect the type of
language your parent employs. General statements won't work as
well as carefully crafted ones that echo your parent's guilt lexicon.

2) RECORD EACH LINE INTO A TAPE RECORDER, USING
THE EXACT INFLECTION YOUR PARENT USES

The closer you get to how your parent really sounds—at least in
your mind—the more effective this exercise will be. (If you have a
friend who's a good mimic, enlist his or her help.) Leave at least two
minutes of silence between each statement. (Some statements may
go on a bit—some parents really riff when they're doling out the
guilt—so group these statements in order to get the real effect.)

3) SIT IN THE PLACE AND POSITION YOU ARE USUALLY
IN WHEN YOU DEAL WITH YOUR PARENT'S GUILT
OFFENSIVES

Put the phone up to your ear or let your body assume the stance it
takes when you are face-to-face with your parent and he or she
plays the guilt card.

4) PLAY BACK THE TAPE

As you listen, let yourself relate to any anger or frustration the
statements may induce. Punch a pillow or tear a piece of cardboard.
Smash down the phone or bang on a counter. If it feels right, you
can even curse your parent out loud for his or her insensitivity and
weakness.

5) IF POSSIBLE, STAY IN THE SAME ROOM, BUT CHANGE
YOUR POSITION TO A RESTFUL ONE

Put some cushions on the floor to support your back. Turn down the
lights, turn off the phone, and lie down. Use whatever relaxation technique you are comfortable with—allow yourself to breathe deeply

and release tension from all your limbs. If visualization is effective for you, picture yourself in a meadow or floating on a raft, or anywhere that you feel peaceful.

6) LISTEN TO THE TAPE SEVERAL TIMES

Each time, let your parent's words flow through you. Take note of your thoughts and feelings, but don't let your body get agitated. Without denying or resisting the sensations, direct your mind to focus on your regular breathing, on the peaceful images you've created. It may take four or five times to desensitize yourself.

7) REPEAT THE EXERCISE WHENEVER YOU
   ANTICIPATE CONFLICT

Perhaps you can have a run-through before that regular Sunday night telephone call or the Thanksgiving visit.

Don't be discouraged if desensitization doesn't always work and you either blow up at your parent or give in. Retraining doesn't happen overnight. You may need to repeat this exercise periodically for quite some time. But if you are determined to hold the line, to not surrender to guilt, you will grow progressively stronger, progressively less "guilty."

Chapter 4

The "Gift" That Keeps On Taking—and Taking: A Word about Anger

Anger makes dull men witty,
but it keeps them poor.—Elizabeth I

It is among the most powerful forces in the human arsenal. It can lend even the mildest person the strength to heave a boulder across the room or turn a gentle soul into a whirling dervish of destruction. We've all experienced it: one moment you're humming along; then, seconds later, a wave of hostility rises from your stomach to your head, clouding your perceptions and causing your brain to burn white-hot. Bad things almost always follow.

Anger sends a shot of adrenaline into our bloodstream, causing our heart to pound, a flush to rise to our faces, and many of our inhibitions to dissolve. Often it moves us to say things we later regret, to act rashly, to substitute emotion for reason—often to devastating effect.

Of course, anger can sometimes be a wonderful tool that brings us closer to our real needs—the battered wife at last getting mad enough to leave her spouse, the long-suffering employee finally getting up the courage to quit working for a verbally abusive boss—but medical science now says that cultivating anger on a long-term basis does a great deal more harm than good. Anger can be a wonderful bridge to self-knowledge, but unless it is a transitional aspect of the process, it can destroy everything in its wake.

That was not always the consensus of medical opinion. Until the past few years, it was thought that the only way to deal with anger healthily was to express it at will. Keeping anger "bottled up" was said to be dangerous; the anger would only seep out elsewhere, poisoning everything, and possibly leading to cardiac illness and stress-related ailments. But recent studies have shown that this theory, referred to by Dr. Martin Seligman as *ventilationism,* has no sound basis in fact. Instead, the opposite appears to be true: dwelling on old betrayals and consistently expressing outrage over them leads to heart disease and more anger.

In one study that Dr. Seligman cites, 255 medical students were surveyed in the 1970s to measure their levels of hostility. Twenty-five years later, the angriest had about five times as much heart disease as the least angry ones. Perpetually angry people have higher levels of cortisol, a hormone released by the adrenal glands in response to stress. Elevated stress hormones are necessary in fight-or-flight situations, but are not healthy on a day-to-day basis. That constant state of agitation leads to heart attacks, coronary disease, strokes, ulcers, colitis, and immune system problems.

ANGER AND CHILDHOOD WOUNDS

Many of us are saddled with a less than ideal childhood we are still angry about. And our bitterness doesn't seem to have a natural statute of limitations. Perhaps your developmentally disabled brother sucked up all your parents' energy, forcing you to be the "good girl." Or you felt your mother blamed the derailment of her career on you. Maybe your father seemed to care only for your sister, the "beautiful one." For some people, these past offenses are sad but distant memories, but they are very much alive for you. Just thinking about them, which you do frequently, makes your mind reel with thoughts of betrayal and humiliation.

This "old" anger complicates our present-day interactions with our parents. Yes, your parents may be annoying on a daily basis, making unreasonable demands and manipulating your feelings, but your smoldering annoyance with them is likely compounded by ancient history.

If you are one of the "perpetually angry"—I estimate about 15 percent of those I work with fall into this category—you have your work cut out for you. There's no use even contemplating a new relationship with your parents until you reconcile old anger. No matter how much you believe you want change, your anger, barely simmering below the surface, will bubble up just at the moment you most need to stay calm. This, I guarantee you, will undo your hard-fought gains.

A MATTER OF DEGREE

People who had a genuinely horrific childhood face a much harder road than the rest of us. If they were, for example, sexually or physically abused by their parents or inadequately protected from such abuse by their parents, made party to their parents' infidelity, or endured significant drug or alcohol abuse by a parent, reconciliation will only come after a lot of hard work. In most such cases, it's a multipart process that involves facing the trauma, allowing anger to surface, developing some degree of empathy for the abuser's sickness, and, eventually, learning to accept the past and move on. Full recovery can take years and usually requires skillful therapeutic intervention.

These situations are often complicated by the fact that the abuser is not contrite and accepts no responsibility. In such cases, the victim is forced to make difficult decisions about forgiveness and reconciliation. Many victims, understandably, decide to sever all contact with the person who hurt them.

You, thankfully, are in a significantly different situation. Chances are that your rage, while vivid and painful, likely can be resolved with a less intensive program. And you have already decided to improve your relationship with your parents, so your path is clearer.

The steps to resolving any kind of anger over injustice are the same as with clinical abuse—recognition, anger, empathy, and, eventually, acceptance—but there is usually no reason that the process drag on for years.

I am not minimizing your anger or suggesting that it has no justification. I am merely saying that *maximizing* it is not going to get you closer to your goal of having a mature relationship with your parents. And resolving your anger has benefits that extend way beyond this discussion: finding a permanent way to cope with the past will free you on every level. In fact, committing yourself to resolving your anger is probably the single most valuable lesson you can learn from this book. It will make every aspect of your life—and life with your parents—immeasurably easier, more satisfying, and less stressful.

COMBATTING THE RESISTANCE WITHIN: PAOLO

Paolo couldn't stand the way his mother, Edie, lived. Just thinking about it as he drove to see her for his once-a-week visit made him want to snap the steering wheel of his Volvo in two with his bare hands. By the time he got out of the car in front of her small house in a suburb of Chicago, his fingers were cramped and sore from squeezing, his neck nearly paralyzed with anger.

She was fifty-six—he was thirty—but she lived like a college student. Her house was decorated—a term he used loosely—with Indian tapestries, a futon couch, and huge throw pillows. Usually, it was a mess, with the pillows on the floor, a smoldering bong of pot on the makeshift coffee table, and plates of half-eaten food everywhere.

Edie, a sweet, confused woman who had never quite gotten the hang of life, had been on disability for years after a slew of careers—dancer, waitress, health-care worker.

"I walk in there, stepping over empty Corona bottles and crusty plates of tacos, and it all comes flooding back to me," he told me the day after a visit that had ended with him screaming at Edie, and her weeping. "I remember being nine years old and being embarrassed to bring friends home. I remember being ashamed of her and so, so mad that she couldn't be like everyone else's mother, just a regular lady driving us to the mall."

On a recent visit, Paolo couldn't contain his anger. Instead of discussing the insurance documents he had brought over for her to look at, he pulled out a plastic garbage bag and began to throw things into it, helter-skelter, shouting at his mother all the while. After ten minutes of this, she locked herself in her bedroom and wept.

These visits with his mother always had reverberations for the rest of his life. In the weeks following a blowup, he would divert his mind by spending hour after hour at his law office. He would take on new clients, even though he didn't have time for them. He would

*"I never cared much for apple pie, and, as for mother,
the less said the better."*

spend as little time at home as possible because he found that he was especially critical of his wife and kids during his post-Edie recovery. "I don't want to take it out on them, so I just stay away," he said. "I feel so terrible about screaming at my mother, but I just can't help myself."

And, of course, he spent hours wondering if he should just stop seeing her. "Maybe I should just hire someone to stop in and clean the place every week and make sure she's alive," he said, his voice full of defeat.

Unfortunately, as I explained to him, taking such a step wouldn't resolve the problem. Edie would still be on his mind, still making him angry in absentia, still preying on his psyche like a helpless, desperate animal.

In addition to exploring the roots of his anger, I asked him to ponder why he was still so angry with his mother after all these years. Sure, his childhood had been pretty bad, but he had survived it and thrived. Why was he still as angry as he had been as a teenager?

Perhaps, I suggested, staying angry with Edie served a valuable function for him. After all, rejecting her way of life so energetically had been one of the motivating factors in his becoming a lawyer. And her use of drugs and alcohol, though never serious enough to endanger him, had served as a warning to him. While many of the kids in the neighborhood had gotten sidetracked by drug or alcohol abuse, he had become a responsible, straight-arrow family man with a great career. Was he sure that he wasn't hanging on to the anger because he believed he needed it to keep himself moving toward his goals? Was he afraid of what would happen if he let go, if he began to distance himself from her and allow compassion for her wasted life to replace his anger?

As Paolo learned, it's not easy to relinquish anger. Outrage can be a near-nuclear source of energy, a habit-forming diet that can power you to great achievement—or make the bitter pill of your own failure go down more smoothly. Have you ever said to yourself,

"If it wasn't for them, I wouldn't be having so much trouble with my own life now"? If you have, you may be using your anger toward your parents as an excuse for your own shortcomings.

No wonder, then, that so many of the people I work with are afraid to let that anger go—they have lived with it as an internal combustion engine for most of their lives. And their anger often has another purpose: they use it to punish their parents, to serve as a constant reminder that they were wronged. They wear it like a tattoo, brandishing it with a vengeance whenever their parents step across the invisible line.

It's important that you examine and acknowledge what's going on. Let me clarify this point: It's not surprising that anger is a mixed bag for you. That's the human condition. But until you accept that you may be nursing some underlying resistance to letting go of that anger, you will never be able to work on your future.

The most common reason people have for clinging to anger is fear. Many of the people I work with spent years ignoring and repressing the pain of their childhood, finally reaching the point, often through therapy, where they could show anger. These people feel they have "earned" their rage, and they are afraid that letting it go will cause them to revert to their old state. They worry they will again become a pushover or a simpering fool who allows a parent to manhandle them.

Others fear that letting go of anger will be letting their parents off the hook. They have cast themselves in the role of vengeful god, responsible for keeping their parents in line with thunderbolts of rage.

Some also hold on to their anger as an excuse for not taking control of their own lives. Staying angry with a parent is a good way to avoid accepting responsibility for disappointments.

Each of these scenarios is understandable but counterproductive. Each equates anger with strength, but anger does not have any relationship to strength—just think of Gandhi.

Strength, one of the core values we're striving for in restructuring a relationship with parents, is a matter of self-revelation and self-confidence. It doesn't rest on the hypervigilance of keeping your parents in line with anger or the cheap thrill of "losing it" whenever your parents do something that brings up old hurts.

In fact, strength in such situations derives from the opposite: being able to keep your calm when your parents seek to enrage, control, or infantalize you. Strength is separating your anger toward yourself from your anger toward your parents. Strength means self-control, not denying old anger but putting it aside to live in the present tense, choosing your words and actions free from the recklessness fueled by adrenaline.

LETTING GO: LEARNING TO FORGIVE—OR AT LEAST, ACCEPT

Just as anger is one of the most potent human emotions, forgiveness is one of society's most important values. It is the basis of both Christian and Jewish thought, and an important aspect of Hinduism, Islam, and Confucianism.

But in recent years forgiveness has become controversial because there is much talk of people who have experienced extreme injustice at the hand of monsters who regret nothing. How can we forgive such people? Isn't forgiveness letting them off the hook? Even if the offense you are "prosecuting" was not as severe as textbook "abuse" (the father who lay motionless on the couch through your childhood, the mother who never seemed happy with anything you did, the gruesome pair of parents who put you and your siblings in the line of fire during their battles), isn't it important to keep pressure on the offenders, to never let them forget what they did, especially if they refuse to acknowledge it?

Well, that depends, again, on your goals. If your goal is to maintain your shield of righteous, impenetrable anger at any cost, then embarking on the course of forgiveness will be unthinkable to you.

Forgiving your parents may also mean you have to face the fact that your childhood anguish does not fit comfortably into the category of abuse, as you had always believed. The revelation that you were not abused in a clinical sense can, ironically, be painful. It's hard to give up the idea that your anger may have outlived its usefulness.

EMBRACING EMPATHY

Forgiveness entails developing *empathy,* defined in the dictionary as "the imaginative participation in another's feelings or ideas." Developing empathy for your parents means that you will have to delve into the motives and circumstances surrounding their mistakes. True empathy means getting into another person's head *and* heart to both understand and *feel* that individual's experience. To some people, this smacks of excusing the offender, a concession they are not willing to make.

I don't believe that developing empathy means making excuses for bad behavior. To me, it is a signal that you are on the road to truly becoming an adult who acknowledges the complexity of life. Yes, some childhood offenses are committed by heartless, vicious, evil souls, but in my experience, that accounts for only a tiny fraction of the pain that erupts out of childhood. Mostly, the mistakes adults make are sad and poorly thought out, born of weakness, bad luck, bad judgment, and a legacy of inadequate parenting that may stretch back for generations.

If you have children, reflect for a moment on all the things they are angry with you for now, and those things that you suspect they will castigate you for in the future. Aren't some of their accusations unfair and others totally off base? Even if they are justified, weren't some of those things beyond your control? Even when it comes to those things you do take responsibility for mishandling, would you not wish for their empathy and understanding?

Nonetheless, I am not trying to push forgiveness on you, merely hoping you will start thinking about it. Nor am I suggesting that forgiveness is an easy, overnight cure for whatever ails you. I am well aware that premature "faux" forgiveness can do more damage than good, and I shudder when I think of all the instant-forgiveness clinics and seminars that promote mass forgiveness. Instead, I am suggesting that working toward a mature, well-thought-out acceptance of the past is key to achieving adulthood.

Here are some very fine books on the subjects of anger and forgiveness. Some are quite old, but they are still wonderful—and available on Amazon.com.

> *Making Peace with Your Parents: The Key to Enriching Your Life and All Your Relationships* by Harold Bloomfield with Leonard Felder
>
> *To Forgive Is Human: How to Put Your Past in the Past* by Michael E. McCullough, Steven J. Sandage, and Everett L. Worthington Jr.
>
> *Forgiving and Not Forgiving: Why Sometimes It's Better Not to Forgive* by Jeanne Safer
>
> *When You and Your Mother Can't Be Friends: Resolving the Most Complicated Relationship of Your Life* by Victoria Secunda
>
> *Family Re-Union: Reconnecting Parents and Children in Adulthood* by Robert Kuttner and Sharland Trotter
>
> *You Can Go Home Again: Reconnecting with Your Family* by Monica McGoldrick
>
> *Anger: Wisdom for Cooling the Flames* by Thich Nhat Hanh
>
> *The Dance of Anger: A Woman's Guide to Changing the Patterns of Intimate Relationships* by Harriet Lerner

I also believe passionately in the restorative power of literature. You can learn lessons from great books that no therapist could teach you. Here are some classics about parents, children, and the anger that connects them, books that I read and reread.

Fathers and Sons by Ivan Turgenev
Long Day's Journey into Night by Eugene O'Neill
Death of a Salesman by Arthur Miller
Fierce Attachments: A Memoir by Vivian Gornick

PART II

PRESENT IMPERFECT

• Chapter 5 •

What You Need to Know
about Your Parents

*To be ignorant of what happened before you were born is to
be ever a child. For what is man's lifetime unless the memory
of past events is woven with those of earlier times?*—Cicero

The key to handling your parents is understanding them. Sometimes, especially when they are annoying you, the very idea of that
is repellent. You don't want to understand their motives; you want
to grumble about them, shrug your shoulders helplessly about how
impossible they are, assure yourself that they're crazy.

That's a completely natural reaction, but it's not useful. The only
way for you to improve your chemistry with them is to know what
forces shaped them. Just as you are shaped by your past (the
humiliation of having your heart broken by that achingly beautiful
girl in junior high school, the jubilance of overcoming a learning
disability, the pain of your parents' divorce), so too are they people
with a past every bit as poignant, surprising, and important as
yours. You need to know that history in order to:

- understand that when they try to manipulate, control, or
  demean you, they are often acting out dramas from their
  past that have little to do with you;
- formulate an effective way to deal with them based on
  their vulnerabilities, sore spots, and "points of entry";
- develop empathy for them so you no longer feel threatened by them and can relate to them as an adult;

53

- find common ground that will make it easier for you to create a more meaningful relationship, a relationship of equals.

HOW TO DIG UP THE DIRT

It Can't Hurt to Ask

As you read this, you may be thinking, *I couldn't possibly just come out and ask my mother about her childhood. That would be too embarrassing for her . . . and for me.* But you may be dead wrong. Your parents may be much more open to direct questions than you think. Many of my clients judge their parents' approachability by their own childhood standards of privacy, fear, and taboo. Because their childhood was scary and full of family secrets, they assume that their parents will be shocked if asked about *their* childhood.

But these two things are not necessarily related, especially not in your parents' minds. Many parents enjoy answering questions about their childhood. To begin with, they're getting older, and as the human brain ages, it tends to favor long-term memory. That means your parents may now remember, perhaps fondly, details of their childhood that they thought they had forgotten. Also, if your parents are the types who demand a lot of attention, asking them these questions will help satisfy that need. They probably enjoy talking about themselves (Who doesn't?) and will be flattered by your interest. You may be surprised at how quickly and fully they open up—provided that you deal with them skillfully.

TIPS

- Choose a comfortable setting for this discussion, a place where they will not feel defensive.
- Think about what kind of interaction they handle best— are they better talking "off the cuff," or do they need time to organize their thoughts and words?

- Be gentle.
- Be nonjudgmental.
- If it will help draw them out, be willing to share some of yourself. Major caveat: be sure you don't one-up them, bring up uncomfortable things from your childhood that involve them too directly, or monopolize the conversation. Remember, this is about them, not you.
- Ask follow-up questions. Don't let them drop an intriguing detail and then move on. If your mother says, "It was really hard for us because my parents were so poor and there were six kids," you reply, "That must have been tough. What was the hardest thing you remember about being poor?"
- Gently dig for stories, not just impressions. Specific anecdotes tell the important truths. Your father may say his own father was a disciplinarian, but what did that mean? Try to elicit a story that demonstrates how strict your grandfather was with your father. Remember, the story he chooses to tell is the one that is the "money," the one that will tell you a lot about what discipline—or lack of it—means to your dad.
- Probe for the opposites. If your dad just talks about negatives ("My mother was very cold; she never said she loved me"), ask if there were positives too ("Did you have any surrogate-parent types in your life? Did you get love elsewhere?"). If your mother only speaks in glowing terms ("I was a superstar in high school"), gently ask if there was any downside ("Did you feel a lot pressure to perform?").

How to Get the Ball Rolling

Always begin with a neutral, nonthreatening observation or question. Then steer the conversation toward the topic you're interested in.

Here are a few opening gambits you might adapt to your situation.

- "Dad, I've always been jealous of how well you X (shave, cook, organize the bills . . .). Did your father teach you that?"
- "Mom, I was looking through some old photos of you and Aunt Jean, and you guys looked so cute and happy in your poodle skirts. And Grandma looked so young and proud. Were things as happy for you back then as they look?"
- "You know so much about the Civil War, Dad. Were you interested in it when you were a little kid. No? Then what were you interested in back then? What were you like back then? It's hard for me to imagine. I'd love to have met you then. What were you like as a kid?"

You may find many keys in their childhood. Perhaps you don't have the expertise to analyze all their answers like a trained therapist (*Her mother yelled at her a lot, so that's why she sometimes pulls that martyr crap with me*), but you can reflect on their answers, and that may give you innovative ideas on how to deal with them. Many clients who delve in earnest into their parents' pasts find a cache of unrealized dreams and aspirations: a father who dreamed of being a professional athlete until a knee injury sidelined him forever; a mother who wanted to go to college but wound up pregnant at seventeen. You may think that you're the only one who had your dreams thwarted, but maybe that's not true. Be careful—you may discover that your parents are much more like you than you think.

Here's a good example from my life. My father was a navy pilot during World War II, stationed in the Pacific. After the war, he and two friends wanted to stay in Hawaii and start a small cargo-shipping company, but my mom, who'd been raising my older sister at her parents' home on the mainland, didn't want to move that far. Dad was an easygoing guy and agreed to come back to New Jersey, but I know he always wondered what would have happened if he had stayed in Hawaii. That little company his pals started became one of the biggest in the Pacific Rim.

Disappointment colors people's lives and can have a profound effect on their families. It can be painful to find out about such things, but it's crucial that you do so if you ever hope to see your parents as fully realized beings.

Knowledge of their past will give you empathy for them. You may find that their childhoods were much more similar to yours than you thought, that they echo the chilliness in your youth or the over-powering expressions of concern that made you feel smothered.

Or you may be surprised to find that their impressions of their own childhood are in direct conflict with what you've heard from other family members or what you experienced in watching them deal with your grandparents. (I've had many clients whose parents describe their own childhood as idyllic, though the clients them-selves remember volcanic fights between the parents and the grand-parents.)

This is all grist for the mill of your empathetic imagination. Remember, just as you want to be respected for your memories of childhood, they too are heavily invested in their childhood stories, despite the fact that those memories may not be entirely accurate.

As you explore the past with them, you may even find buried clues that will help you help them get in touch with some of their more tender, vulnerable memories and experiences.

A Father Lost and Found: Jo-Ellen

Jo-Ellen had never had much of a relationship with her stepfather, Kurt, but she was determined to change that. Her mother had mar-ried him in 1990 but had died a few years later. Jo-Ellen, a twenty-eight-year-old artist, missed her mother terribly and desperately wanted to incorporate Kurt into the life of her young son, Harry, who didn't have a grandfather on the other side of the family.

But Kurt, fifty-five, was a distant man who, despite saying he wanted to have a relationship with Harry, seemed terribly uncomfortable with him. Jo-Ellen struggled with the situation because Harry, a sensitive four-year-old, sensed Kurt's coldness and was hurt by his rejection. Jo-Ellen found herself getting angrier and angrier with Kurt.

"But then one day, I took Kurt and my son to the park, and as we sat on the bench watching Harry play, I asked Kurt if it brought back any memories of when he was a kid. He was quiet for a minute, and then he said that he didn't have many fond memories of his childhood. I asked why that was, and he told me that his mother had been a concentration camp survivor and that all he could remember was that everyone treated her like she was fragile glass. He didn't recall being taken care of at all; all his memories were about his father taking care of his mother. I asked him about his own son, David, whom he rarely talked about. He said that he had adored the kid, but that in the divorce, his first wife had moved out of state with David and gradually turned their son against him.

"It struck me that his childhood had been pretty painful, and full of mixed messages. It helped me understand why he found it hard to relate to Harry. And it made me more patient with him."

Eventually, Jo-Ellen began to focus on uncovering the aspects of Kurt that had attracted her mother, instead of his failings. She read books about the Holocaust. She forced herself to meet his chilliness with warmth, sensing that beneath it, he really did want the connection. After all, he had chosen her mother, a live wire if ever there was one, and the couple had been very much in love during their short time together. She decided that Kurt's stony exterior was a defense against getting hurt again; he had, after all, been through a long life full of pain and disappointment, culminating with her mother's premature death. But she was conscious of not overwhelming Kurt with her affection. Instead, she maintained a steady level of calm, welcoming acceptance.

Her approach created a chain reaction. As Harry saw her grow more open to Kurt, he let down his defenses, which, in turn, slowly thawed Kurt. There was no miracle, no overnight catharsis, but over a couple of years, Kurt grew warmer toward Harry, and the two developed a strong bond.

When They Won't Talk

Some parents will not give up the details of their early life. No matter how many ways you try, no matter how gentle you are, they clam up. Don't be discouraged; silence speaks volumes. If your parents are unwilling to discuss their past with you, there is probably a good reason. Perhaps they've blocked it out due to a trauma. They may have been raised to think they were so average —"nothing special"—that there wasn't much worth remembering. It's also possible that they just don't recall that much, that their memory is slipping, and they're too embarrassed to admit it. If any case, their feelings of self-worth are probably pretty stunted, and that's something you should be aware of, because it probably had a lot to do with how they treated you as a child, and how they treat you now.

Parents who won't talk don't let you off the hook, though. There are still ways you can "crack" them, ways you can get some insights into their past.

Talking to Their Friends or Relatives

Yes, it can be awkward to talk about your parents with their friends or siblings. But if you are gentle, and clearly express your motive— genuinely wanting to get to know your parents better—you may find they are very responsive. Chances are that at least one of the older people you ask will be experiencing the glow of improved long-term memory, so they may be able to recall many illuminating details. Even if they were not there at the beginning of your parents' lives, they may have heard stories they are willing to share.

The key is to choose the most approachable friends or relatives, the ones who seem to have both warm feelings for you and an innate understanding of and empathy for your parents. Avoid those friends or relatives who are petty or are having conflicts with *their* kids. Pure motives are very important here. Avoid putting them in the middle of your conflict with your parents, however; opt for a casual, loving exchange.

TIP

If you are able to convey genuine caring, you may even get your parents' friends or relatives to admit that they, too, find annoying the very things that drive you to distraction about your parents. Imagine that!

For my client Aimee, such an exchange led to a revelation that set the tone for reconfiguring her life with her folks. "My mother adores her two brothers, who live in California," she told me. "All my life, I wanted to know if they had any insight into her and if they understood why I found her so difficult sometimes, but I figured that if I ever confided in them, they would be defensive and say that she was perfect and wonderful. But one day when I was visiting them, I made a low-key comment about how she was really getting on my nerves, and they laughed and nodded in total agreement. I was shocked . . . and thrilled. We finally had the discussion I'd always wanted to have. They told me they loved her, but that they had always found her hard to handle. Just hearing that made me better able to deal with her, made me feel less alone."

Photographs and Letters

In many families, there is an old box at the top of someone's closet stuffed with old photographs. These photos can be great conversation starters with your parents and their friends, but if you reach a dead end on that score, the photographs can talk for them. Study old snapshots carefully, and you will see the milieu in which your parents grew up, the way they carried themselves as children, and the distance between them and *their* parents.

When you look at these pictures, keep in mind that families tend to keep the photos they like best, the ones that put them in the best light, so viewing family photos with your parents or just talking about them will enable you to gently find out if things were as rosy as they look in the pictures.

But even if you never get the full picture from these pictures, going through them will give you a greater sense of your parents' humanness. Seeing images of them as children and young adults will remind you that they have their own complicated past to deal with.

Hit the Books

Even if you can't get your hands on photos, you're still not defeated in your detective work. Go to the library and research where your parents came from. No matter what era they grew up in—the Great Depression, World War II, the buttoned-down 1950s, or the swingin' 1960s—the cultural history that swirled around them during their childhood influenced them. Reading about their time can give you great insight into their worldview. You may also find it helpful to look up the books they read, the music that topped the charts in their "day." Not only will that help you understand their orientation, it will give you something to talk about with them or with people who knew them back then.

TIP

You can look up the *New York Times* Best-seller List and the *Billboard* charts on microfilm at most libraries. The Internet is also an invaluable source. You are looking for the books and recordings that were popular in the year your parent was eighteen.

BOILING DOWN YOUR RESEARCH

After all your research is done, on the flip side of your childhood narrative questionnaire, jot down the following:

The three formative conflicts/traumas/disappointments your parent suffered that had nothing to do with you.

1)

2)

3)

The three most important things you learned about your parent's past.

1)

2)

3)

The three things about your parent's past that you think have the most to do with how he or she deals with you today.

1)

2)

3)

Like your personal narrative, these lists should stay, at least metaphorically, in your back pocket. They are not excuses for your parent's behavior today; nor are they intended to fuel your guilt. They are notes to your adult-self, memos to remind you that your parent's behavior today is deeply informed by experiences that took place long before you entered the picture.

Chapter 6

Your Fantasy Parent
Doesn't Live Here Anymore

Liza loved her friend Tara, and she *really* loved Tara's folks. Angelo and Loretta lived in a rambling wisteria-covered house in Santa Barbara just a few blocks from the beach. He was a jovial abstract painter who had recently taken up high-end carpentry; she taught literature at the local university and had a warm smile and a way of making everyone feel smart. They were in their sixties but loved running on the beach, inventing barbecue recipes, and discussing books and politics long into the night. Liza had gone with Tara on a visit to Santa Barbara a couple of years ago, and it was a treasured memory for her.

That's why Liza was so happy when Tara again invited her to come along on another vacation with her parents. But her mood plummeted within hours of the invitation. Instead of savoring memories of her last visit, she could only think of the last time she had flown to Boca Raton to see her own parents, who were as materialistic and judgmental as Tara's parents were artistic and easygoing. And Liza's parents seemed to detest each other. At the beginning of each visit there was, as always, false gaiety—the hugs at the airport, her mother preening in a new outfit—but by the time they reached the condo, her father had found something to pick on her mother about, invariably something petty and mean. When her mother wasn't shooting back insults at her husband, she was brushing the hair out of Liza's eyes and asking her about that nice money manager who'd stopped calling her. "Not that you're not a beautiful girl," Liza's mother said, "but I don't think there's anything wrong with a little Botox."

It went on like that for seventy-two excruciating hours—her father exploiting any opening to demean her mother and her mother prying into Liza's personal life with the doggedness of a federal prosecutor. Liza bore it silently for a couple of days and then exploded, ripping into both her parents. That hadn't solved anything; her mother wept, and her father locked himself in the den.

Why can't my parents be normal? Liza thought. Her mind drifted back to an afternoon in Santa Barbara, when Tara's mother had planted a kiss on her husband's head as he spoke with pride of Tara's younger brother, who was in the Peace Corps. The memory shot through Liza's chest like a bullet. *Why can't my parents be like that?* she thought.

Many of the people I work with spend a lot of time bemoaning their luck-of-the-parent draw. Even if they profess to love their parents, they can't stop dwelling on how different (read: better) their life would have been if their parents had been better educated. Or richer. Or more adventurous. Or less nervous. Or more generous. Or more imaginative. Or more disciplined. Or less depressed. Or, or, or . . . They dream of parents who prefer the cafés of Paris to the faux cafés of Disney World. Parents who kiss passionately in the kitchen. Parents who are like the parents, well, on TV shows from the 1950s.

I hear this complaint from people whose parents are basically well-meaning (if flawed) as often as from those who consider their parents to be downright venal. Having an ideal of this sort is a common, understandable human reaction to unhappiness and frustration, but it is one I would advise you to throttle *right now* because it is poisonous to your relationship with your parents. If you can't accept that your parents will never be the fantasy figures you have concocted, it's futile to try to alter your behavior toward them. If your interactions with them are colored by your fantasies—and your anger over how they have fallen short—you will never be on solid ground. Dealing in a productive way with your parents entails facing *and* accepting who they are.

To look at this from a fresh perspective, consider how your secret (or not-so-secret) expectations can adversely affect your children. Any child-development specialist worth her salt will tell you that nursing an absurdly high benchmark for your child—he will turn from an awkward seven-year-old into a brilliant centerfielder; she will morph from a belligerent slacker into the valedictorian—will undermine your relationship with that child. The child will feel shame because he cannot fulfill your expectations . . . and anger because you don't accept him as he is.

The same goes for your parents. In hanging on to anger about your parents, you are letting yourself get stuck in a common childhood stage that is very painful. Unhappy children often nurse a fantasy that their parents are not *really* their parents, that they were born to another "perfect" couple and then, horribly, left in a wicker basket on the doorstep of the awful people they are now forced to call Mom and Dad.

Children generally outgrow this stage, but some adults desperately cling to a version of it that keeps them in a state of perpetual longing for those perfect parents. Such fantasies provide facile explanations for what has gone wrong in your life ("I wouldn't be such a mess if my parents had been kinder/richer/smarter . . .") and make sense of your social displacement and embarrassment. Blaming your parents for who they are is a seductive way to abrogate *your* responsibilities, but it creates an emotional swamp you will not be able to climb out of.

Accepting who your parents are—*really* are—can be a painful process, but when you do that, you will be ready to make progress in changing your relationship with them. Once you accept them as they are, you can accept that they are not a part of you, that you are wholly separate. Only then will you be free.

1. GETTING REAL

You must first face the fact that other people's perfect parents are not as perfect as you imagine. I can count on one hand the number of "perfect" parents I have dealt with in twenty-five years. Some people idealize their parents, but that is just the flip side of longing for the fantasy parent, another one-dimensional fabrication. Recognizing and accepting imperfections in our parents is the first step in truly growing up.

Tara's parents are a case in point. In Liza's eyes, they represent everything her parents are not: loving, creative, hip, unneurotic. They are iconic figures, taunting her with their unattainable perfection. The truth is that, while enchanting, they are, like the rest of us, deeply flawed, a truth that Liza chose to ignore because it would have undermined her recriminations of her own difficult parents.

I encouraged Liza to ask Tara some probing questions about what their marriage was really like. Tara was extremely forthcoming: since Angelo quit painting full-time, he's been drinking too much, which worries Loretta. And over the years he's had a few bouts of infidelity—he and Loretta had even separated for a couple of years back in the 1990s. Liza thought Tara was the carefree product of perfect parents, but the truth was more complex: Tara had spent three years in therapy trying to reconcile the facade of her parents' marriage with its reality.

2. MOURNING

Letting go of a fantasy is very painful and can make you extremely sad. There are two things to grieve here: that you didn't get the parents you feel would have helped you become who you want to be, and that other people's parents, who you once thought were infallible, are only human.

Sometimes formal mourning helps. In recent years, there have been techniques developed to codify this process. There's no reason why you can't adapt them to this situation. You can draw a picture of your dream parents, either in your mind or on paper, or snip photos from newspapers or magazines that evoke those fantasies. You can name your "rightful" parents with magical, lyrical names and give them the characteristics that you feel would have made all the difference in your life.

If your fantasy parents are real people, it's time to bury them as well. Putting them to rest may entail an actual ceremony, burning those drawings or clippings, perhaps, or lighting a candle in a house of worship. Feel free to cry if it helps; you've nurtured these fantasies for a long time, and letting go of them can be difficult. But bear in mind: you are not saying good-bye to people; you are saying good-bye to your fantasies. What is being laid to rest is a piece of your internal resistance, the part of you that still defines yourself in terms of your childhood and your parents. Saying good-bye to that is liberating and is your pass into the land of the unencumbered.

3. GIVING 'EM THEIR DUE

Now you must draw up a list of your parents' strengths. Most parents, other than the few true monsters, have strengths, but we tend to shove those qualities to the bottom of the barrel. The annoying things that our parents do—and Lordy, there are plenty!—seem writ as large as billboards, whereas their good qualities become invisible to us.

The list that follows presents some attributes you might consider giving your parents credit for. This list is not inclusive by any means. Your parents probably are deficient in many of these qualities but strong in others. No parent is all bad or all good. Remember: conceding that your parents have some strengths doesn't mean you're whitewashing their weaknesses. It simply means that you are growing to recognize your parents as complex and contradictory beings. Check off as many of the following as you can.

My parents:

- Show affection
- Have achieved important things in the face of adversity
- Expect great things from me
- Can be a lot of fun
- Have great taste

- Are proud of me in their own way
- Give me room to breathe
- Are cultured/well read/politically aware
- Stand up for themselves
- Are generous
- Love my kids
- Make few demands of me
- Have a social consciousness
- Have a good sense of humor
- Never give up
- Have dignity and pride
- Are always there for family members
- Take care of themselves
- Put their own needs aside to raise a family
- Want me to be happy

4. CREATING A NEW STORY

Once you've let yourself embrace your parents' strengths, it's time to marry these positive qualities with their history to create a compelling story. Now you must create an alternative narrative for your parents based on truth, not fantasy. Your fantasy parents may have been aristocratic Connecticut Yankees who gave you a trust fund and a set of first-edition Dickens, or groovy Bay Area anarchists, but your real parents have attractive qualities as well. Whether your father was an Armenian file clerk and your mother a midwestern dairy worker or you came from the tough inner city or a bland suburban wasteland, your parents have had a life of tribulation and desire fit for a novel. Get to know them. Listen to their stories. They are living, breathing, evolving entities who, like you, are fighting for survival.

5. GETTING FREE

The final step is declaring that your parents neither define you nor defeat you. In a nutshell, you must attain a state of mind where you don't take your parents personally. Whatever they did or did not do for you in the past is only *one* reason you have become the person you are. Your parents are imperfect, but you can learn as much from their mistakes as from their successes.

If you can bury your fantasy parents and make peace with your real ones, you will be much happier, much healthier, and in a position to take control of your relationship with your parents. And if you do prevail in this struggle, the triumph and the rewards will be yours, not theirs. You didn't make it because you had good parents whom you emulated or bad parents whom you eschewed; you made it because you pushed yourself. Regardless of who your parents are—or are not—you are a wholly different being, responsible only to yourself for what you are and what you will become.

Chapter 7

The Relief of Having
Reasonable Expectations

Expectation, the mere mention of the word, evokes strong feelings in almost everyone. "Here's what I expect from you, and I won't be satisfied with less." "You've disappointed my expectations once again." "I expected more from someone like you." These statements can be scary if you're on the receiving end, and most of us have been at some point in our lives.

But expectations are unavoidable in lots of situations. With kids, for example, abandoning clear expectations for behavior is a recipe for disaster. Oftentimes, children who are not expected to achieve will not do so, and those who are not expected to show respect and civility for others will not develop the empathy and self-control necessary to be happy, productive adults.

Having expectations of children can also be extremely dangerous—when they collide with reality or are influenced by selfish motives. Barraging your infant with flash cards to ensure his readiness for Harvard or giving full reign to your disappointment when your twelve-year-old tells you she wants to quit soccer can do enormous damage in the long run.

The same goes with having unconstructive expectations of your parents, though the damage done in this case is mostly to you. When you let your "perfect parent" fantasy, instead of your pragmatism, dictate your expectations, you doom the enterprise of change to failure.

WELL, THAT'S THE WAY I'VE ALWAYS HEARD IT SHOULD BE: MADISON

Madison had always dreamed of being a mom, and when, at age twenty-nine, she and her husband, Brad, had a gorgeous baby girl, Heather, she was thrilled. Part of her fantasy had always included her mother, Rena, who she hoped would be the perfect grandmother, helping with the housework and taking care of Heather so Madison could go to the gym and start getting her freelance commercial art business back on track. Madison knew that Rena hadn't been a superattentive mom during her childhood—she had been more interested in her career as a landscape architect and had struggled with a failing marriage—but Madison somehow expected this would change when she had Heather. She dreamed that Heather would be the conduit to a sort of closeness that she and Rena had never had. Rena would support her in ways she had not when Madison was growing up; she would morph into the earth grandmother to make up for the past.

But Rena didn't seem to have memorized the script. Instead of becoming the grandma of Madison's dreams, she had a very different concept of her new role. She was charmed by Heather and visited fairly frequently, but saw no reason to be particularly helpful to Madison on the home front. To her way of thinking, this was "her" time, time to enjoy her granddaughter. She didn't want to change the baby's diaper or do the dishes while Madison fed Heather, as Madison had fantasized. She simply wanted to pop in once a week after work. She expected Heather to be diapered and fed so she could play with her for an hour or so and then—leave. She expected Madison to be there throughout her visits with Heather, just in case the child needed anything. She wasn't even very watchful about things like extension cords or kitchen cabinets that could threaten the baby's safety. That's what moms are for, she said gaily.

Madison stewed about the situation, and of course it grew worse. She endlessly planned to confront her mother, picturing how she would weep and tell her mother how much she longed to be close, how she had dreamed that her mother would support her need to reconnect with her career. That would melt her mother's heart and make Rena realize that she had been wrong and selfish. If not, she intended to limit Rena's visits. That would show her. Unless she wanted to really pitch in, she wasn't welcome.

But Madison's game plan was based on expectations that Rena was very unlikely to ever fulfill. Her mother had in fact been very clear about her own needs, boundaries, and desires from the beginning. It wasn't that Rena was unsupportive of Madison's desire to go back to work part-time, but she figured that she had made it on her own back when it was much tougher for women, so why couldn't Madison? She simply didn't see herself as a child-care alternative. She adored the baby but, after raising four kids herself in the midst of molding a career, believed it was her job to enjoy her grandchild, not look after her. Her own mother hadn't helped at all with the kids, hadn't even been much interested in seeing them. What Madison saw as selfishness, Rena saw as healthy self-possession. Compared to her own mother, in her mind she was an A-1 grandma and a good role model for Heather of an independent woman.

No amount of pouting or heart-rending sobs would change things, as I explained to Madison. The only constructive course of action was to start to have more realistic expectations of her mother. It was very painful; she would have to come to grips with the fact that her mother would never be the earth mother of her fantasy. "I thought I had dealt with that disappointment in college, realizing that I had always felt cheated because we weren't close, but having Heather just kicked all that up again."

Once she readjusted her expectations, however, she came up with a more practical approach: she hired a teenager to baby-sit one afternoon a week when Rena came over. That way, Madison was able to work on her art without worrying that the baby wouldn't be minded. She didn't need a high-priced sitter—Rena was there, after all—just a youngster to make sure Heather wouldn't get hurt. In fact, Rena was so happy with the solution that she split the tab for the sitter. Free of the tension she had sensed from Madison, she upped her visits to twice a week.

No; Heather didn't wind up being the conduit to a fabulous new mother-daughter bond, but once Madison stopped dwelling on her unrealistic expectations of her mother, she was able to focus more on the real joy in her life: planting kisses on Heather's soft curls.

No, Rena never gave her the grandmotherly "payback" Madison had dreamed of to make up for Madison's less-than-idyllic childhood, but, little by little, Madison was able to appreciate some of the unexpected joy of Rena *not* being a supergrandma. For instance, unlike some of her friends, she never had to worry that Heather preferred her mother to her, nor did she have to deal with a mother who always thought she knew the best child-rearing techniques. She herself could be the wonderful, engaged mother Rena was never interesting in being, and that gave her enormous satisfaction. For her part, Heather seemed to accept the situation gleefully, enjoying both her mother's style and her grandmother's style.

It was not the storybook ending that Madison had once expected, but it took the pressure off the two women's relationship, which automatically made it more satisfying—as well as taking little Heather out of the equation. Making her daughter a pawn in her relationship with her mother would have passed on the legacy of unfair expectation, a move that Madison eventually realized was not healthy for anyone.

Chapter 8

The Urge to Merge—
and the Need to Diverge

The deep psychological connection between us and our parents may be the topic of a thousand textbooks, but it is still a great mystery. It begins with birth—the helpless infant cries, gets picked up and fed by its mother—and snakes through countless interactions for the rest of our lives. We want closeness; we want distance. We slam the door; we pray there will be a knock on it. We crave unconditional understanding; we find ourselves unable to give the same.

Let's face it, we will never, none of us, ever fully figure out the bond with our parents. But that doesn't mean we can't better understand the basic dynamic at work. Without that understanding, the mystery tends to overwhelm us, whether we are fifteen or fifty. Understanding doesn't solve everything, and it doesn't preclude the need to change the aspects of our parental relationships that are standing in the way of our happiness, but it makes our path a good bit clearer.

Yes, it starts with a baby. You. As an infant, you are completely dependent on your mother for food and nurture. It is, as Victoria Secunda writes in *When You and Your Mother Can't Be Friends,* "the most perfect of unions, every need met—shelter, protection, love, food—all suffused by physical closeness to mother, the warmth and comfort of her skin, the soothing reassurance of her voice, her adoring smile and touch."

Despite their helplessness, babies are, by definition, narcissistic creatures. They sense no boundaries between their caregiver and themselves and believe that their cries magically make their parents appear. They are little "need machines," forcing the world to conform to their requirements for survival.

The process of growth and development represents a long cast-out-of-Eden arc away from perfect babyhood. As children grow, they begin to want, at least partially, to separate from their parents. But they also desperately want to return to the safety of the womb. If the parents are capable, they realize that readying the child for this independence is their most important job.

It's a complicated process. Talented parents know how to mix love and security with risk and exploration. Such a mix enables most children to internalize the message, creating in their own minds a "good mother" who can allow them to strike out in the world with self-confidence.

But some parents don't have the right stuff to promote healthy separation. They may be insecure due to their own childhood experiences, terrified of being left alone, or perhaps just clueless. And some children are better at separation than others by temperament, seemingly born fearless; others are, from infanthood, desperately afraid to let go.

Difficulties in separation underpin much of the unhappiness I see in the people I work with. They struggle fiercely for a strong sense of self because they never adequately separated from their parents. Fortunately, it's never too late to separate. In a nutshell, that is the goal of this book, the goal of a hefty majority of the therapy I do. No matter how limited your parents were or how hard your childhood was, it is now up to you to repair the damage and create a functioning whole, independent of your parents' needs, projections, and insecurities.

For many of us, paradoxically, this involves taking control of the very relationship that has kept us in an uncomfortable box: our relationship with our parents. For years it has been a psychological version of Mr. Toad's Wild Ride because you had no goal, no theme for making changes. Now you have a litmus test for all your decisions: Does what you are doing—or plan to do—help you build a separate entity? If not, don't do it.

• Chapter 9 •

You Say You Want a Revolution. But Are You Your Own Worst Enemy?

Many of the people I work with have spent years blaming their parents for not "letting" them separate—for crowding them, for fussing over them, for demanding too much of them. Often these people don't make real progress on this front until they realize that their most powerful enemy is their own resistance to separation. They say they crave freedom, but they do plenty to sabotage their efforts to get it. They go toe-to-toe with their parents time after time, often provoking the conflicts, but in the end they always give up, sometimes with a theatrical sigh, telling themselves that the solution is worse than the problem. Or they take the role of the martyr, bemoaning their emotional enslavement but, deep down, thinking that they look pretty good in a hair shirt.

The fact is, overlinked parent-child relationships are not without their comforts, and they are sometimes hard to give up, even when you know that those comforts eventually bite you in the behind.

Why? To begin with, there is the comfort of familiarity. We may be in a destructive pattern with our parents, but it is one we know very well and may prefer to the scary thought of forging an independent life. Second, our parents offer pleasure and pain, often in the same package. They dole out compliments, money, and approval while withholding love, limiting our independence, and manipulating us for their own needs. In a world of doubts, insecurities, competition, and financial stress, our parents sometimes offer a refuge, albeit with strings attached. Even the most mature among us sometimes want to be taken care of, want to escape back to the nurture of the nest—even when we know that nest is lined with barbed wire.

Another tendency that contributes to this push-pull is the repetition compulsion, which Freud wrote about. Although you'd think that people would run away from such childhood trauma as being held too tightly and not being allowed to establish an independent self, the opposite tends to be true. Freud believed that we repeat those patterns as adults, unconsciously, because when we were childen we were, by definition, passive; now, as adults, we initiate the same conflict over and over to convince ourselves that at least we are in control, even if the outcome is unpleasant.

There is no shame in wanting both to separate and to stay merged. It's an eternal dilemma for many of us. Freud believed that we could stop the repetition compulsion merely by understanding the original trauma, but many people have found that that "ah-ha" moment is not enough. Even after they understand how a lack of separation made them feel powerless as a child, they still, as adults, find themselves trapped in a battle of internal resistance.

In my mind, there's only one way to truly reconcile the conflict: you must stop fighting it. There is no magic revelation that will make it go away. Instead, you must learn to tolerate it, to look your resistance in the eye, acknowledge that it will probably linger, and yet choose strength and, ultimately, freedom.

How? Your best defense against your own resistance to change is a permanently heightened awareness. Once you get into the habit of actively acknowledging the duality of your feelings, you will start to get comfortable with these contradictory impulses instead of running from them. Just because your feelings are in conflict doesn't mean you have to fold and repeat your usual negative behavior patterns. These are, after all, just feelings. I don't believe this is truly a compulsion, as Freud did. You aren't Son of Sam with an imaginary evil dog whispering orders in your ear that you must obey. You are free.

When you feel such conflicts arising—by now you know the signs—stop cold and ask yourself these questions:

- What will I gain if I change this behavior? What do I fear losing?
- Why is my usual response (giving in, stewing with anger, just letting things go) "easier"?
- Are my actions in these situations in turn making it difficult for my parent to change? Is there any level on which I might actually want that?
- Is the "devil I do know" really better than the "devil I don't know"?
- Have I already jumped ahead in my head to the part where I say to myself, "See, she always does this, she'll never change"?

A bit of good news about meeting resistance head on: the first time is the hardest. Once you start confronting, accepting, and, finally, combating your resistance, the new patterns come more easily and feel more natural. Deciding to consciously stop repressing your conflicting feelings will free up energy to make real changes.

Resistance is like having your arm in a sling. It's not healthy to ignore that it's there, yet you can't let it keep you from dancing.

• Chapter 10 •

Seeking a Second Opinion

Perhaps you are confident that you see your dynamic with your parents through a clear lens, but remember: parent-child chemistry is loaded with baggage that can obscure your judgment. I often spend many, many sessions with a frustrated client, hearing the step-by-step details of how he and his mother interact, but when I finally get the two of them in my office together, I see that the son has forgotten to mention—or may not see—many important nuances of their relationship.

Misha, a forty-nine-year-old, highly successful architect, spent a great deal of time complaining that his mother was pushy and intrusive. He told me the sorts of things she would do: call him six times a day, show up at his office at the end of the day because "she was in the neighborhood," buy him virtually an entire wardrobe each Christmas.

But he never mentioned to me what I saw immediately when his mother came into the room: that she was extremely beautiful, only seventeen years older than he, and a compulsive talker. She literally couldn't shut up, and her agony about this disability—I call it that because her compulsive talking clearly was beyond her control—was evident. There were moments when I could see she was struggling to be quiet, but whatever psychological or physiological condition she was suffering from made that impossible.

Misha was clearly mortified by her, especially when she rattled on, interrupting him constantly. His response, which I realized once I saw her was the backbone of how they related to each other, was to scream "Mother!" in a voice straight of the movie *Psycho*.

When Misha and I talked later, he was shocked to hear an outsider's take. He hadn't thought much about her beauty, or about how young and inexperienced she was when she gave birth to him. Nor had he thought of how having such a gorgeous, young mother who was terribly overinvolved with him might have affected him. The most important thing he had missed, though, was how useless his cries of "Mother!" were as a way to modify her behavior, how it only made her prattle on more intensely. Worse, by responding to her in that way, he was slipping back into childlike patterns.

Misha benefited enormously from getting a second opinion (let's call it an "S.O." for brevity's sake). Understanding why he had such a strong visceral reaction to his mother and why she had caused him so much sexual embarrassment over the years enabled him to tackle some of the problems he was having with women. Seeing his mother less often and bringing along a friend also alleviated the tension. Eventually, he even developed a set of behaviors that brought his mother's disability under control when he was around. Instead of slipping into his Norman Bates imitation when his mother began to blabber, he would put his hands on hers with a moderate amount of pressure and say, "Breathe with me, Mom." They would breathe deeply together for several moments, which would release her, at least for a while, from her compulsion to chatter.

I acted as Misha's S.O., but help like this doesn't have to come from a therapist. Sure, it's great if you can get your parent to come to therapy with you for a session or two, but that can be difficult to arrange. A smart, observant, well-meaning friend can be just as effective.

Now I know what you're probably thinking: *I can't subject a friend to this. It's too embarrassing. Besides, why would any of my friends care about my problems with my parents?* However, in my experience, you are wrong. In fact, when clients do this—when they think seriously about which friend would be most honest and helpful and then ask the friend to perhaps have lunch with them and their parent—they are universally met with kindness . . . and plenty of enthusiasm. For the most part, friends love to meet the parents of people they care about. It helps them achieve intimacy and fill in a few blanks.

Besides, it is very flattering to be asked to help. If you've ever sat on a jury, you know that jurors, a ragtag group of citizens of all stripes, often evolve into human beings of enormous stature the moment they are charged with deciding a case. No matter who they are, they invest the deliberation with great dignity and compassion. It's human nature to rise to such challenges. So consider how someone you respect and trust will feel if you ask him or her to help; it's likely this individual will put a great deal of energy into helping you.

HOW TO CHOOSE THE RIGHT PERSON

The most important criteria are that the person be perceptive, honest, and free of prejudice. You are, after all, trying to get an unbiased take, not just have your own view reinforced. So don't choose a best buddy who still bears wounds from being beaten by her parents, or a needy soul who seeks your approval and will do anything to make you happy. And be careful about asking the person to whom you have complained bitterly about your parent for the past several years; he may have a hard time being objective after all he has heard.

Choose someone tough but loving. Someone who you know has the courage to say things that people (read: you) don't want to hear.

This is why my client Cassandra chose her friend Keisha to meet her mother, a chronic worrier who makes Cassandra crazy: "Keisha's a coworker, but we also have a solid relationship outside the office. She's not my best friend and her background is a little rougher than mine, but that's one of the reasons I chose her. She isn't like Lena, who thinks of me as a little sister, and she isn't like Anton, who had very distant parents whom he's really down on.

"Keisha is the sane one in the office, the one who never blows things out of proportion and yet doesn't let anyone get away with that Emperor's New Clothes stuff. She's the one I go to when I don't trust my own reactions. She's never afraid to tell me—or anyone—the unvarnished truth, but she isn't a grandstander; she makes the truth go down easily. She calls things like she sees them, and she has a way of looking at problems productively. She's not a drama queen. And when she talks about her own mother, who sounds like no day at the beach, she seems to have a healthy perspective on it. She stands up for herself but still gets laughs out of it."

ESTABLISHING THE GROUND RULES

Tell your S.O. that what you are trying to figure out is whether you are overreacting to your parents—or underreacting. Make it clear that you want complete honesty. You want insights into your own behavior as well: Do you stiffen when you are with your parents? Is your tone shrill? Do you make things worse? Set your parent up? Cringe at the slightest criticism? Do you get a faraway look in your eye or nod vaguely as your parent starts that annoying riff?

Just as I advised you in the section about your past to write your personal narrative as though you were an alien reporting in to your high commander, you should give the same advice to your S.O. Tell him not to spare your feelings or cut your mom a break. You are looking for insights that you have missed because you are too close to the situation.

SETTING UP THE MEETING

The idea is to get your parents—and you—to be as relaxed and natural as possible. You don't want to put your parents in a situation that will make them wary; it will either exaggerate their behavior or mask it. The same goes for you; you must be committed to letting your S.O. experience the actual dynamic that exists with you and your parents.

It may take more than one meeting with your S.O. to get everyone to be themselves, but trust that your friend will be patient. Usually, it doesn't take that much time for the old patterns to surface.

If it's more comfortable for your parents, you might consider having more than one friend with you to dilute the tension and take the attention off your S.O. You could have a dinner party and invite your parents, or if you regularly have dinner at your parents' place, ask them if you can bring a friend. You could invite your parent to lunch and have a friend or coworker join you. Perhaps there's an office event or a celebration to which you can invite your parents and your S.O. Or try an afternoon at the mall. Elaborate ruses usually backfire, but you can always try a "chance" meeting with your parent and your S.O. if that is likely to bring out the most natural reaction from your parent.

GREASING THE WHEELS

Loosening everybody up is a good idea. And there's nothing wrong with a bit of alcohol, provided no one has issues related to it. Suggest a glass of wine, a cocktail, or a beer. Good food can also be an icebreaker. But make sure you are not creating an artificially comfortable setting in which your parents are not themselves; the same goes for you. You want everyone to feel comfortable enough to act naturally.

WHAT TO DO IF YOUR PARENTS LIVE FAR AWAY OR THEY ARE UNCOMFORTABLE WITH STRANGERS

Thank goodness for tape recorders. Remember the one you used for your guilt exercise? Well, pull it out again and tape a phone conversation with your troublesome parent. You can also use a "pickup," sold in most electronic stores. It's a small, inexpensive suction cup that plugs into the back of your phone and lets you record your conversations. Or use your answering machine to tape.

A benefit to taping versus a face-to-face meeting is that your father or mother will not be on his or her best behavior, trying to impress your S.O. Be sensitive to the time that you are calling. Has your mother just woken up? Is your father just coming in the door or on his way out? Be cautious about goading your parent into unusually bad behavior or smoothing things over because you are embarrassed, knowing your S.O. will hear the tape. You must be committed to the truth.

GETTING FEEDBACK FROM YOUR S.O.

After meeting with your folks or hearing the tape recording, your S.O. can give you feedback by filling this questionnaire.

1. What "hit" you most about my mother/father/both?
2. Did I prepare you for that?
3. How would describe my parent?
4. What was the best thing(s) about the way we interact?
5. What was the most negative thing(s)?
6. Did I contribute to the bad vibe? How?
7. How did my parent react/feel during the interaction?
8. Did the way we get along remind you of any character on TV or in the movies?
9. Was my tone of voice positive or defensive?
10. What about my body language? (Of course, this is not evident from a tape.)

11. Did I seem genuinely engaged?

12. Did you feel I was sending mixed messages?

Second opinions are not binding. They are not a setup to make you feel like you are being too hard—or too easy—on your parents. They are just a great way to get valuable information that will help you formulate a game plan.

Remember: the closer you can get to assessing your interactions with your parents calmly and objectively, the more successful you will be in altering your behavior in ways that will promote a more adult dynamic.

• Chapter 11 •

Button Up Your Panic Buttons

Unfortunately, we're all acquainted with the uncomfortable feeling of having our buttons pushed. Whether it's the boss shooting us a sharp look across the table at a meeting, the kids disrespecting us in front of someone we're trying to make a good impression on, or the rival at work telling us how much better his car/kid/house/marriage/life is than ours, the physiological reactions are all too familiar to most of us: heat rising from the collar, a vise grip squeezing our temples, a fireball of rage and shame and inadequacy and injustice blazing in the pit of the stomach.

It's ten times worse when it's our parents pushing those buttons. They occupy a special place in our pantheon of irritation and outrage. For some reason, we cannot process their transgressions without subjecting ourselves to an inordinate amount of suffering—either in silence or by expressing ourselves loudly and angrily.

Their transgressions set off a chain of events that seems impossible to stop. The sweaty brow, the itchy palms, the clenched jaw: all these things are merely precursors of the inevitable feelings of anger, guilt, frustration, fear, intimidation, and humiliation, right? Then—pow!—comes the yelling, the stalking off, the wall of silence that envelops you.

"'You pushy, manipulative, tyrannical scum . . .'
Scratch that. 'Dear Mom and Dad . . .'"

You probably think that as soon as this cycle starts, all is lost; that there's no derailing this train, that you have to ride it into the wall. You think it's like a law of physics: your reactions are pre-ordained and unchangeable. Your folks bait you; you react. Boom. It seems as immutable as the sun rising each morning in the east.

The reason it seems impossible to change this dance is because the feelings our parents trigger are very deep and primal, hard-wired into our emotional makeup. And, consequently, our reactions are often unconscious.

But what if you could sever the age-old connection between the moment when your parents push those buttons and the moment you process their actions as irritation, threat, offense, and manipulation? What if instead of completing the destructive cycle of action and reaction, you were able to insert a step that changed the whole equation? What if there was another way to interpret your parents' provocation, a way that would short-circuit your negative reactions?

What I am suggesting is this: at the moment when those visceral, physical changes kick in, you consider them as *warning signs.*

They are your body's way of telling you that you are under siege. They are a good thing, a tool that can work for you as reliably as a fire alarm. Nothing more. They need not be taken as a signal that you are out of control; with a little work, they can be a signal that you are *in* control.

Just as you can touch the stove for a split second and pull your hand away before you are badly burned, or know to turn around and exit a dark alley when your instinct tells you it's unsafe, so can you learn to reinterpret your parents' provocations in a way that will protect you, will make you feel strong instead of weak. If you can begin to think of those physical signals your body is sending you as an early-warning system, you will no longer be caught in a cycle of rage and despair you have no control over.

When you let your reflexive responses dictate your reactions, you will, without fail, be stuck on the treadmill. But when you are able to carve out a small, calm space for yourself between your parents' provocations and your response to them, you will be able to deal with them in a way that will get you where you want to be, not where your parents are dragging you.

This pause, this space between their provocation and your response, may be short—even momentary—but it is crucial. It's within these few fleeting seconds that your efforts to rework your relationship with your parents will truly be born. There's a great deal that must be accomplished in this small space of time, so you'll need a step-by-step plan that's easy enough for you to adapt to a variety of circumstances. At first, these steps may take more time than is "natural" (be prepared for a few awkward silences when you first put this plan into action), but as you train yourself to detach your parents' provocation from your instinctual response, you will be able to go through the steps more quickly. Soon this new pattern will become second nature, supplanting your original, destructive interaction. To the button pusher, the change will be subtle, but to you it will be profound.

Your old pattern:

1. Your mother makes a provocative statement.
2. Your physiological signals kick in.
3. You respond to those signs instinctually (yelling, freezing up, striking out with a nasty comment, slamming down the phone).
4. Your mother makes things worse (yells back, shuts down, counters with an even nastier comment, redials your number furiously).

Your new pattern:

Step 1. You spot the warning signs that tell you your mother is about to initiate a conflict.
Step 2. Your mother makes a provocative statement.
Step 3. Your physiological signals kick in.
Step 4. You acknowledge them silently and interpret them as a call to action.
Step 5. You analyze what your mother wants and why.
Step 6. You decide what the productive response is.
Step 7. You make that response.
Step 8. You move on to neutral territory.

WALKING ON THE WRONG SIDE OF THE STREET: KEIKO

"My mother and I get along pretty well, but once a week or so she blindsides me," said Keiko, a thirty-five-year-old brand manager for a liquor company. "There we are, having a pleasant conversation, maybe over lunch or as we're walking up the street, and suddenly, the whole feel of the conversation shifts. Suddenly, she's acting like everything I do is wrong—my attitude, my clothes, my work ethic. I know it's nonsense, that I have a great career, that I have a good relationship with my boyfriend, but as soon as she pushes that button, I go numb. I'm walking and breathing, but I can't feel a thing. And she talks until she runs out of gas—and until I can hear my heart beating like a drum in my chest. It takes me an hour afterward to get over it."

To alter this pattern, I told Keiko she had to do a better job of recognizing what was actually happening with her mother, Renee. She needed to raise her awareness level. During your next conversation, I instructed her, become superaware of how the dynamic builds. Don't focus solely on the moment the conflict erupts, I told her, but several minutes before, when the warning signs kick in. Parents generally telegraph that they are about to push your buttons. Such incidents are usually preceded by a "setup," a predictable series of actions that culminate in a final statement or question that sends you over the edge. Typically, such a setup includes indicators such as raised eyebrows, a change in tone of voice, long pauses, throat-clearing, the reiteration of meaningless phrases ("hmmmm" and "my, my" are popular). These are signs that your parent is about to move in for the kill.

A week later, Keiko reported back: "We were coming out of a Starbucks one afternoon, and I was telling my mother about work. Talking about my boss and how she had a tendency to be very nitpicky, and how all of us in the office deal with it. And then I saw it! I saw the change! The smile faded from her lips, and her face got really tense. She broke eye contact and started looking straight ahead. And then she started grilling me, acting as though it was *my* fault my boss was so picky, maybe it was what I was doing, and maybe I wasn't applying myself at work."

"Does talking about your job always set her off?" I asked. "Is that the subject that starts the pattern?"

"No, that's what's confusing; sometimes it's when I'm talking about guys and dating, or dealing with my friends."

"Is there a link somewhere? Think back on the last three times you two went at it—what sort of point were you making at the time?"

Keiko thought about it for a moment. "Well," she began slowly,

"I was being offhand about other people criticizing me, I guess. Once I was talking about my boyfriend, Lionel, how he bugs me for not caring about housekeeping and how I don't take it seriously, and she started in on me about how maybe I *should* care, maybe he had a point, that if I wanted to keep a guy I'd have to pay more attention, that I was careless, et cetera.

"Another time I was talking about my friend Ivanya, how she always dresses so perfectly and how she ribs me about being a slob, and my mother got that same look and then started in with how I don't care about my appearance, how I wear jeans too much. She just went off on me."

"And her rant is always preceded by the same set of physical changes on her part?" I asked.

"Yeah," she said, "I guess it is—that suddenly blank-slate face."

Having identified the warning signs (step 1) and prepared herself for the provocative statement (step 2) that set off a set of physiological responses (step 3), Keiko was ready for step 4, acknowledging these responses.

"The reaction starts in my fingers," she said, recalling how she felt as the conversation got tense outside Starbucks that afternoon. "It's a cold, numb feeling that travels up my arm. Then I start to hear a ringing in my ears. Her voice gets kind of echoey. Then I feel kind of like I'm shrinking. Like I'm a mute. Like I'm disappearing. It's the worst feeling in the world."

I urged Keiko to adjust her thinking a bit. "It may feel like you're disappearing, but I read it differently. For you, that numbness is as strong a sign as a whooping siren. It's the unique feature of your personal alarm system."

Keiko understood that letting those involuntary physiological effects flow through her was the part she needed to work on, so we made a list of actions that might help:

- controlled breathing;
- unclenching clenched fists;

- opening the chest by squeezing her shoulder blades together;
- visualizing a heat source deep within the body that is warming up all the appendages.

A few weeks later, Keiko returned with a progress report: on a sunny afternoon in the park, Renee had started in on her about her boss again, saying that "as a human resources person," she could tell that Keiko was "sloughing off."

"I totally saw it coming this time," said Keiko. "So I was ready. When the numbness started, I thought of the wood stove in my parents' summer cottage, how if you sit by it, the soft heat just sort of consumes you, and the smell of the hickory smoke fills your lungs."

Keiko says this worked for a while, but Renee continued to harp, which eventually broke down Keiko's defenses, but it wasn't nearly as bad as usual.

With the image of the warm fire working for her, we moved on to the next step. To get out of such situations unharmed, she needed a better set of responses to short-circuit her mother's criticism. That meant she would need to understand where her mother was coming from (step 5).

"My mother is really very insecure, I think," she said. "She's supersensitive to any criticism and always thinks everything is her fault." She reflected on her mother's childhood narrative: "Her own mom really hammered her, told her she was lazy and untalented and that no guy would want her, and I think she really believes it deep down. I think that whenever I mention that someone is giving me a hard time, she assumes that I deserve it, just like she assumes she deserves it. Consciously, she thinks I'm great, and most of the time she acts that way, but any mention of me being criticized really triggers her insecurity. Even though she knows that I have a great career and a good relationship with a guy who values me, she starts to freak out if I suggest, even jokingly, that anyone is judging me. At that moment, she sees me as an extension of her, I guess.

And I get numb because for that moment, at least, I worry that she's right, that I am failing. I know it's not the truth, but I've got my own insecurities. Mostly they're under control, but she gets to me. She makes them worse."

To move on to step 6—deciding on a productive response—I suggested Keiko try some reassurance with her mother. This tactic might quiet her mother's inner dialogue as well as make her mother understand that Keiko didn't share her self-doubt. Acknowledging her mother's insecurities might allay them somewhat; following that acknowledgment with a strong statement about how Keiko was a separate person would be a sign that she would not allow her mother to project those fears onto her. At the same time, such a statement would strengthen Keiko's own resolve not to be paralyzed by her mother's fears.

Keiko came back a few weeks later and told me: "My mother and I were shopping, and I found a blouse I really liked. As I was deciding whether to buy it, I told her I vaguely remembered that I had one sort of like it in my closet. I joked that Lionel says I'm such a pack rat and so forgetful that there could be a chest of gold doubloons in the back of my closet and I wouldn't know it, and—boom!—I saw 'the Look.' Then she said, 'Well you are a terrible pack rat, but maybe Lionel was trying to tell you that you're a spendthrift. Men get really worried about that kind of thing.' She started pushing every button she could get her hands on, but instead of letting the freeze go through me, I visualized the wood stove again and that really calmed me.

"Then I interrupted her by putting my hand on her shoulder. I said, 'Mom, there's no need to worry that Lionel is criticizing me. He was only expressing fondness—that is part of how we interact. I know you were criticized a lot as a kid, so you're really worried when anyone criticizes me and you're just trying to protect me, but the criticism you got as a kid was wrong. You didn't deserve it. There wasn't any need for you to doubt yourself, and there's no need for me to doubt myself. How about this? If I mention that someone criticized me and you get worried that the criticism is justified, just ask me if I'm as worried about it as you are. I promise I'll tell you if I'm worried. OK?" Keiko had to ask twice if her mother was OK with it, but Renee finally said yes.

A few days later, a similar situation cropped up. Keiko mentioned to her mother that Ivanya called her a stick-in-the-mud for not going to a party, and Renee suggested that maybe Keiko was antisocial, which was a "good way to lose friends." But Keiko knew what to do as soon as her mother pushed that button.

"Mom, remember our deal? If it worries you that someone criticized me, you promised to first ask me if it worried me as well, instead of assuming they have a point. Now I'll pretend you did ask, and here's my response: No, I'm not worried about losing friends because I didn't go out to the party. Ivanya and I are very close; she was just trying to goad me into partying. She wasn't criticizing me. She loves me. And I love you. Now let's get a coffee and enjoy the rest of our day together."

• Chapter 12 •

Keeping Your Eye on the Prize

We all love being right. Even better, we love being told we're right (preferably loudly and within earshot of people we hope to impress). We love it when others realize we are right and they are humbled. Conversely, and somewhat perversely, we derive a hit of pleasurable righteous indignation in knowing we are being dealt with unfairly. One of our deepest (and more self-destructive) fantasies is that those who have wronged us will realize how unfair they have been and beg our forgiveness. "You were right," they will say, eyes brimming with tears, shoulders slumped in humiliated resignation. "Can you ever forgive me?"

Well, dream on. As I said, this is a fantasy. Ain't gonna happen. And in no part of your life is that scenario less likely to occur than when dealing with your parents. No matter how sure you are that they are in the wrong, no matter how well documented the litany of their offenses, the likelihood that they will one day realize that they have treated you unfairly and, after confessing all this tearfully, will work to change their behavior is very, very small.

Face it—too much of their self-image is on the line for that to happen, not to mention that they are already struggling to face (or ignore) the fact that you are no longer a child they can control. Add to that the scary knowledge that their life is drawing to an end, and you've got to admit they have a lot going on.

Plus, they don't think they're wrong. In fact, they don't think they've ever been wrong! And you can't shake them from that position with dynamite. While you are working frantically to get them to admit they are all wrong, they are trying just as hard to get you to admit that *you* are wrong. You may as well be trying to open a door by pushing on it from opposites sides. It isn't going to open, no matter how hard each of you pushes. And, the harder you push, the more likely it is that one or both of you will get hurt.

Nevertheless, many of us have an irresistible urge to prove our parents wrong—at any cost. We argue the same points over and over, and they counter in the same nonsensical way over and over. That's why fights escalate, why grudges linger, why we end up moaning that "nothing ever changes."

If you truly want to break this cycle, you will have to learn that proving you are right—even if you could do it with graphs and charts and expert witnesses—means nothing. Spending all that time on such a futile activity only distracts you from what you're here to do, which is to create a new, productive relationship with your parents. Your goal is to find alternate behaviors and mind-sets that will illicit reactions from them that will, in turn, enable you to deal more comfortably, humanely, and kindly with them while maintaining appropriate boundaries. As I said earlier, it's up to you to be the adult.

To do that, you must keep your eyes on the prize. By that I mean you must focus on the goal at hand: changing your behavior and reactions. If you get distracted by your need to be right, you will only wind up frustrated and angry, and back on the treadmill. The prize is *not* that moment of revelation when your parents suddenly see that they have misjudged you or imposed upon you or unfairly acted the martyrs or abused you all these years. The prize is inching ever closer to an adult relationship with your parents.

LOOK, DAD, NO ARGUMENT: KENNETH

Kenneth's father, Larry, was a former jock who had wanted to go to law school but instead wound up in a factory job to support his three kids. Kenneth was the oldest, the only boy, and also a jock. He managed to make it to college on a tennis scholarship and later flew through law school. Larry never told his son he was proud of these achievements, but Kenneth just assumed this was the case. He knew his father wasn't a demonstrative guy, but that was OK. What Kenneth couldn't figure out was why the conflict between them was out of control. Shouldn't his dad be beaming with pride over his accomplishments?

Kenneth felt that his dad continually set them on a collision course, almost as if he were picking a fight. No matter what the subject, Larry knew better. Once, when Kenneth took his parents out for a fancy dinner for their anniversary, the conversation turned to a recent U.S. Supreme Court ruling that had been on the front pages. Things were going well until Larry complained that "Supreme Court Justice Ashcroft" wasn't doing enough about terrorists. Kennth said, "Dad, you mean attorney general. Ashcroft is the attorney general." Kenneth was stunned when his father argued with him. "Dad, I'm a lawyer," Kenneth said with a chuckle. "Trust me on this one." But Larry wouldn't budge. Finally, out of frustration, Kenneth raised his voice. "Dad, you don't have a damn idea what you're talking about." He even got a passerby to confirm that he was right, but his father stuck to his guns. They finally dropped the topic, but Larry sulked for the rest of the evening.

"What was I supposed to do?" Kenneth asked me later, still fuming. "Pretend he was right? I refuse to patronize him." I asked him to think about his father's narrative and how it overlapped with his own. His father was a competitive, immature guy struggling with inner conflict: he was proud of his son and, at the same time, envious. After all, his son was a handsome, successful corporate lawyer.

He was sixty-four, overweight, and miserable in a blue-collar job. He might even be borderline depressed.

"I'm not suggesting you pretend he's right when he's wrong," I told Kenneth, "but you should realize that there are less confrontational ways to deal with him, ways that take into account that he's coming into the situation a bit defensive. Knowing his narrative, you might assume that, unconsciously, he wants to provoke you, like an old stag challenging a young buck. You don't have to buy into that."

The first thing I told Kenneth to do when his father pushes those buttons is to follow the protocol from chapter 11. Acknowledge the physiological reponses. Note that heat is rising from your collar and that your hands—already balled into fists—are starting to itch. Realize that these are warning signs, red flags that tell you to slow down your breathing and switch from emotional energy to adult control. Remind yourself that your father is reacting this way because he's threatened.

Also remind yourself of your main goal: resolving such conflicts in a strategic manner that will satisfy your desire to have a calmer, more adult relationship with him. Even if he's going to act like a child, it's your responsibility to make sure that cooler heads prevail.

For starters, I told him, breathe slowly and more deeply. Then try softening him up with an affirmation, not a contradiction. Something like this: "Yeah, Dad, that's an easy thing to mix up. In fact, Ashcroft kind of looks like Rehnquist, one of the Supreme Court justices. One of the guys at the firm says the only way he can keep them straight is to think of the *R* in *Rehnquist* standing for *Robes*."

Kenneth's immediate goal is to diffuse the confrontation without "yessing" his father. Anger is the least effective response, and Kenneth's attempt to prove he was right ran counter to his larger goal. It's a lesson many a politician has learned, or has perished: don't let yourself be taken "off message" by emotions or diversions. The important thing is to keep focused on what you want to accomplish in the moment and in the long term.

Kenneth realized that he had to force himself to have a strategic response instead of a knee-jerk reaction: How can we get out of this bad situation he put us in without either of us losing our honor or our temper? How can I move us closer to a low-tension relationship without forfeiting my integrity? Note that I suggested Kenneth inform his father of the tip about how to tell the two lawyers apart. That nuance was purposeful; it let Kenneth get his information across without sounding like a know-it-all. By pretending that he, too, needed help, he made it easier for his father to swallow his mistake, and it also created a bond of vulnerability between them.

This may not be your fantasy scenario, I told Kenneth. It doesn't deliver the gold medal–winning rush of seeing Larry drop to his knees and say: "You know, son, you're right. I'm an idiot for having mixed up those damn lawyers and then argued with you about it. Gosh, I'm a pill. Can you ever forgive me?"

But it's a model for realistic problem solving; a workable, repeatable solution that can prevent blowups and save face for everyone. And it doesn't involve lying. For Kenneth, with his sharp, lawyerly mind, it had an elegant simplicity. As conflict nears, let the answer to one question guide you: Is my response bringing me closer to the prize?

Chapter 13

Building Fences 101:
The Art of Creating Boundaries

Let's begin with a pop quiz. What do these three parents have in common?

- A sixty-nine-year-old mother who riffles through her forty-one-year-old son's underwear drawer.
- A fifty-year-old father who tells his twenty-nine-year-old son about his extramarital affairs.
- A seventy-one-year-old mother who calls her thirty-six-year-old daughter at work five times a day.

Yup, you got it: the phrase *off limits* makes them cock their heads quizzically, like a dog annoyed by a high, faraway whistle. And these people are, unfortunately, everywhere. When I probe beneath the surface of tense relationships between parents and their grown children, the culprit is almost always a lack of clear boundaries.

Too many parents walk all over their adult kids: they come and go and come as they please, unable to differentiate between your home and theirs; they say whatever they want, giving unsolicited advice and making snide comments; they waste your time and needlessly churn up your emotions. The ensuing chaos hurtles you back to the dark side of childhood. Just as children get anxious when parents are unable to set clear boundaries, adults desperately need to have some control over where the property lines are.

But let's get something straight: the responsibility for such behavior lies as much with you as with them. As a child, you could not be expected to stop them when they transgressed your borders; as an adult, you *must* do this.

It won't be easy. If you've functioned this long without clear boundaries, it can be scary to challenge the status quo. But many people compound the difficulty by plunging in without a realistic idea of what limits to set and how to establish them. Instead they wait for pressure to build to untenable levels, then throw down the ultimatum gauntlet, setting absurd, impossibly tough limits. ("I never want to have dinner with you again. I'll send the kids over in a cab once a month, but count me out. Forever.") Such limits cannot—and should not—be maintained, and when you go skulking back, your credibility is tarnished, as well as your self-respect.

HOW FAR AWAY IS FAR ENOUGH?

In their book *How to Manage Your Mother,* Nancy Cocola and Arlene Matthews draw a parallel between how forests grow and how people thrive with respect to their parents. In the woods, the seedlings that burrow too close to the parent tree are cut off from sunlight by the older tree's leaves and are "poisoned" by toxins from the roots of the mature tree. Seedlings that burrow too far from the parent tree also have problems; they are left unshaded and are unable to thrive.

Keep this in mind when you are conceptualizing the boundaries you are trying to set up between you and your parents. Parameters are not merely ways to repel contact; they are ways to regulate it for everyone's comfort and well-being. Simply throwing up an electrified fence between you and your parents is not our goal here. We are trying to carefully build a strong-yet-flexible membrane that will fend off excessive intrusions without sending your mother or father flying off into the woods, screaming with rage.

MANAGING RESISTANCE—YOUR OWN: CRAIG

"Sometimes I feel like a walking cliché," said Craig, a forty-five-year-old gay man who was having trouble getting his parents out of his personal life. It wasn't that his mother, Ruby, and his father, Earl, had exiled him when he came out to them ten years before; on the contrary, they used the fact that he wouldn't ever get married or have children as an excuse to lavish much of their time on him. His sister had long ago moved across the country and had plenty to worry about with her three kids, but Craig remained their exclusive property. They called him daily, and nothing was off-limits to them. They felt free to ask him about his love life as well as the minutiae of his job as a stage manager at a small theater, and expected him over for dinner twice a week. Every season they bought three subscriptions to the opera and to the ballet, which meant there was a seat for Craig, of course.

By the time Craig came to see me, he was fuming. He had tried to be polite—ducking their calls and changing the subject when they grilled him about his relationships and his job—but that had only made them pump up the volume. They had started calling twice daily and taken to sending him expensive gifts (cashmere sweaters, a digital camera). Craig got the jitters every time the phone rang or someone knocked on the door.

I asked him if he had considered sitting down with his parents to talk about this issue, to tell them that he needed space to breathe. The suggestion made him go pale. "That would kill them," he said. "They base so much of their self-image on how cool they think they are for tolerating a gay son. They would just die if they had any sense that I didn't want to be a unit with them. They don't have much to say to each other at this point, and having me around makes that much easier for them to take. I couldn't stand the thought of throwing them off balance at this late stage in their lives."

Those are certainly significant considerations, I said, but what about your own reluctance to give all this up? In addition to your anger, you may be worried about how you'd feel if you could get them to back off. You haven't had a boyfriend in a long time, and lately you've been wistful when friends of yours have paired off. You tell me that you'd do "anything" to get them to leave you alone, but are you sure that you don't have some internal resistance to that outcome? Who wouldn't? From what you say, those opera tickets are pretty great.

Consciously, you may hate it when your parents disregard your boundaries, but that doesn't mean you aren't hoarding some unacknowledged resistance. Most of us are. Our parents' excessive attention may satisfy impulses deep within. We may feel comfortable with the familiar push-pull, or perhaps we aren't truly ready for full separation. We may unconsciously enjoy having our parents so close to us; it may make us feel wanted, even cherished. I find this particularly true of clients who don't have alternative nuclear families, that is, their own partner and children. Hey, it can be lonely out there, and at least the folks still care—even if that means they take liberties that compromise our independence.

What Craig learned, eventually, was that until you're ready to face the warring impulses of wanting to separate and wanting to stay attached, and commit to erecting real boundaries despite them, there's little use declaring that you are mad as hell and not gonna take it anymore. Without resolving those issues, you'll just find excuses not to set limits, or continue to blame your parents for their intrusions. You'll continue to be a powerless child.

Hey, you *are* mad, just as mad as you were when your mother decided that those flowers on your kitchen table were dead and headed toward the garbage pail, or when your stepfather called his bigwig buddy at your firm to tell the guy you deserved a raise. But you may also be full of sadness over the impending loss of your parents' overinvolvement.

Welcome to the world of conflicting impulses. I have faith that you will learn to live with them. And I have faith that when the fog clears, you will choose to pick up your hammer and get to work.

LESSON 1: DUST OFF THOSE CHILD-REARING MANUALS

If you're a parent, you probably know how important it is to set reasonable, consistent boundaries for your kids. This runs counter to many of the trends in our modern acquisitive society, but if you haven't yet figured out that giving your children "all the things you didn't have" and letting them run roughshod over you is a terrible idea, you are probably in big trouble. Setting reasonable limits for children is one of the most loving gifts a parent can give. Adjusting to external limits is how children learn about the world, and, eventually, they learn to control themselves by creating their own internal limits. The great irony of parenting is that true love means knowing when *not* to give in, when to say no, even if it hurts.

There are many similarities between child-rearing and "parent-rearing" in this area, and although I don't know of any books that focus on setting limits for your parents, there are plenty of good ones for dealing with your child. I urge you to adapt those lessons (see my favorite books listed in the bibliography). But be aware that there are some profound differences between dealing with your children and dealing with your parents. Lucky for you, though, the differences are mostly in your favor.

- With small children, parents are always worried about making mistakes that will scar the kids for life. Will saying no discourage them from exploring the world? No need to worry about this with parents. For better or worse, they're long past the impressionable stage.

- Children quickly grow out of whatever stage they're in, thereby making limits you have set obsolete, sometimes within days or weeks. Your parents, on the other hand, evolve more slowly (or, in many cases, not at all, alas!), so once you set limits with them, the benefits will be long-lasting.
- Unlike your kids, who test you by wheedling, hoping unconsciously that you will set limits to make them feel safe and help them develop self-control, your parents really *are* trying to get you to cave in. No need to over-think their agenda or worry if you're doing the right thing. Just start mulling precisely what sort of fences will make them good neighbors.

LESSON 2: CONSISTENCY IS KING

Here's where child-rearing and parent-rearing are identical: consistency matters. A lot. Setting limits and then enforcing them sporadically does more harm than good.

Being inconsistent with your parents is even more dangerous than being inconsistent with the kids; your folks are older and wilier, and will immediately sense that you are not committed to the limits you have set, and will push you even harder.

When you are conceptualizing the limits you intend to set, keep in mind that you will have to enforce those limits virtually for as long as your parents live. You will have to stick to your guns, unless there are health issues or other problems that intervene. That may seem scary, but after a short while such enforcement will become second nature. Still, you will not be able to relax, or you will weaken the message you have worked so hard to send.

The good news is that a healthy proportion of parents will stop struggling against these boundaries, just as most children accept limits. After a period of consistent enforcement, parents realize that pushing you is not going to help them achieve their goal; they know that no matter how much they push, you are not going to back down.

Think of these boundaries as a dam that you have struggled to build. Once it's up, you must consistently check the stress points. Otherwise, the waters will wipe it out. You don't have to rebuild the darned thing every day, but you do have to monitor it regularly, and closely. The tide won't magically recede just because it's been held back for a long time by the dam, and you wouldn't expect it to.

In the same way, you must accept your parents' basic nature and understand that they will continue to want to get their way, to surge against your "dam." They want you to give them what they want—attention, adoration, obedience—even if that is damaging to you. You must stop blaming them for feeling this way—do you blame a forest fire for burning the trees in its path?—and concentrate on constructing boundaries that will protect you.

LESSON 3: PASSWORDS TO CONTROL

Codifying your limits into some sort of mantra can be extremely helpful. Repeating a phrase aloud or in your head can free your mind from the fears and distractions that disrupt concentration. In the traditional Hindu usage, the meaning of the mantra is secondary to the relaxing effects. When dealing with your parents, you might want to have both a private *and* a public mantra, with different purposes.

The private mantra is for you alone. It reinforces the commitments you have made, strengthens your shield against guilt, and becalms any feelings of anger. It enables you to relax and keeps you from getting distracted by whatever your parents might throw at you.

The public, or parental, mantra is a phrase that is carefully constructed to establish your boundaries verbally. Begin with a generous affirmation of your parents' good intentions (even if you're not sure about this) and then end with a clear signal that you will not be manipulated or even discuss the matter further. The repetition (use slight variations, so you won't sound like a broken record) will help you "stay on message."

Some private mantras my clients have found helpful:

- I love her, but my privacy comes first.
- He's upset because I'm no longer under his control.
- I know she is trying her best.
- This is the only way she knows to show me she loves me.
- I want him in my life but on my terms.
- She's acting this way because she's afraid of losing me.
- He treats me in a way that reflects who he is, not who I am.

Some parental mantras they have used:

- "Dad, I know you don't like the way I dress, but I like it and I am not going to change it no matter how many times you complain about it."
- "Mom, I love that we both like good food, but please do not put food on my plate. If I want to taste what you ordered, I will ask."
- "Mom, I always admired your decorating taste and how proud you felt when people came into our home. I need you to respect my need to feel the same way about my home."
- "Folks, I am happy to discuss politics with you, but I will not let you impugn my choices. I expect you to give me the same respect about my opinions that I give you."
- "I'm glad we live in the same town, Mom, and that we have the opportunity to see each other frequently, but I still need you to call before you drop by."
- "Pop, it is so nice that you always buy gifts for my kids when you go out of town, but Joey has issues with his

weight, so I must ask you to bring something other than food."

I won't sugarcoat how exhausting it can be to master the art of building good fences. You're too smart for that. It is among the most draining techniques in a repetoire of new behavior. But once those fences are up, and you feel confident that with a doable expenditure of energy you can maintain them, there is no more satisfying change.

• Chapter 14 •

Getting Your Spouse
in Your House

Marriage, or any domestic partnership, is a remarkable and often harrowing ride, a leap of faith in its purest form. Creating a unified, functioning entity out of two individuals with their own dreams and values is a mammoth task. To successfully negotiate money, kids, career, real estate without tearing each other apart is a minor miracle.

Dealing with our parents in the midst of all this doesn't make things easier. Sure, parents sometimes provide financial or emotional help, but that often comes with strings that add stress to your marriage. Their demands, criticism, and bottomless pit of needs can bring an already simmering pot of marital discord to a boil.

Among the many strains put on a marriage, I believe that difficult parents are the most likely to create discord. Dealing with a delinquent child often brings couples together; they see themselves as a team, mutually responsible for the problem. And if their marriage is healthy, they work in tandem to find a solution.

This isn't merely good for the marriage; it's good for the problem: when children see their parents working together, they quickly realize that it's useless to try to play them off each other. On the other hand, if couples start to assign blame ("Well, we know where the kid got *that* from"), the whole effort falls apart.

Unfortunately, such teamwork rarely seems to be in evidence when it's a matter of dealing with "delinquent" parents. That's partly because there's an implicit belief in many marriages that "*your* parents are *your* problem." Instead of consciously formulating a shared plan to deal with troublesome parents, one in which each partner has clearly defined tasks, boundaries, and a chance to articulate feelings, couples tend to divvy up parental responsibilities in a way that creates a gulf of isolation, guilt, and blame.

There is plenty of humor based on the old saw about the dreaded mother-in-law poisoning marriages, peppering popular TV sitcoms from *The Honeymooners* to *Everybody Loves Raymond*. But it isn't just a cliché. Nor is the infuriating "mama's boy" simply a myth. And we all know a "daddy's girl" princess whose father undermines his son-in-law at every turn until the guy just explodes.

These stereotypes of spouses at each other's throats over out-of-control parents can be funny—on television or on the movie screen. But when it's you who is trapped in the cycle—either because your spouse won't join with you in forging a new relationship with your parents or because he won't face that it's his folks who need to be dealt with—it's not amusing. It's lonely.

Yes, you can successfully tackle parent problems alone, and you may have no choice, but it's not the optimum scenario. Not only is it tougher for the person who shoulders the burden, but it doesn't do much for your marriage either. The resentment that builds up over time is very hard to overcome, even many years after parents are gone.

I'm not suggesting that joining forces is easy. Often two partners have very different takes on the situation, depending on whose parents are the problem and which, if any, coping skills each partner has. But if you can fight the tendency to divide, and be conquered, no matter whose parents are the problem (or if both sets are!), you will find that dealing with either your parents or your spouse's parents is immeasurably easier. And your marital relationship will emerge stronger.

How do you begin to create a finely tuned parent-management team? First you have to know precisely what's going on in your head and your partner's head. In separate sections of this chapter, you'll find strategies if:

- you need to get your spouse on board to deal with your parents;
- his parent are the problem, and you want to find a way to deal with them as a team.

Read through both sections, no matter whose parents are making your lives difficult. Even the parts that don't seem directed at you are designed with you in mind—to give you insight into how your spouse is thinking. Culling what's going on in your partner's head is half the battle.

I'M OK, BUT MY PARENTS AREN'T

Shame Kills

Dealing with your bad parents may make you feel angry or guilty, but dealing with your *spouse* about your parents probably makes you feel embarrassed or ashamed. Let's face it, the only thing more depressing and humiliating than being a grown-up still embroiled in a childish relationship with parents is seeing that truth reflected in your partner's eyes.

This seems to be especially true for men, who labor under society's expectation that they always be in control, be manly, and not be childlike in any way. There is no more lethal cut than to call a man a mama's boy. Knowing that your wife thinks you're a wimp with your parents is a source of endless—and justifiable—shame.

Women are not exempt from shame on this score. They suffer from societal expectations as well, especially now that they have achieved greater parity in the workplace. At work, they are tough and decisive; at home, talking on the phone to the folks, they are eight years old again, caught with their hand in the cookie jar.

These men and women are their own worst enemies when it comes to getting help from their partners. They reflexively shut down or alienate their partner at the very moment they could be relying on them for support. Or they complain about their parents and berate their partner for not being helpful, but do very little to get their partners to understand how to help them. They grow defensive ("Don't you dare say that about my mother!"), wrathful ("Don't even mention my father's name in this house!"), or morose ("There's no use even talking about this").

Why? Because that's the behavior pattern associated with shame. More than any other emotion, it triggers a "flight" mechanism that sends you into a tailspin of denial. Guilt tends to make people fold, meekly giving in even when such behavior is self-destructive; shame tends to make them run away from the problem and throw up

impenetrable emotional barriers. And the person left on the wrong side of that fence is their partner, who feels confused, helpless, and upset—or just disgusted.

If you stop running for a moment, however, you may recognize that beneath your shame is a feeling of hopelessness. Whatever your behavior—whether you systematically deny that you're having trouble handling your parents and snap at your spouse to quit bugging you about it, or moan about the problem constantly and castigate your spouse for not solving it—beneath it all you probably don't have much faith that anything *can* be done. Anger at your spouse is most likely a product of your frustration.

The end result is isolation. You cut yourself off, and you cut your spouse off. This, in turn, exacerbates your feelings of hopelessness, turning the process into a never-ending cycle of despair.

The Lonely Dance of Isolation

Why do we push our spouses away when we need them most?

- Regulating intimacy makes us feel powerful—at least we can control *someone,* even if it's not our parents.
- Our problems with our parents make us feel unworthy of closeness and support.
- We choose to think that isolating ourselves shows "strength," and that sharing shows "weakness."
- We worry that being honest with our partner about the problem will make it more "real" and thus more difficult to ignore.
- We're afraid our partner will tell us the problem is even worse than we think.
- We want to avoid the embarrassment of having our partner criticize our parents, so we unconsciously slip into "automatic parent protection" mode, even though it's the opposite of what we really feel.

All these thought processes are counterproductive, but completely natural. Like mold, they fester in the dark places but wither when exposed to light. Once you bring them out into the open, they lose their power over you.

Building Bridges: Learn to Communicate, Not Complain

Grousing about your parents to your spouse is almost a parlor game for some couples. And while it's true that venting can release tension, it can also grate mightily on your partner's nerves. You may tell yourself that all you're looking for is a sympathetic ear, but remember that hearing the same diatribes every night is not sexy pillow talk. Worse, it never solves anything.

There's another pattern that few people are conscious of: Lisa complains about her parents to her spouse, Ted, but never makes any changes in her behavior toward them, unconsciously hoping Ted will get frustrated enough by her inaction to confront them. Setting Ted up as a stalking horse lets Lisa avoid acknowledging her anger.

This dynamic may be satisfying for Lisa in the short term: Ted may actually force a change in her parents, and even if he doesn't, at least he will have made them feel bad and made Lisa feel as though her spouse has made a valiant attempt to protect her (probably closer to her real motives). In the long term, however, it will sow greater marital discord. Indirect communication of this sort is never a good thing, and eventually Ted will feel used. His anger will likely boomerang back on Lisa because she has not taken responsibility for her feelings *or* her problem. Also, Lisa's parents will blame Ted for the strained relations. Just as important, Lisa will never derive the benefits of owning her anger and the satisfaction of taking steps toward becoming a real adult.

The bedrock of any partnership is calm, undefensive communication. This must stretch from the initial stage of sharing your feelings to the final stages of implementing a game plan. Underlying all good communication is a commitment to being pragmatic instead of merely venting: you are communicating emotions as well as ideas but always with an eye to solving problems. Many people think they are communicating when they are really just wallowing, rehashing their frustrations, and sinking into the attitude that no new behaviors are worth trying. This creates more marital problems. Communicating must entail progress, at least in how you deal with each other, if not in how you deal with your parents. Even if the innovations you explore don't solve the problem, the process of coming up with a joint game plan can pay dividends for your partnership.

Sisters Clare and Lucinda have spent a great deal of their adult lives—and *way* too much of their energy—trying to deal with their parents, Horace and Lupe, who are divorced. Each uses a complex set of manipulations to control their daughters. Horace's weapon of choice is health crises, including high blood pressure and a weak heart, employed to get his daughters to rush to his bedside at a moment's notice; Lupe withholds praise and tries to play the sisters against each other, bestowing expensive gifts on one while depriving the other.

The sisters do a fairly good job of supporting each other (though sometimes their mother's bribes are pretty hard to resist, and they wind up at each other's throat), but neither of them has been able to find a way to deal with their husbands on the issue. Gerry, Clare's husband of five years, had a terrible family life. He "dumped" his folks long ago and regularly urges Clare to do the same. He has little patience or sympathy for her pain and walks out of the room when she tries to discuss it. Often they wind up in a screaming fight when there is a phone call from one of her folks. "He says I'm setting a bad example for the kids," she said, tears in her eyes. "He says I'm teaching them that people can just walk all over them." When her husband makes these comments, Clare gets flustered and speechless, and runs from the room. Gerry ignores her, and eventually they patch things up. But nothing ever gets dealt with.

Len, who has been married to Lucinda for almost a decade, has an entirely different attitude. He blames Lucinda for "not just giving her parents what they want" and laughs off their manipulative ploys. "I can't understand why he doesn't get it," said Lucinda, "why he thinks this is all a big joke. When I tell him that giving in to them just makes them want more and more and makes me feel smaller and smaller, he says, 'Well, just do it and then mix yourself a cocktail. They're just a couple of old pains-in-the-neck. What's the big deal?' He makes me feel like an idiot for trying to change anything."

The sisters were desperate for ways to deal with their parents, but I was more concerned with higher stakes: their marriages. Even if the progress they made with their parents was negligible, getting their husbands on board would be the greatest contribution they could make to their marriages—and to their children's future. Such a model would serve as a template for many other difficult situations they might face down the line, like serious illness or financial crisis.

Here is what I told the sisters about how to discuss parent problems with their spouses:

1. Couch your discussions of parent problems as tasks to be solved, not mere complaint sessions. ("You know I'm struggling not to lash out at my mom when she criticizes me. Do you have any suggestions?") Recasting stories as solvable problems is much more palatable to partners than merely whining. ("Let me tell you what happened to me today; maybe there were other ways I might have handled the situation.") Asking for help has a magical effect on partners, bringing them into the fold, and cuts through isolation like a sword.

2. If you are looking for something specific from your spouse during conversations about your parents, ask for it gently but directly. Don't wait for him to somehow know what to do or say, to sense what you want from him by the mere arching of your eyebrow or your imploring tone. He won't. Even if what you want is small and

easy to do, give it to him straight. Don't be coy. Use a loving, unaccusatory tone, perhaps aided by some gentle touching. ("Honey, I hear you say that I'm being oversensitive about my dad, but please withhold judgment for the next ten minutes. I'll try to put this in context in a nonemotional manner. Please be patient with me.")

3. Let your spouse know that you intend to make changes in your parental relationship on a significant level. Trust me, he will react quite differently as soon as you demonstrate a willingness to take the bull by the horns. The prospect of helping to formulate a game plan gives your partner an active role, rather than merely being a sounding board for the same intractable problems night after night.

You Are the Team Captain

The "divide and be conquered" strategy may be a dead end, but that doesn't mean this program for change is a fifty-fifty deal. The fact is that you must take the lead, not because they are your parents but because it is your emotional freedom that's at stake. In the end, you need to know that it was *your* will and self-discipline that began the cycle of change. That is the only way you'll achieve true separation from your parents. Your spouse can be an invaluable ally but, no matter how well meaning, cannot implement this strategy *for* you.

Consider it a crucial investment in the future of your marriage. In my experience, marriages are fortified when one partner takes primary responsibility for a situation that is more closely related to himself (parents, job, relationship with a friend), while seeking strong collaboration with a partner.

Generally, it's a good idea to design your program so that you are the point person in dealing with your parents, with your spouse providing backup and support. But there are times when you may decide to work in concert, perhaps in a good-cop, bad-cop scenario. This is perfectly acceptable, as long as you're doing it because the two of you have decided that it's the most effective way to deal with your parents, not because you're too timid to take the reins and prefer to turn over the bad-cop role to your spouse.

Assigning Tasks

Being a strong leader means getting input from the troops and, after considering all options, clearly doling out duties. A leader also reassesses progress and makes adjustments if necessary.

Your spouse is your invaluable lieutenant. You need his insights into the situation when you're formulating a plan, and he must be kept intimately informed about strategy and progress. Most important, he needs to know that you need him throughout the process. "Help me!" or "Just give me support" is not a helpful request. Instead, give specific instructions. For example: "If my father drains his scotch while I'm trying to talk about the situation with him, please rush to refill it so he doesn't have an excuse to go to the liquor cabinet and stop the conversation." Or: "If I start to get emotional, please don't comfort me. Instead, take over from the exact point I left off until I can compose myself."

Here are some other variations:

- "Please let me ventilate about my father for two minutes a day and then remind me gently that I asked you to stop me after that."
- "When my mother starts complaining about not having enough time with the kids, please let me tell her quietly about our new policy, and then, if she starts to raise her voice, step in and tell her that there's no negotiation."
- "If you see my face get red when my parents start to bicker, kick me gently under the table to remind me to get up and go into the other room for a moment, like we planned."

The Power of the Recap

Long live the postmortem! When it comes to dealing with your parents as a team, nothing is more important than reviewing your progress, especially after you and your parents have had a dust-up.

The key is to be positive and forward-thinking. This is not a blame session; it's a joint strategy session.

TIPS

- Wait until you're alone, in a comfortable setting.
- Start by thanking your spouse for helping.
- Ask concrete questions. ("Do you think they heard my message? What makes you think so? Was I shrill? Did you like that thing I did with my hands?")
- Set goals for next time. ("You chime in a little earlier," or "I need to stop nodding my head like a bobble-headed doll," or "We both should keep our voices lower.")
- Have a sense of humor. Remember that this can be a good time to build bridges in your marriage and reinforce the sense that you're in this together.

The Power of Appreciation

There is nothing as mighty as the heartfelt thank-you. And nothing bonds a marriage more strongly than telling your partner that his support, patience, and counsel are not only appreciated but indispensable. It's easy to roll past the gratitude part when you're intent on making changes with your parents. Don't. Even if you are unable to "fix" your parents, getting your spouse to participate is an enormous victory. It means you are truly a team and have learned shared skills and strategies that will pay off in many other aspects of your marriage, from dealing with the kids to attaining your financial dreams. In the long run, creating that kind of partnership is as valuable as anything you hope to achieve with your parents.

Giving thanks graciously—and frequently—to your spouse, no matter how small the contribution, is the cornerstone of such a relationship.

I'M OK (AND SO ARE MY PARENTS), BUT HE (AND HIS PARENTS) AREN'T

Maura had been with Keith for nearly three years when she came to see me. In most ways their relationship was wonderful. She had no complaints about how Keith, a thirty-five-year-old lawyer, treated her—he was kind, gentle, and generous, and he adored her. But his relationship with his mother, Coco, was simply "too heavy" for Maura, a thirty-four-year-old music teacher, to cope with. "His father died when he was seven," she told me, mixed emotions gathering on her brow like a storm, "and his mother raised him alone. When he was twelve, she got remarried, but the guy turned out to be a real pig. He was beating her, so she and Keith had to run away. They lived in crummy hotels for a year until his mom got on her feet. It was really traumatic for both of them, but it brought them ridiculously close."

The result was that mother and son had forged an intimacy that was impenetrable to outsiders. They had a shared language of jokes and memories that made Maura feel completely left out. When Coco called, which she did at least twice daily (and she lived only a mile away), Keith's conversation took on the whispery, slightly telepathic quality of a man talking to a lover.

At first, this devotion impressed Maura. Her family was emotionally cold; her parents had been married for nearly forty years but acted more like cellmates than partners. She spoke to her siblings only once a year or so. "I loved the fact that Keith was so able to express love and respect for his mother. He was still awed by the courage she showed in raising him. And I was too, at first. It really was a great story, all those years she scrimped and saved, working as a court stenographer, eventually sending him to Stanford."

Besides, Coco defied the overbearing mom stereotype by being gentle and modest. And she welcomed Maura, calling her "darling" right away and showing her the warmth that her own mother had never been able to show.

After a year or so, though, Maura began to get uneasy with Keith and Coco's symbiosis. The closer Maura got to Keith, the more aware she became of his mother's manipulations. For instance, Coco, a delicate woman who weighs less than one hundred pounds, seemed always to get ill whenever Keith and Maura were about to go on vacation, which meant that either they canceled, or Keith called her a few times a day while they were away, which left him preoccupied with Coco's illness so he couldn't enjoy the vacation. Once, they canceled a long-planned trip to Morocco because Coco was sure she had a lump in her breast and couldn't get a doctor's appointment until after they were scheduled to leave. "I tried to be sympathetic, but afterward I found out that she had done that a half dozen times. When I suggested to Keith that there might be something *else* going on, he defended her vehemently."

Coco also understood the seduction of food and creature comforts. She would regularly leave a dazzling array of meals, in individual containers perfect for freezing, on their doorstep, and whenever she visited them, she always pulled out the iron and pressed a few of Keith's expensive shirts. "He doesn't want me to do it," she said, conspiratorially, to Maura, "but I just love ironing. It's so relaxing." Maura, an indifferent housekeeper who preferred eating out, was flummoxed: "I'm not gonna do a Suzie Homemaker thing to compete with her. Besides, I love her cooking, too. Still, it all makes me uncomfortable."

But Coco made it hard to get angry with her. She poured on the sugar, buying Maura small, meticulously chosen pieces of antique jewelry and rare recordings of Chopin, Maura's passion. And Coco was a master of the guilt sonata as well. Whenever she sensed that Maura was losing patience with her, she dusted off yet another poignant tale of raising Keith: how she snuck in to bake a birthday cake in the hotel's crummy kitchen or how she spent her spare time hand-tinting photographs so he could go to summer camp for a week.

For more than a year, Maura wavered. She loved Keith, but she feared that his inordinately strong connection to his mother would always come between them. She tried to talk to Keith about this issue, but she was always afraid of sounding like a shrew, harping on "Coco, the saint."

Besides, whenever she got near the topic, Keith simply assured her that his relationship with his mother was "totally worked out."

He said, "All it means is that I am capable of respecting women. I thought that was what women always complained about, that men aren't able to show emotion or loyalty. The guys you have to worry about are the ones who *hate* their mothers." He even hinted that he wanted to marry Maura—*if* she could "accept" his closeness with Coco.

Maura was confused and sad by the time she flopped down on my couch. Recently, she had become friendly with another teacher at her school who had dated Keith during college, and talking to her had made Maura even more uneasy. "She just rolled her eyes when I told her I was seeing Keith. She said she had dated him for a year but had dumped him when she realized that Coco was his 'true love.' I didn't know what to think. Keith had told me this girl was a narcissist, that she had to have all the attention all the time and that's why they broke up. I don't know who to believe. I know I'm not OK with things as they are, that I don't want to marry him if I'm always going to feel as though his primary connection is with her."

I'm not going to lie to you. Trying to wake a partner up to the fact that there is something seriously wrong with the way he deals with his parents is one of the most complicated and delicate of all parent-related problems. It is even tougher to resolve such issues than it is to get your partner on board with a plan to manage *your* parents—the problem we discussed earlier—because it's likely that your partner has not acknowledged that there *is* a problem. If he had, you'd probably have put your heads together to solve it by now, or you'd at least be on the same page, working as a team.

Dealing with logjams of this type takes a great deal of patience, honesty, and empathy. First, you have to know what you're dealing with. In general, partners who have unacknowledged problems with their parents fall into three categories: the ragers, the guilt collectors, and the blissfully overindulged. These are not mutually exclusive categories, of course—many people are hybrids (Keith, for example, is both overly indulged and saddled with plenty of childhood guilt)—but most people who aren't ready to face these problems fall somewhere along this continuum.

Rage against the Machinations

Ragers are often so angry with their parents that they cannot see how that anger is hurting them. They may have plenty of contact with their parents—perhaps even taking care of them full-time—or none at all. Either way, they resent their parents bitterly, have not resolved their childhood issues, and have not found a way to love the good things about their folks while putting the awful things in context. Their anger blinds them—to why their parents still arouse such fury in them, to the part they play in this unhealthy dynamic, to the complexity of their parents' inner lives, to any behavioral changes they could make that would blunt that anger.

People at the far end of the rage spectrum have given up, cutting off all contact with their parents. Unfortunately, that rarely solves the problem. Anger, like human teeth and bones, is remarkably resilient; it can survive, virtually intact, even when it's buried deep. Distance can provide some relief—you can't punch your dad when he lives on the opposite coast—but the acid eats away at your insides nonetheless.

You may be surprised to know that of all three groups, the ragers tend to react fairly well when a partner intervenes with their parents. If you have enough courage not to be intimidated by your partner's anger—and have some good techniques under your belt—he may even let you do some bridge building. Why? Because most angry people desperately want to make things better, to be able to express some affection toward their parents and to be loved in return. These people may not be able to transcend their pain on their own, but they may be willing to let you establish a beachhead—if you proceed very carefully. (This, of course, only applies if your partner's parents are open to you, and not too angry at him.)

Do Your Due Diligence

Even if your partner says that he's angry with his parents for present-day misdeeds, there is a very good chance he is still stuck on stuff from the past. He'll probably deny that, but if he's deeply angry, be suspicious. It's up to you to thoroughly, if gently, research his past. Use movies or books as a jumping-off point to get him to talk about his childhood (see chapter 5). Gently interrogate his siblings. Watch him with his parents and note when and how ancient history seems to poison their interaction. Piece all of it together and come up with a clear idea of what old hurts he is bringing into the present.

Be Supportive, but Don't Be a Cheerleader

You are naturally protective if the person you love is treated badly by her parents. You want to show her that you understand and support her. Like the parent who makes a show of "punishing" the sidewalk in front of a child who has just fallen down, saying "Bad sidewalk!" you want to express your indignation at whatever hurts her. But merely echoing her anger at her parents isn't very productive. You also need to find ways to establish a workable détente between her and her parents.

To do this, put your energy into finding safe common ground upon which she and her parents can "meet." This may mean creating family traditions that don't dredge up bad memories (Flag Day brunch—you cook), or forging new conversation patterns (instead of letting her argue politics to the point of hysteria with her history-buff father, step in to ask her father to explain to you the history of nuclear proliferation and the cold war). By inserting yourself into the family dynamic, you can help transform it into a forward-looking, nonconfrontational one. This is an example of triangulation, the process by which a third person enters an interpersonal dynamic and takes the heat off the intense one-on-one. You are there to defuse conflicts, demonstrate how the old assumptions are out-of-date, and provide new, trustworthy information.

Show Your Partner the Parents He's Never Known

If your spouse is "permanently" angry with his parents, chances are he has never let himself see them as complex beings. Operating on old assumptions from his childhood, he has likely reduced them to cardboard bad guys or has built up a reservoir of bad feeling so huge that he can't see past it. You must "expose" his parents' humanity.

This doesn't mean you grasp at straws ("Well, at least they have good personal hygiene") or argue with him ("They're not really that bad"). In fact, it's not about *telling* him anything; it's about *showing* him that his parents are complicated people with vast pasts, people who are worth knowing better.

Again, refer to techniques discussed in chapter 5. Ask his parents about their past in front of your spouse. Elicit stories, especially ones that may have some bearing on your partner. You can probably get them to talk about things they never would discuss if he asked; after all, if he is angry with them, they probably aren't too happy with him either. You can act as a conduit through which your partner and his parents can get to know each other.

One of my clients, Anna, was able to help her husband, Tomas, make huge strides with his parents when she asked her father-in-law what it had been like when he lost his job in the early 1970s. That had been an awful time for Tomas; his father had plunged into alcoholism and despair, sowing the seeds for the anger between them. Anna, a wise woman, simply waited until the day the conversation rolled around to mention how tight the labor market was. Then she turned to her father-in-law and said, "It must have been pretty terrible when you lost your job. What was it like? What did you do?" Listening to him tell her how painful it had been, how much of a failure he had felt like, and how badly he had treated his family rocked Tomas. After hearing his father's point of view after so many years, Tomas found it harder to remain locked in his bitterness. Eventually, he was able to tell his father how bad that period had been for him, which went a long way toward thawing their thirty-year chill.

Remember: The best way to help an angry spouse deal with his parents is to maintain civil communication with them yourself. Adding a relatively neutral party to the mix—provided you show him your loyalties lie with him—may eventually enable him to soften his stance and force both antagonists to climb off their high horses.

Slave to Love

Unlike the ragers, who at least never cause you grief by putting their parents first, guilt collectors tap into your self-doubt and have a tendency to bring out the worst in you. To an outsider, a guilt-tripping parent is so obvious that it invites ridicule. When a partner is enslaved by the needs and desires of his or her parents, it's hard not to burst out with, "Are you out of your mind? Don't you see that she's just laying it on thick to get you to do what she wants?"

Worse, a "guilty" partner seems *wimpy,* which is a real passion killer. This cuts across gender lines. Many men who are involved with a woman whose parents hold sway over her often wind up feeling emasculated by their inability to "save" their spouse. Even "evolved" guys who understand that it's not their job to rescue their mate often feel cheated—because they dreamed of a wife in control of her life, one who wouldn't fold under pressure.

A woman whose partner is deeply enmeshed with his parents struggles with a different set of disappointments: she may be repelled by what she sees as his lack of strength and backbone. When she fell in love, she didn't bargain on getting a guy who turns into a preschooler whenever his mom or dad walks into the room, someone who thinks it's not a vacation unless Mommy and Daddy come along. Most women are instinctually turned off by such behavior because it is not "manly."

Such feelings invariably come to the surface in a relationship, wreaking havoc. When Larraine told me of the daily phone calls between her boyfriend, Jack, and his mother, she mimicked him calling his mother "darling Mummy" a dozen times in a baby voice. Of course, he didn't really address her like that, but in Larraine's mind, that was the subtext. It's not surprising that her resentment and disrespect seeped into their relationship and eventually helped destroy it.

Although guilt collectors may seem like victims, be aware that some of them cultivate the dynamic, either consciously or unconsciously. Some create a situation in which they are the heroes, "saving" their parents. I have a client, Jeremy, whose ego is very invested in supporting his parents financially, even though they could manage on their own. He insists they live in his converted attic, which is very tough on his wife, who has logged half a continent of miles going up and down those steps. Jeremy says he feels put-upon by the arrangement, and he frequently complains about the financial strain, but he plays a major role in maintaining this unhealthy situation.

Obviously, this is a complex situation, as are most guilt-loaded interactions between parents and children. If you, as a spouse or partner, are trapped in these webs of emotion and responsibility, you no doubt feel helpless. Obviously, this is a situation in which a therapist can be invaluable, but often partners are resistant. As I've said before, there is, alas, very little you can do to help someone who doesn't believe there's a problem.

But you can change *your* behavior or at least change the way you think about the situation. In the end, you may decide that the dynamic is too much for you to endure and you want to terminate the relationship. Or you may decide to tough it out, accept that there is nothing you can do, and consciously decide to focus only on your partner's more appealing characteristics. There is, however, a middle path that involves subtly altering your behavior to create an atmosphere conducive to change.

Describe What You See—
but Don't Be a Broken Record
If you have never pointed out the destructive dynamic between him and his parents and he seems genuinely unaware of it, you should make him aware of what it looks like from your perspective.

But beware—this must be done very carefully. (If he knows that he is trapped in a spiral of guilt, he will likely resent you for telling him what he already is all too aware of.) You might consider sittting down with him and describing how, as an outsider, you view the way he interacts with his parents. Note I use the word *describe,* which is defined as "to trace or traverse the outline of."

- Use nonjudgmental language (imagine you are an alien being who is viewing the dynamic from an objective standpoint).
- Stay calm.
- Don't have a snarky or pouty attitude.
- Express understanding of how common this dynamic is; screen yourself for condescension.
- Have specific examples ready.
- Don't use psychobabble.
- Avoid ultimatums ("if this doesn't change, I'm going to leave you").
- Show you are willing to work as a team to change things.
- Suggest there are practical alternatives.

Be Glad You're Not Your Partner

The most important thing to remember when you're in this situation is that, no matter how conflicted and annoyed you are, your partner is really suffering, even if he or she doesn't acknowledge that anything is wrong. Being a slave to guilt is a special kind of hell, one that reduces life to two unsavory choices: do what your parents want and feel awful, or don't do what they want and feel awful.

I am not suggesting you feel sorry for your partner, just that you examine your emotional response to the situation. Anger and repulsion are the two most common reactions to partners who are "enslaved" to their parents, but if you nurse these feelings, refuse to use a different set of thoughts to override them, your only choices are to end the relationship or shut up and suck it up.

Depersonalize

Stop for a moment and remember that your partner's relationship with his parents existed before you came on the scene. It's not a reflection of your intimacy or trust; it's the result of a long-standing lack of separation between him and his parents, a complex web of childhood experiences and insecurities.

It may sometimes seem that your partner is weighing your worth against his parents' and deciding that *they* are more important, but that's not what's happening. In fact, it's much more likely that you are more important to him than anyone has ever been, and his feelings for you have likely put him in great turmoil. That turmoil may be so painful that he can't directly confront it, so he's plunging even more deeply into denial. This ball of tangled thread is huge and complicated, as we've discussed in earlier chapters, but in order to help him you need to take three steps back, stop focusing on your own pain, put your ego in the drawer for a while, and concentrate on new behavior that will produce results.

Differentiate between His Problems with
His Parents and *Your* Problems with Them

Making this distinction can be difficult. If his parents regularly manipulate him with guilt, it's likely that your interactions with them are problematic as well. They may marginalize you, criticize you, or talk sweetly to your face as they dish you to your spouse privately or try to work their guilt magic on you.

These behaviors can be wrenching, and I don't suggest for a moment that you ignore them. (For an excellent discussion of this problem, see Susan Forward's spirited book, *Toxic In-Laws*.) I know how deeply wounding it can be to see that your partner is incapable of defending you against his parents, and I don't advise you to blindly accept this situation, but until you're able to differentiate between the two problems, it will be nearly impossible to make things better.

In other words, when your partner's parents give you the cold shoulder because you refuse a dinner invitation, or overnight-mail you a box full of cosmetics that sends the clear message that they think you're not "taking care" of yourself, it's ill-advised to use that moment to initiate a conversation with your partner about how *he* shouldn't come running when his parents guilt him into driving them to airport. The likelihood that such a conversation will degenerate into accusations, angry defenses, and stupid non sequiturs is, well, about 100 percent. Not very good odds, if you ask me.

Choose a time of relative peace to bring up your concerns. You might want to begin with something like this: "I've noticed that you seem conflicted by all the demands your parents make on you. You obviously care about them and want to fulfill some of their needs, but are you sure you need to fulfill all of them? Would you be willing to collaborate on some strategies to find a middle ground?"

You can try an approach like this even if your relationship has suffered through years of irritation (yours) over lack of backbone (your partner's). Yes, you will have to moderate your approach to take the past into account, but there is no reason you can't just decide to stop harping unproductively and start laying the groundwork for functioning like a team.

Teach by Example

Hate to see your partner manipulated by his parents? Then make sure you banish guilt—giving it or giving in to it—from your life. Make it explicit: if your partner tries to make you feel guilty over something, anything, or if you find yourself pulling the guilt routine with him or the kids, say, "I'm uncomfortable with this. I don't want to have any coercion in my life. I don't like it when your parents do it to you, and I don't like it when I see anyone else do it. I've made a commitment to myself not to give guilt or take it."

Provide Alternatives to Giving In

People who are excessively vulnerable to guilt tend to see things in black and black. They believe they have no choice but to relinquish their will to their parents. They can't even imagine ways to compromise.

One of my clients, Dan, developed a good system with his wife, Karen, who felt very guilty about her sweet but needy parents and often found herself doing everything for them: their paperwork, their shopping, even their worrying about their other kids and grandkids. Dan was tired of fighting about this issue, so he used the couple of months following the birth of their first child as a pilot program to show Karen that there were compromises she could make that would enable her to help her parents without being racked with guilt if she didn't always say yes.

He chose—smartly, I think—to do this in a lighthearted yet highly organized way, avoiding drama-soaked confrontations or abstract complaints of the past. Instead, he developed a practical, highly visual system to make Karen think about how her overvigilance to her parents' needs was hurting her and affecting their family.

He informed her parents that he would be "playing Karen's part" while she got her strength back, that they should call him with any problems. His idea—one I've used with many clients since—was to create a "guilt bank," a floating check-and-balance system that would keep track of how much assistance was flowing out. The underlying principle was that her parents had a preset limit of "guilt credits" available each month, which they could spend in any way, but once these credits were used up, the bank was closed and all assistance would stop. That made him budget what he did for them. He hoped to show Karen that there was a fixed "balance," that she was not an endlessly renewable resource.

Karen was a thrifty sort who thrived on the challenge of limits, so he figured that the idea of budgeting her favors would appeal to her. Seeing an accounting on paper of all the tasks she had done for them would also bring home the message that she could say no a third of the time, say, and still be doing a lot for them.

With panache and humor, Dan decreed that there were fifty points in the account. He then assigned values to all tasks: shopping, chauffeuring, accompanying them to the doctor's office, even taking their phone calls after 10 p.m. The assigned values reflected

Dan's desire to pare down the time spent in service: if they asked him to pick up a prescription for them, it would cost them ten points, but if he told them the pickup would have to wait until he was on the way home from work that evening, only eight points would be deducted from the account. This way, he wound up doing a reasonable amount of what they asked without wondering if he was doing "enough." The "enough" had been decided—it was fifty points' worth. Plus he and Karen had some good laughs, turning the exercise into their own private game show.

Give Up Unrealistic Expectations

No, neither Clark Gable nor George Clooney let his parents push him around (I checked). And Barbara Stanwyck and Sharon Stone didn't for a moment let their parents mistreat their husbands (no surprise that these ladies knew how to keep the folks in line). But what's the point of nursing fantasies about your husband finding his inner "macho man" when dealing with his parents or your wife turning into a "tough broad" with her folks? Such unrealistic ideals are bound to stop you from constructing doable, forward-looking strategies. Your partner is human. He or she probably has many strengths, but dealing in a mature fashion with the parents isn't one of them. At least not yet. If that is untenable for you, which I can understand, especially if your partner turns a blind eye while his parents treat you badly, you may decide you are unable to continue in the relationship. This is a painful thought, I know, but the only character in this play you can control is you. Having unrealistically high expectations of your partner, ones that are dashed over and over, is just a way of prolonging the agony.

Can your partner change? Yes. Can your partner change enough to make you happy? That's less of a sure thing. I wouldn't count on your partner metamorphosing from a timid man afraid to disappoint his folks into a Rambo-like figure striding into his parents' condo, bullwhip in hand, ready to tell them he's getting off the guilt train here and now. To begin with, those patterns have deep origins. And despite your ministrations, change has to come from deep within.

Change rarely comes in a single blinding revelation. Do not dismiss the importance of incremental improvements. Many of the strategies in this book can be adapted to win small victories. For most of us, escaping guilt is a gradual process. What you need to think about is what *you* can live with.

Her Heart Belongs to Daddy

If you are involved with one of the blissfully overindulged, be aware, there is no magic pill to transform a pampered prince or princess into a self-reliant adult. You may want to shout at your partner, "Stand on your own two feet!" but this is a very difficult pattern to break because everyone involved in it—everyone but you, of course—seems pretty darned happy with things as they are.

You may see as clear as day that your partner's relationship with his parents is a devil's bargain, but to them—your partner and his parents—their dynamic is a symphony of needs being met. Your partner probably believes he has a perfectly functional lifestyle. He may be in complete denial about what he is missing: the thrill of being financially and emotionally independent from his parents. Many people like this have developed a defense mechanism that is hard to break through. And why *should* they want to break through? Self-knowledge would mean giving up their comforts.

For you, this situation can be excruciating. Trying to realize a mature love with someone happily ensconced in his childhood dynamic (sometimes even in his childhood bedroom!) seems futile. A man who falls in love with a woman whose father still "takes care" of her finds himself in a creepy Freudian-tinged competition that can be especially "sticky" if her father is wealthy; a woman who gets involved with a man whose parents "subsidize" him may find he has unrealistic expectations of what it takes to make it in the real world with a family. Maura, for example, felt she was the tolerated mistress in the long-standing love affair between Keith and Coco, a situation she eventually felt was too much for her to handle.

Before you tackle a problem like this, you must understand a basic tenet: allowing oneself to be overindulged goes way beyond money; it is an elemental state of mind, usually involving two impulses:

- *The desire to maintain the visceral essence of childhood.* You want to hold on to the enveloping feeling that your needs are being taken care of by beings put on earth to serve this purpose, that is, your parents. Sometimes there are intense psychosexual bonds as well
- *An underlying insecurity.* You may not think that you can take care of yourself. This belief can be a function of personality or a result of long-standing childhood conditioning.

Although it is difficult to fight these impulses, they can be conquered. Luckily, some people locked in this kind of relationship with their parents nurse some internal doubts about whether they should seek more independence, despite what they say and do. Society sends plenty of positive messages about independence and self-sufficiency. You may think your partner is inured to these messages, but subliminally, they may be nesting in the back of his or her mind. The key is for you to amplify those messages without becoming shrill or defensive.

Be Direct
If you feel that your partner's overreliance on his parents is getting in the way of you two having a more intimate relationship, say so. Wait for a nice evening meal to bring up the topic. Don't be snotty or accusatory, and resist being sarcastic about how coddled your partner is. Take responsibility for your feelings, but be positive. Try

something like this: "I want you to know that independence is very important to me. I know you enjoy the things your parents provide for you, but when you take them it makes me feel as though we aren't creating a separate unit that can go it alone. I'm glad you have such a strong bond with your folks, but I want us to work toward greater independence. I've been thinking of some ways to do this, but let's put our heads together to come up with some we can both be comfortable with."

Make Sure You Can Part with the Creature Comforts Provided

You may hate how pampered your partner is and wince at how he is under his parents' sway, but if he's sharing the benefits with you, it's sometimes not easy giving up the perks: that help with the mortgage, the subsidies for the kids' summer camp, those vacations at the cabin. Alas, you have to choose. You can't say you resent his immaturity and covet the fruits of his extended childhood. Want to know how to plant the seeds for change? Quit taking. But don't be petulant about it. "I appreciate that your parents invited us again to their house in Aruba and want to pick up the tab for our airfare, but I've decided I would prefer to go on a more modest vacation we can pay for ourselves. Perhaps your parents would let us go to Aruba at another time—alone—and we could repay them with some sweat equity on their house there."

Create Alternate Rituals

Being taken care of like a child is often a matter of routine. People who are overly involved with their parents in this way often come from tradition-bound families where ritual is crucial. If you have suffered through a decade of yearly nativity plays at your in-laws' house (that darned shepherd's costume pulling under the arms again) or withstood every Fourth of July weekend of your marriage at their cottage in Nova Scotia (no plumbing so we can all "get close to mother earth"), you probably know what I'm talking about.

Be aware that ritual is a powerful binding force, one that may be holding your partner deeply in thrall, without him even realizing it. He may unconsciously fear that becoming more independent from his parents will lead to a loss of those rituals, that connection.

Instead of trying to tear your partner away from family traditions or refusing to participate:

- *Help your partner create a new set of family traditions, independent from those his family already engages in.* Avoid competing; innovate instead. Celebrate entirely different holidays (Bastille Day, Boxing Day, the anniversary of your first date), or think up commemorations of traditional holidays that more closely mirror your adult interests (a pre-Christmas midnight champagne snack à deux, an annual Labor Day scavenger hunt with your best friends and their kids).

- *Invite parents to participate in these new traditions— on your terms.* Yes, I know you'd prefer to make them private, and I urge you to do so, if you can, but don't despair if it's not possible at this time. (Keep your eye on the prize.) Regardless, the great thing about creating new traditions is that you "own" them, as a team, especially if they take place on your turf. So you can afford to be generous. Be careful to resist the urge to marginalize the troublesome parents. You and your partner should offer them a prominent role in the proceedings. (Always be aware that both your spouse and her parents may feel that these new traditions are undermining their old ones. Tread lightly.) Here's where your empathy comes into play: endow parents with status in your new tradition to soothe their egos. Perhaps his mother, the decathlete, would like to be asked to coordinate all the sporting events for a new Memorial Day family track-and-field competition; if his father is a great cook, he might want to become your "guest chef" or organize a group expedition to the market.

Encourage your spouse to come up with responsibilities to give his parents a sense of belonging—without giving them total control. That will give him a chance to experience the pleasure of acting like an adult in relation to his parents, to enjoy being in control of that dynamic for a change.

Chapter 15

Role-Playing with the Punches

Movies and television shows are mere imitations of life, but who among us hasn't experienced those moments when we are sucked in by the naturalness and conviction of an actor's performance? It all seems so *real*—a whisper on the veranda triggers a twang of sexual heat, that good-bye kiss sends tears running down your face.

But no matter how convincing the scene seems, you can be sure—regardless of what you glimpsed on the cover of a tabloid about "instant chemistry" between the stars—that it didn't just "happen." That moment was the product of many hours of rehearsal.

Knowing that, why should you expect to feel relaxed when you start talking to your parents in a wholly new way? The courageous act of becoming the person we want to be with our parents is virgin territory, and having a vague idea of what you want to accomplish is not enough. Actors don't just plunge into a scene, so why should you? Realigning your relationship with your parents won't come any more "naturally" than belting out the lead in *Lion King*. No actor worth his salt would try it cold. He would tell you that he needs to rehearse for a while to "inhabit" the role.

Before you can play that role, you need to do some role-playing, which is rehearsing behavior in order to make it more natural and less fraught with fear. It's important for several reasons. It will help you

- construct a new lexicon, new body language, and new dialogue rhythms;
- become desensitized to your parents' responses;
- explore ways to head off guilt-barrages and other manipulations.

THERE'S NO RIGHT SCRIPT

Role-playing is not a way to "script" more satisfying interactions with your parents. Alas, that never works because your folks are wily, adaptable creatures who have not read the script, would not follow the script if they *had* read it, and will respond in ways that are guaranteed to mess up even your best-rehearsed line-reading. Instead, role-playing is a way of becoming comfortable with "guided improvisation," that is, keeping in mind your general goals for the interaction, having on hand a variety of well-thought-out ways to achieve those goals, and training yourself not to get distracted by whatever curves your parents may throw. The idea is to alleviate your anxiety level by

- analyzing the traditional patterns of your interactions with your parents;
- constructing a flexible set of new, focused responses so you will not be blindsided by your parents' responses (whatever they are);
- training yourself to be comfortable improvising in a variety of conditions, steering the discussion where you want it, even in the face of anger, contradiction, and guilt tactics.

GETTING INTO THE ROLE

1. Sit in a darkened room, armed with your trusty tape recorder. Conjure up one of your regular conflagrations with your parents, either from the past or from your imagination. This can be a well-considered confrontation as you tell them you are making a change (moving across the country for a job, no longer coming to dinner every Tuesday night, once again dating someone they despise) or simply one of your usual spontaneous blowups (your mother berates a waiter in front of you; your father starts ranting about how badly behaved your kids are).

2. Turn on the tape recorder and begin to dictate dialogue between you and your parents *as it usually ensues.* Do both parts— yours and your parents'. Be honest; render the frustrating, endlessly repeated interaction as it tends to unfold, with missteps on both sides. Make sure you play out the scenario through at least four back-and-forth volleys. Remember to approximate the intonations and tone of voice of all characters in your little drama. The goal is to re-create an actual conflict. I know this exercise may seem silly, but don't worry if you suddenly flash on Norman Bates from *Psycho,* doing both his own dialogue and his dead mom's—no one is listening.

3. Transcribe the dialogue. Replay the tape and get it all down on paper. Now you have a "script" from which you can design some more positive variations.

4. Reread your parents' part on paper. Try to see between the lines: What are they really saying? Are they scared? Threatened? Competitive? Reflecting their own unhappiness?

5. Turn on the tape recorder again. Read your parents' opening volley aloud, then stop for as long as it takes to theorize how—taking into account what you think is the underlying motivation for your parents' behavior—you could more effectively have dealt with the burgeoning crisis. How could you have kept the conversation from degenerating into a full-blown argument while still making your

point? Remember to *keep your eyes on the prize,* focusing at all times on limited, realistic goals.

6. Act out your parents' response—or multiple responses—to your newly thought-out approach. As smart folks with their own agenda, they will undoubtedly try to foil your efforts. You know them well enough to anticipate what they will counter with.

7. Come up with a variety of responses suitable for each of the responses you imagine your parents would come up with. Focus on not being distracted by their provocative comments. As White House advisers tell the president, "Keep on message."

PLAYING ALONE OR WITH FRIENDS

Now that you have a set of rewritten scripts to substitute for your old, stale ones, you can role-play by yourself or with help. If possible you should do both. The more you practice, the sooner you will feel comfortable with your new set of behaviors.

When role-playing by yourself, you can practice dialogues in the car or as you walk the dog. Speak into your cell phone if that's generally how you speak with your parents. The tape recorder comes in particularly handy when you are role-playing alone; just record your parents' parts and leave gaps for you to ad-lib your own responses.

Role-playing with a partner can be fun—I'm not kidding. It can provide an opportunity for laughter at the most unexpected moments. (You'll probably need some of that by this point.) In chapter 16, "Laughing through the Apocalypse," you'll learn how to appreciate the inherent humor in your situation. Role-playing is a good way to experience this. Listening to someone pontificate with your mother's grandiosity or whine like your dad may be painful, but it may also strike you as poignant or amusing. It's OK to laugh, and don't forget to laugh at your own verbal tics and tired routines as well. Seeing the humor in these situations means you are gaining distance, which is a key element in moving beyond a "stuck" relationship.

SWITCH-HITTING

Enlisting someone to help also allows you to try what I call *switch-hitting,* that is, flipping roles so that you put yourself in your parents' shoes. That way, you come closer to truly identifying with them. By taking on their dialogue and letting yourself hear how your words sound coming out of someone else's mouth, you will raise this exercise to a much higher plane. Not only will you be able to fine-tune your parents' probable reactions, but you will get an instant injection of empathy. Internalizing how scary it is for your parents to experience the "new you" will, when the time comes to play this scene out for real, enable you to spot immediately what they are feeling. Armed with that knowledge, you will know how to deal with their emotions in a humane yet firm fashion. Most important, seeing guilt-provoking emotion on your mother's face or anger in the taut line of your father's mouth will not ambush you. You will be expecting that reaction.

CASTING YOUR COSTAR

Your Spouse or Partner

The most obvious choice is your significant other. This individual knows your parents well and can easily help you construct realistic dialogues as well as anticipate your parents' points of resistance. A supportive partner can also help you be less self-conscious about role-playing.

However, in some cases your partner may not be the best choice.

- She may have given up on dealing with your parents—or hers. Many people don't believe that it's worth the effort to try to change things. You've got enough on your plate without trying to change her mind.

- He may be uncomfortable with role-playing. Some people, men especially, feel silly pretending in any context. Bullying him into helping is a bad idea, and it can really backfire. For role-playing to be effective, you need someone who is really loose and game.

Friends

You might consider asking your Second Opinion to help with role-playing. That person obviously knows the situation and has interacted with your parents, which makes it easier to ensure that the scenarios you construct will be realistic. Perhaps you are afraid that you have already asked too much of your S.O., but remember: Most people like to see things through to the end once they have made an initial emotional investment. Having made that investment, your S.O. will likely be delighted to accompany you a little farther down the road to change.

Don't overlook the ham. If you can't get help from someone who is familiar with your folks, try that pal who is always "doing" voices, the one who is a genius mimic and has a talent for drama. What hams lack in familiarity, they make up for with ability—they *love* to act. Tell them you're asking them specifically because they are such great actors, and they will probably work their heart out mastering your parents' every inflection and gesture.

Siblings

Brothers and sisters also know your parents well, and whether or not they are working on changing their relationship with them, they can be of great help in your efforts. Unlike the long, wrenching discussions between siblings wrestling with troubling parental issues, role-playing can be great fun. It can give you and your sibling(s) a chance to gently make fun of your parents (don't get too nasty), without having to delve too deeply into childhood dynamics. It can actually bring you closer to your siblings. Besides, most of us have a sibling who would *love* the chance to "play" one of our parents.

WHAT YOU WANT FROM YOUR "SCENE PARTNER"

Feedback on a role-playing exercise is especially valuable if it is very specific. "You looked uncomfortable" doesn't tell you much that is useful. Instead, ask for feedback on how convincing you sound and how relaxed you look. "Your hands looked nailed to your sides, you didn't smile, your lips were tight, and you never looked at me" makes it very clear what you need to work on.

Give your scene partner this questionnaire to fill out.

Please describe my:

- Facial expression (smiling, grimacing, tight-lipped)
- Body language (crossing arms across chest, hands on hips, twisting hair)
- Posture (ramrod straight, lounging on the furniture, shoulders hunched)
- Tone of voice (high-pitched screechy, disc-jockey mellow, kindergarten-teacher condescending)
- Inflection (confrontational, timid, firm)
- Sounds (tsk-tsking, tongue clicking, sighs)

On a scale of 1–10, rate how well I:

- Stayed on topic
- Repeated myself enough (but not too much)
- Was gentle but firm
- Listened attentively to their responses, didn't interrupt except to get things back on track
- Used positive language

- Displayed empathy
- Thanked them sincerely for listening and being open

BREATHING AND RELAXATION

You'll know if you're role-playing effectively if you start to get worked up when you do it. Just going through the motions without allowing yourself to feel some of the intense emotions that come up in your conflicts with your parents is a waste of time. You have to be willing to risk something; you have to get into character to get something out of this exercise.

In chapter 11 we talked about the pivotal moment when your parents push your buttons and how almost instantly your breathing gets labored or your palms begin to itch or your temples throb. If you are role-playing effectively, you will feel at least a twinge of that.

To keep such physiological reactions in check, experiment with controlled breathing. It allays anxiety by feeding extra oxygen to the brain. Scientists now believe that deep-breathing and standing-relaxation techniques are the best self-preservation mechanisms we have. See the bibliography for some good books on this topic. And read the next chapter to learn how to make your physiological reactions work for you rather than against you.

Chapter 16

Laughing through the Apocalypse

With the fearful strain that is on me night and day if I did not laugh I should die.—Abraham Lincoln

Laughing is probably the last thing you feel like doing when your parents are driving you insane, but that is precisely the reaction you should have sometimes. Throughout the ages, much humor has been derived from the antics of bumbling dads, meddling mothers-in-law, and overindulgent parents of all sorts. Think Shakespeare, Jane Austen, Woody Allen, Philip Roth. From *Sanford and Son* to *Meet the Parents* and *The Royal Tenenbaums,* relations between adult children and their mothers and fathers have been a rich topic in popular culture. There is good reason for this: almost everyone periodically finds themselves in situations with their parents that walk the line between harrowing and hilarious.

One of my clients, a top executive at a huge entertainment company, brought his mother to the Grammy Awards. After introducing her to some of his colleagues, he brought her over to say hello to Mariah Carey. His mother took one look at the singer's gown—cut down to her navel—and asked in a voice tinged with disapproval, "Do you work for my son?"

"No," said Carey. "I'm an entertainer."

"I'm sure you are, my dear," said his mother, turning on her heels.

Did you laugh when you read that? I certainly did when my client told me that story. He was mortified by how his mother had

148

acted, and I was trying to be sympathetic, but I couldn't help myself—a little guffaw just slipped out. And you know what? When he saw me laugh, he started laughing too. In fact, we both laughed so hard tears came to our eyes. I still smile now every time I think of his five-foot-two-inch mom in her spangly pantsuit giving Mariah Carey the cold shoulder.

My point is that learning to see your parents' foibles—and your sometimes overblown reactions to them—as humorous, at least on some level, is healthy and extremely productive. Seeing that your life resembles a not-ready-for-prime-time reality show can be as efficient as the SWAT explosives unit at diffusing any bombs your parents throw at you.

And learning to laugh to yourself at your parents—yes, it's something you may have to learn—will also provide you with great material to share with friends and family. That's important, because telling funny stories about your zany parents is a good way to drain the drama and heartache out of your dealings with them. And that's a giant step toward putting it all in perspective and eventually dealing with your parents in a sane, strategic manner.

With whom should you share such stories? Well, for starters, your Second Opinion will enjoy hearing you talk about your parents with humor. He or she already knows the players and what's at stake, and—if you have chosen your S.O. carefully—will be overjoyed to hear that you are dealing with the conflict in a less loaded way. Everyone loves a good story. There is no greater tension reliever than being able to transform an annoying interaction with your parents into a ruefully funny story to tell your partner as you both lay in bed at night. The person you love probably has heard his or her share of horror stories, listened to you complain endlessly, probably with good reason, about your burden. If you can occasionally rework the drama into a comedy, it will make listening to your complaints much easier the next time around.

I realize that recasting the drama between you and your parents into a comedy is not always easy. Laughter requires distance. Unless you put some space between yourself and the situation, learn to float above it and look down at the dynamics from a safe place, you will not be able to appreciate the inherent humor, however black, in the situation. If you allow yourself to be stuck in the role of victim, you will feel threatened and angry instead of bemused and in possession of a good story for your friends.

Imagine your family as a sitcom. Even though you may react to that suggestion by saying, "But the things that go on between me and my parents aren't funny; they're tragic," remember that, on paper, the friction on *Everybody Loves Raymond,* or *All in the Family,* could have been tragedy, too. The guilt in those shows is thick and unwieldy, as are the insults and humiliations. But the writers work hard to tap into the universality of suffering, which can be funny in a poignant, human way. They tried to find the humor in misplaced pride, in petty self-interests, in love gone awry. That is how I want you to view the friction between you and your parents, at least from time to time. What role would you play? What actors would you cast as your mom and dad? What would your character do differently? What funny lines would you give yourself? Where would the laugh track chime in?

You might also create a parental humor support group with some friends and swap tales of your parents' silly behavior. Avoid complaining; concentrate on the nutty narratives. Not only will such sessions alleviate an unbelievable amount of stress, but they will show you that you are not alone. They may even show you that some people have parents even crazier than yours.

Humor can exist in the most painful and difficult of situations. In urging you to find the humor in your situation, I am not suggesting that you mask your darker feelings—merely that you not be overwhelmed by them. The key is to accept that your parents can be simultaneously annoying (or humiliating or sad or manipulative) *and* funny. And that you can sometimes be funny or at least lighthearted in your response to them.

There is a big difference between *manufacturing* humor (it will always feel phony and hurt more than it helps) and *cultivating* it if even the faintest whisper of humor lurks in any situation. That is a gift that will last you for many years. As Mark Twain said, "Against the assault of laughter nothing can stand."

・ Chapter 17 ・

Making Your Body Say
What You Mean

I bet you'd be horrified if you could see a film of yourself as you "get into it" with your parents. I can almost guarantee that your body, like the Incredible Hulk's, undergoes a stunning metamorphosis: you may arch your back, hunch your shoulders, or draw your head into your shoulders like a turtle. Perhaps you cross your arms across your chest, gripping your biceps savagely.

Or are you one of those people who squeeze into the corner of the couch, rolling up into a progressively smaller ball as the conversation proceeds, by the end of it almost invisible?

To take control of the situation with your parents, you must control your own body. You need to realize that changing your body language with them can be one of your most effective tools of persuasion, because body language is, for the most part, subliminal. Your parents may not know what's different about you, but they will register this change deep down. And when that happens, they in turn are likely to change in unexpected ways.

NOT THROWING YOUR WEIGHT AROUND: CONNOR

During their many arguments, Connor had spent much of his adult life trying, in vain, to physically intimidate his father, Arthur.

Connor, a forty-seven-year-old aerospace engineer, was a couple of inches taller than Arthur, a difference that was even more pronounced now that the older man was in his late sixties and had shrunk a bit. When Arthur would rise to his feet to badger Connor about his investments or his kids or his house or any of the dozen of pet complaints he had, Connor would jump to his feet as well and stand close enough to his father to smell the old man's stale cigarette breath. His voice would be loud and challenging as he argued back. Naturally, things would get worse from there.

Connor's height advantage was not helping him win these arguments; in fact, getting "physical" with Arthur only made him more irascible. Neither man would back down, and their arguments sometimes escalated to the point where Connor was afraid one of them was going to really lose his temper one day and throw a punch.

There were a lot of things Connor had to learn about dealing with his father, but I urged him to start with a change in his body language. To initiate that, I suggested that Connor and his father stop meeting for lunch at Arthur's condo—too easy to get into one of their classic toe-to-toe altercations there—and instead meet at a restaurant. That way they were both more likely to remain seated, if not calm.

I advised Connor that when his father began the usual litany of criticisms, he was to immediately focus on what he had identified as the prize: moving the conversation away from his father's complaints and toward more enjoyable topics, shared interests like bonefishing or political history.

We came up with some body language that was more likely to help Connor achieve that goal. When his father started on one of his annoying rants, Connor would *not* rise to his feet and bellow back; instead, he would slowly and sympathetically nod as his father tore into him. He would keep his mouth pleasantly impassive and look directly into his father's eyes. He would not look away with embarrassment or try to stare the older man down. He would try to look as though he was listening respectfully—without betraying his feelings about what was being said. In fact, the goal was to not have any feelings at that moment. He was to adopt the body language he knew well from his job; I told him to imagine he was stuck in a very boring meeting, a very boring meeting he had to appear to be extremely interested in. Connor would let his father prattle on while he thought about what he was going to buy his wife for their anniversary.

Connor tried this strategy a week later and was astonished by what happened. Within three minutes, he said, his father ran out of steam. It was the shortest confrontation they had had in decades. Then, as we had planned, Connor reached across the table and gently, lovingly put his hand on the sleeve of his father's jacket. "Yes, Dad," he said, "I hear you. And I'll definitely keep what you said in mind. I think it's really important."

Before his dad could say anything, Connor then reached into his briefcase and pulled out a magazine on adventure-fishing. "I saw this," he said, pulling his chair closer to his father, "and I thought of you." Connor says they spent the rest of their lunch happily discussing the merits of fishing rods and native guides.

Connor stuck to this routine—never rising to the bait when his father yammered on, always nodding in a vague, sympathetic way while making eye contact, always producing a positive diversion as soon as his father seemed to run out of things to complain about. After about six months, he realized the combat scenes were happening less and less frequently. And then, one day, there was no confrontation at all. His dad had given up.

"I took all the fun out of it for him, I guess," Connor told me the day after he and his father had their first tension-free lunch. "I guess if I wasn't going to give him a good fight, throw my weight around, and tell him he was wrong, it really wasn't worth his while."

FIVE STEPS TO MAKING YOUR BODY SAY WHAT YOU WANT

1) ANALYZE THE PROBLEM

Meditate on what your goal is when dealing with your parents and then think about how your physical message is undermining that.

2) DIAGNOSE

Become aware of how you carry yourself when you are with your parents. Do you shove your hands in your pockets? Sit as far away from them as possible? Loom threateningly? Avert your eyes? Pay particular attention to your posture, the position of your hands, your facial expressions.

3) FORMULATE A PLAN

How can you alter your body message to achieve your goal? Should you sit closer to your mother on the couch? Put your hand on her shoulder firmly to stop her from complaining about your father? Should you pull yourself up to full height at the dinner table when your dad starts to grill you, instead of trying to sink under the table? Is it time to stick your chin out and fix a steely glint in your eyes? Or is it better to concentrate on controlling your breathing and look off (slightly) into the distance? Don't forget to consider how your parents generally react to physical stimuli. Do they crave hugs? Hate contact?

Remember that you have many options: standing or sitting, smiling or keeping your face blank, keeping your hands quietly in your lap or waving them around, hugging your mother or whining at her. Make sure you consider all your options.

4) EXPERIMENT

Careful planning is good, but sometimes it takes a few trial runs to figure out what works. So have a few backups. It may seem logical that your mother would respond better if you angle your body toward her forcefully, but people don't always act logically, and that may wind up only exacerbating her negative behavior. So try something else—perhaps getting up to straighten the sofa cushions when she's driving you nuts. Don't be discouraged if the first thing you try doesn't work; don't let that scare you back into your old routine.

Connor, for example, figured that Arthur might be jolted out of his litany of complaints by a gentle touch, but he was a little afraid to actually lay a hand on his father, who had never been much for showing physical affection. So we came up with an alternative: Connor would touch Arthur on the sleeve of his jacket. Sure, there was risk involved—Arthur might have drawn away angrily—but if that happened, we had yet another alternative: the next time, Connor would lean forward and rest his arms firmly on the table to communicate the same message to Arthur, that he had indeed heard his father's complaints and it was now time to move on.

5) ONCE YOU'VE GOT IT, STICK WITH IT

If you have children, you know how important it is to be consistent. Once you find something that works, keep doing it. More than any other kind of change you can make, physical changes are received by your parents in a deep, unconscious way. Just as your body is "speaking," their body is "listening"—even if they don't know it. If you can be consistent, they will, in a relatively short time, subliminally let go of your old, ineffective language and adjust to your new posture.

Chapter 18

Toning Down Your Tone of Voice

Most of us are aware of *what* we are saying in tense situations, but many of us are clueless about *how* we are saying it. I have lost count of the number of times during conferences with clients and their parents that it has become apparent that an aggressive tone of voice is the detonator in conflicts.

TONING IT DOWN: ELISE

"All I said was that repeating herself endlessly was not making the situation any better!" In a counseling session with her mother, Adrienne, forty-three-year-old Elise, a preschool teacher, was giving me the play-by-play of their latest fight. Their arguments had settled into a very predictable pattern. Adrienne was always offering advice and opinions, sometimes pretty wacky, and then repeating them when Elise ignored her. Eventually, Elise would tire of her mother's carping and hiss a response that was innocuous on paper but volatile in practice.

This time, they had been at the mall and Elise had forgotten where she'd parked the car. Her mother had trailed after her in the parking lot, offering suggestions ("Maybe we could ask people who are pulling out if they've seen a light blue Honda"). Frustrated by her mother and her own forgetfulness, Elise finally shot back.

"The tone she used was absolutely humiliating," said Adrienne, sixty-six, a retired accountant, her voice still quavering with fury. "I repeated myself because she was disregarding my suggestions. I thought maybe she hadn't heard me." True to form, Adrienne then burst into tears.

Let's be clear on the facts: (1) repeating herself is a problem of Adrienne's, one that irritates Elise no end, and (2) Adrienne didn't

"What the hell do you want?
You know this is my busiest day, Mother!"

really think that Elise hadn't heard her. But neither of those truths is the point.

The point is that using a dismissive tone with her mother wasn't helping Elise achieve her goal: getting her mother to stop offering silly suggestions and to stop repeating herself.

When Elise and I were alone later, I cautioned her not take her eyes off the prize. Ignoring her mother's exhortations and then, at the breaking point, turning on her and spitting out a retort laced with bile was probably her *least* effective strategy.

I suggested that she act preemptively. First, separate the wheat from the chaff, I told her. By that I meant she should listen for *any* valuable suggestion her mother might make. Sure, most of what her mother offered in such situations was way off the mark, but I had noticed that Elise tended to dismiss *all* her mother's comments out of hand, never bothering to search for the nugget of wisdom that was sometimes there. Finding that nugget would go a long way toward satisfying her mother's deep-seated need to be helpful.

Should she find that nugget, I told Elise, she should stop in her tracks and immediately thank her mother in a *gentle voice,* perhaps tossing in a warm grasp of her mother's arm: "That's a great idea, Mom. If I can't find the car in a couple of minutes, I'm going to do just what you suggest."

Should her mother continue to babble—a likely scenario—Elise should not suffer in silence. I advised her to stop again, turn to her mother, perhaps laying both hands on Adrienne's shoulders, and very calmly explain that her suggestions were not helpful at this time. The best tone of voice in such potentially explosive situations is a near-whisper. The key is to *banish the edge that so often creeps into our voice when we are annoyed.* Use loving gestures even if you are feeling the opposite emotions; *cultivate the tone of voice you use with children or your pets during a tender moment.*

Remember: the goal here is not to express *your* frustration; it is to modify your parent's behavior. Use whatever tone and words you believe will mollify your parent, but don't be patronizing—that's just another way of expressing hostility and is sure to make things worse. Summon up your acting ability—we all have it. Take a tip from the Method acting technique made famous by Marlon Brando and Al Pacino: use experiences from your past as a way of generating real emotion. Even if you are feeling angry and frustrated, channel the calm, loving feelings you have toward your favorite aunt or Rusty the Wonder Dog. "I know you're trying to be helpful, Mom, but right now I need to really concentrate so that I can remember where I parked the car. What you can do to help me most is be quiet for a moment."

If that doesn't work, I told Elise, stop Adrienne again and repeat the admonition. The important thing is to keep the tone of voice identical—a calm whisper—instead of pumping up the volume and escalating the situation. There is a very good chance Adrienne will eventually stop. And without tears. Why? Not because she has magically turned into a fantasy mom, but because Elise's new approach foils Adrienne's unconscious need for the blowup that Elise has in the past always rewarded her with. Yes, Adrienne cries when Elise snaps at her, but the interaction is satisfying her on some level. Maybe she needs attention, even if it's negative attention. Or maybe she grew up in a household where such interactions were common. Regardless of the reason, the key for Elise is to remove that satisfaction. By gently stopping her mother and signaling that no matter how many times Adrienne tries to provoke her, it will not happen, Elise greatly improves the odds that Adrienne will eventually change her modus operandi. (It took almost a year, but she did. Adrienne eventually learned to censor herself in those situations, reluctant to endure yet another patient "talking-to" from Elise.)

Be aware that the gentle tone is not always appropriate. For Elise, it was effective, but you may need to modulate your tone in a different direction. Perhaps you need to stop swallowing your words with a bullying parent and speak clearly, forcefully, and slowly. Or maybe you need to stop being so intense and start using a casual, bemused tone.

The key is to experiment—and become acutely attuned to the sometimes subtle ways your tone affects how your parents react. Keep a journal to track the effectiveness of your changes in tone. Haul out that trusty little tape recorder and practice. And remember, consistency is crucial.

• Chapter 19 •

Reaching for the Words That Reach Them

Be honest: Can you imagine *any* situation in which telling someone that they're driving you crazy would be the best way to get them to stop what they're doing? Would it work with your boss? Does it work with the kids or your spouse? In my experience, it has always led to an argument, hurt feelings, or long, uncomfortable silences. Yet many of the people I work with hurl that phrase at their parents weekly, if not daily. You'd think they'd realize by now that it's about as effective as throwing bacon on a grease fire.

The words you use are profoundly important when you are trying to open people up to change. As with tone of voice and body language, the actual words can be as important as the substance of the message you are trying to convey.

I will bet that you use a limited vocabulary when you deal with your parents in times of stress. You may think you are being extraordinarily articulate, making complete sense, and speaking from the bottom of your heart, but the words and phrases you use, over and over, may, ironically, just serve to aggravate the situation. You may inadvertently be using provocative or even incendiary language that undermines your goals; furthermore, your repetition of these words or phrases may grate on your parents like a broken record, which just makes them tune you out.

There are many things we all have said at one time or another that needlessly alienate our parents.

- We stick with accusatory language that always lays the blame at their feet. "If you just wouldn't . . . ," or "Well, that's because you . . . ," or "I can't even talk to you."
- We use psychobabble (often combined with a generous side order of blame—a real winner). "You're paranoid," or "You're projecting," or "This problem all stems from your obsessive-compulsive disorder."
- We speak to them as though they were children. "Now if you'll just sit for a little moment and think clearly, I think you'll agree with me," or "Now there, I don't think you want to be so angry," or "Maybe you're just a little cranky today."
- We use "ultimatum" language. "If you don't shut up, I'm just going to walk out that door," or "I am not going to stand for this any longer," or (my favorite) "One more crack like that, and I'm never speaking to you again."

The psychologist Susan Forward has made a life study out of developing "nondefensive communication," ways of short-circuiting the destructive treadmill pattern of *attack-defense-retreat-escalation* that characterizes many emotionally loaded interactions. This technique is particularly valuable when dealing with parents.

My version of nondefensive communication has two variations, depending on whether you (1) are trying to establish new behavior patterns with your parent or (2) are fending off an unwanted attack by them.

THE LANGUAGE OF CHANGE

If you are trying to establish a new pattern, it's important that you use "sharing" language. That means words like *we, let's, together,* and *compromise.* Imagine that you are at work (especially if you work in a project-oriented office) and you are thrown onto a team with someone you generally don't agree with and don't think is particularly smart. What do you do? Surely, you're savvy enough to know that at the first team meeting you don't start out by using incendiary language. You don't say, "Well, I'm not going through the hassles you had on your last project, that's for sure. That was a disaster." Nor do you say, "Let me lay out the rules for this collaboration right now, missy." Of course not.

Instead, you ease into it, with your ego in check and an unflappable smile on your face. You know you will have to subtly convince your coworker that at least half of your good ideas are *her* ideas, because even if it means less glory for you, such an approach paves the way to a smooth collaboration. You refuse to get angry when she baits you. You carefully cajole her out of any ill-conceived ideas she might cook up (no amount of harmony is worth looking stupid in front of your boss), but you are careful not to create a tense working relationship that would make your boss think you aren't capable of handling a "difficult" coworker.

In the end, it's all about language: "Your idea for that supply chain problem is brilliant, and the best thing about it is its flexibility. It really invites creative thinking. It really sparked me to think of ways we could make it amazing. With your idea as bedrock, we could blow the boss away."

This workplace model works very well with parents when you are trying to institute change. Nondefensive communication requires a commitment to not lose your temper or even raise your voice. You are setting limits and laying new ground rules for how you intend to interact with them in the future, but you are doing so in a calm way, using collaborative, ameliorative language that expresses understanding and empathy. For example: "Mom, neither of us seems to be getting the most out of our visits together. I think we need to come up with some creative compromises. Here are a few of my top priorities, and the ways I'm going to change my behavior. After I finish, please take some time to comment on them and then tell me how you're feeling. No need to get all churned up. We can definitely work together to find a more satisfying system."

THE LANGUAGE OF DEFENSE

When you are fending off an attack, you must remind yourself that on a basic, often unconscious, level your parent is not trying to get a "real" response, even if he seems to be repeatedly pressing you for one. He is simply trying to engage you on any level he can, even if that engagement is extremely negative for both of you. It's a fool's game unless you realize you can't "win" and change the rules. There is no right answer in those situations, no answer that would satisfy him, short of telling him what he wants to hear . . . and in many cases, even *that* wouldn't silence him.

The key is to stick to nonjudgemental, "mirroring" language ("I can see that you're very upset" or "I'm sorry you feel that way") that expresses empathy—up to a point. Be consistent and unshakable in your refusal to snap at the bait.

DO THE RIGHT THING: TAD

"My father has made a second career out of pushing me to the end of my tether," said Tad, a thirty-eight-year-old musician. "He's a sort of evil maestro of the form. Every time I talk with him, he finds a way to bring the conversation back to the same question: When am I going to get a real job? Over and over. I ignore him and change the subject to a decent gig I've had or maybe a great movie I've seen, but he always demands an answer about when I'm going to 'stop fooling around with the keyboards,' and 'put my nose to the grindstone.'"

"He knows I'm worried about money and that I want to get married and start a family, so he plays on that. In return, I get more and more sarcastic. I hear myself sounding shrill, and sometimes I wind up yelling at him, 'How many goddamn times are you going to ask me that question? I've worked all my life to escape the tired little life you've chosen for yourself. Is that too hard to grok, or are you a cretin?' I know that's a stupid response, but I don't how else to deal with this question."

I suggested that Tad try an approach that included a new tone of voice and some new language. Changing the subject obviously wasn't working. Neither was calling his father names. His father was obviously someone who was comfortable provoking conflict, so what was the point of getting into a conflict with him?

My idea was to test whether Tad could find a style of language and a variety of response that would better satisfy his father. We talked for a while about his dad, Aaron, a former machinist who had never been very happy in his job and had been on disability for many years. Yet he was proudly blue-collar, which was a subtext of the conflict between them.

In unconscious reaction to Aaron's working-class, tough-guy turns of phrase, Tad had worked hard over the years to make his speech more precise, even refined. When he talked to his father, that impulse jumped into hyperdrive until he sounded like a snotty college literature professor. He recommended books on musical theory that Aaron clearly wouldn't be interested in, and seemed not to notice that his rarefied language and sophisticated tastes alienated his father.

I urged Tad to realize that his father had many conflicting thoughts and impulses. Aaron was not a simpleton, and he wasn't just annoying Tad for the heck of it. To begin with, he had some justification for worrying about Tad's future, and Tad had to acknowledge that part of his defensiveness stemmed from knowing that his father had a point. Also, Tad was living a footloose life that his dad, with three kids to support, had never been able to experience, which probably triggered some jealousy. Then there was Aaron's sense of mortality; Tad was the oldest, and none of the other kids had managed to marry and reproduce either. To top it off, there was that high-falutin' lingo that Tad slung around like a French deconstructionist.

It triggered feelings of inadequacy in Aaron. All around, a bad combination.

So Tad tried something new.

Aaron: So when are you going to "buckle down" and get a real job, kid?

Tad (*calmly and gently*): I'm working very hard on my music right now.

Aaron: Hell, that's not a real job. I mean one that comes with a paycheck. Something honest and regular. There's no shame in that.

Tad (*calmly and gently*): Definitely no shame in that, Dad.

Aaron: A real job would give you some roots, a way to support a family, like you keep saying you want.

Tad (*calmly and gently*): No doubt about that, Dad. There is that advantage to it. I want you to know that I do a lot thinking about it. I take this problem very seriously.

Aaron: I'm ashamed of you when my friends from the block ask what you're doing.

Tad (*calmly and gently*): I'm sorry that you feel bad, Dad. I know how much you don't like to be embarassed.

Aaron: Then why don't you stop embarrassing me? What is it going to take to get you to settle down and make something of yourself?

Tad (*calmly and gently*): Well, I've decided I'm going to continue devoting myself to my music, even though it's a tough path, but I do see that you're upset about my decision, and I'm really sorry about that. You're certainly entitled to have your opinion about what I should do with my life. And from your point of view, I can imagine why you think my choice doesn't make sense. I want you to know that I'm not just tossing what you're saying in the garbage; I'm not ignoring you. I know you think you know what's best for me, and you must be awfully pissed off that I don't do what you think I should."

Aaron was silent. What more was there to say? It became clear to him—a feeling that was reinforced by subsquent similar conversations—that Tad was no longer going to bludgeon him with rhetoric or lash out defensively. There was not going to be any class warfare. Instead, Tad kept the interchanges brief, unfettered by sophisticated defenses or diversions, and full of measured empathetic language. Most important, he purposefully deprived his father of an emotional payoff that just perpetuated their destructive dynamic. After a few months, they were able to move on to other subjects.

• Chapter 20 •

Diversion: Learn to Love
the Bait and Switch

We are all products of a culture in which honesty, communication, and directness are prized. The old-fashioned values of tact, suppression of emotions, and avoidance of unpleasant realities—what was once labeled "good manners"—are now considered manipulative and psychologically destructive. Such behavior is characterized as the root of much of the unhappiness in the world, from depression and phantom stomach ailments to suicide and spousal abuse.

In general, this is a good thing. Confronting problems directly without resorting to gimmicky tactics, phony sentiments, or bait-and-switch dynamics tends to be more effective, even though truth-telling may cause some discomfort.

That said, there are times when diversion is a valid way to deal with your parents. As long as you are aware of what you're doing and not using such techniques at the wrong time, that is, when you should be cutting to the chase by making boundaries explicit, there is nothing nefarious about breaking the rhythm of your parents' most irritating behavior by throwing a chew toy into their cage from time to time.

Although I don't like to overemphasize comparisons between your children and your parents, in this case, such an exercise can be instructive. Do you think twice about waving a colorful toy in your two-year-old's face when he is about to melt down over not getting the right kind of cookie at the coffee shop? On the contrary. If the toy stops the kid from wailing, you breathe a sigh of relief and secretly congratulate yourself for being a wizard of child management.

The same rules apply when dealing with your parents. Diversion shouldn't replace real limit-setting with parents, but, when used judiciously, it can be a valuable tool. Not every unpleasant incident with your parents has to be turned into a "lesson." Some things are simply better avoided, either permanently or at least until you are ready to deal with them.

In some cases, you may decide to use the following strategies as a stopgap measure because you are focusing on altering other, more heinous interactions with your parents. This sort of prioritizing is healthy; you must concentrate on one issue at a time or risk feeling overwhelmed. In other cases, you may decide that using these diversions helps you eliminate these minor annoyances. Why turn those into major battlegrounds? It's wiser to save your energy for the really significant sources of friction.

Diversions fall into two basic categories, both of which require some planning.

VERBAL DIVERSIONS

You know all too well what your parents' pet peeves and enthusiasms are, and this is the time to take advantage of that knowledge.

Does your mother always have a hilarious, catty fashion analysis of passersby? Then always be ready with a tidbit to toss her way when you sense she is about to bug you about getting your boyfriend to marry you. Wouldn't you rather bond over the tacky woman in the shoe department who really shouldn't be wearing that micromini?

Does your father love to talk about his golf game? Then subscribe to a golf magazine so that when he starts to complain about your mother in that unbearably bitter tone, you can divert him with a discourse on Tiger Woods's short game.

Wouldn't you rather get the negative focus off you, even if it means listening to your parent launch into a diatribe?

PHYSICAL DIVERSIONS

If I had a dollar for every client with a parent who picks lint off her sweater or straightens his collar, I would be writing this book from a cliff house in Fiji. That goes double for smoothing cowlicks, pulling the hem of a shirt to get out the wrinkles, and whacking the client's back to get him to stand up straight.

These actions are really irritating, but you're younger and faster than they are, so take advantage of that. Instead of grinning and bearing it or snatching your parent's hand away angrily, learn to dodge the wandering fingers. Is your mom moving toward you to turn down that polo shirt collar? Get to your feet and start stacking the newspapers for the recycling bin. Is Dad circling to pinch your cheek? Bob and weave like a prizefighter. Consider it part of your aerobic cross-training.

Or you can turn the situation around. Start focusing, with equal good intentions, *bien sur,* on his or her sartorial shortcomings. Unless your mother is a perfectly groomed socialite and your father a blue-blazered yachtsman with a valet, they've likely got a little lint or dandruff of their own. Don't wait for them to start in on the inadequacies of your grooming (you don't want it to be tit for tat); get picky a bit on your own. If they get testy, remind them in a gentle, loving tone that you just want them to look their best.

• Chapter 21 •

Let Them Be Your Savior—
or at Least Think They Are

Whenever possible, I meet with my clients' parents. Among the questions I ask them is "On a scale from one to ten, how do you rank yourself on helpfulness and supportiveness?" You wouldn't believe how many of them quickly give themselves an eleven. This is truly remarkable because when I ask my clients to rank their parents in that way, their reponse is often a variation on this theme: "I'd give them a three or four. They think they're being helpful, but most of the time, they do more harm than good."

Sound familiar? These parents range from the excessive types (they send massive stuffed animals for your kids even though you live in a two-room apartment, flood your e-mail in-box with advertisements for cut-rate memory vitamins, beg you to let them take you for a makeover and some new clothes) to the ones who blithely ignore your needs entirely, all the while bragging to anyone who'll listen about how they wish *their* parents had been as helpful as they are.

Despite such protestations, to you it's probably painfully obvious that for many "helpful" parents, the top priority is to get their own needs met. And, wouldn't you know it, such parents tend to be easily offended when you don't take their smallest suggestion, no matter how delicate you are about refusing. So you wind up twisting yourself in knots to fend off their "help," which ends up sending them away in a huff.

There are myriad reasons why parents act like this: fear about mortality and your independence, frustration with their lives, an inability to quit seeing you as an extension of themselves, and even just plain loneliness, but there is no question that such behavior puts great strain on your relationship with them.

Is there a solution? Sometimes. I call it *saviorizing*. Executed properly, it can transform your parents' fantasy about being helpful into—yes—real help. Saviorizing is, technically, manipulation—it entails tapping into your parents' ego-needs to come to your rescue while you are guiding them toward an undisclosed goal of your own design—but it is a *positive* manipulation. It respects their stated intention of helping you and, in the end, will help sow good feelings on both sides.

Be warned that saviorizing can be a bit bumpy in the beginning. Your parents have likely made it perfectly clear that they prefer to "help" you their way (pop-in visits at inconvenient times, another reindeer holiday sweater that can't be returned). They may be none too happy to give you the sort of help you, in fact, actually find help-ful. But don't balk if they are a bit put out. Stand your ground; the situation will get better. Eventually, they will get a contact high from the joy you derive from actually being helped. When you shower them with gratitude and positive reinforcement—a crucial part of saviorizing—they may experience more pleasure than they ever imagined. Everyone likes to be hailed as a savior (and, after all, it isn't much fun for them to see that little face of yours puckered with disappointment when you take the reindeer sweater out of the box).

Like all the other techniques in this part of the book, saviorizing requires you to keep your eyes on the prize—in this case even more doggedly than usual. If your parents are of the "I'm just trying to help" persuasion, you are probably fed up by now and go to great lengths to reject any "help" they offer. You may have tried, futilely, to explain to them that they aren't helping at all. You may even have tried to point out that their "help" is really self-indulgence in disguise (bad idea). Or you just suffer in pained silence.

But that hasn't improved the situation, has it? Well, it's time to focus again on your goals, not on proving that you're right and that your parents are wrong. If you use your insight into your parents' personality, history, and modus operandi, you may be able to create a scenario in which their joy at being your savior motivates them to help you in real ways.

THANK YOU FOR NOT INTERRUPTING: LYNN

By the time she came to see me, Lynn was on the brink of ceasing to speak in her mother-in-law's presence ever again. Hilla, sixty, a top-flight advertising copywriter, had driven her to this point by constantly interrupting Lynn. Whenever Lynn spoke, which wasn't often because she is shy under the best of circumstances, Hilla would cut her off, interjecting with an anecdote, a piece of unsolicited advice, or an off-the-cuff pronouncement. Often she discoursed on how Linn's shyness must be a problem at work, and gave tips on how her daughter-in-law could be more assertive. The irony of the fact that she interrupted Lynn to give tips on assertiveness escaped her; for Hilla, the only thing that seemed to matter was that she was the star of the show.

Every family event was excruciating for Lynn, especially the times when it was just Lynn, her husband, Tom, their six-year-old daughter, Wendy, and Hilla. Tom had long ago learned to deal with Hilla's interruptions by interrupting her right back, but Lynn, whose parents had been good listeners, was humiliated into silence. She refused to let Tom defend her—that would be too wimpy—but she couldn't bring herself to be rude back to her mother-in-law. Besides, she really didn't like to see Tom slip into such behavior himself. "The woman will not let me get a word out," she said. "She sees conversation as combat, a battle she is determined to win. And there's no way I'm going change that."

Lynn was unwilling to confront her mother-in-law, so I encouraged her to dangle some other incentive for Hilla in order to change her behavior. As we were brainstorming the possibilities, Lynn happened to mention that even Wendy's interruptions—the constant "why" questions every kid of that age asks—had lately been upsetting her, in part because they so reminded her of Hilla. As she told me this—ping!—she realized that recruiting Hilla to help break Wendy of the bad habit of interrupting might be the ticket. It was clearly an opportunity for saviorizing.

The next time Hilla came over for dinner, Lynn took her aside and told her that she and Tom were concerned about Wendy interrupting them and not listening patiently. She said they had begun a two-pronged approach: gently but firmly pointing out when she was interrupting the grown-ups, and setting a good example by trying very hard not to interrupt each other. Would Hilla join the team to help them out?

"Because she's so young," Lynn told her mother-in-law, "we're doing our darndest to exaggerate to her how important it is to let others finish before we begin talking. We're going to great lengths to show lots of respect for other people's opinions. We'd be very grateful if you'd help us out. You know how much Wendy adores you." Lynn was well aware that she was appealing to her mother-in-law's self-image as a helpful, kind person.

Hilla wasn't offended by Lynn's request because, like many people, she isn't very self-aware and doesn't see herself as an interrupter. Instead, she was delighted to be included in the team effort to help Wendy.

Freed from her fear of being rude to her mother-in-law, Lynn was able to deal with the situation. When Hilla interrupted her during a family dinner later that week, Lynn was able to smile and wink at her, gesturing toward Wendy, who, being an adorable six-year-old, piped up with "How come Grandma is allowed to interrupt and I'm not, Mom?" Hilla immediately stopped talking and mouthed a meek "Sorry." Lynn was much more comfortable reinforcing her mother-in-law's recent good behavior rather than having to point out the rudeness of her past interruptions.

Lynn knew, of course, that Wendy wouldn't always be around and that she eventually would have to deal with Hilla's interruptions more directly, but this was a good start.

Several weeks later, when the two women were in the kitchen, Lynn turned to her mother-in-law and thanked her for helping instill good listening habits in Wendy. Then, placing a gentle hand on Hilla's arm, she added that she too had come to appreciate being listened to by Hilla. "I know I'm shy and that probably irritates you sometimes," she said, "but I really feel that lately you've let me speak my mind more. You are lucky that you speak so fluidly, but I really need people to let me finish a sentence. I just want to tell you how much I appreciate your not interrupting me. Thank you. You've really helped me."

• Chapter 22 •

Disarm Them with Honesty

How can being honest qualify as a "trick of the trade"? Yes, I know it seems not to make sense, but bear with me for a moment.

Many of us have spent our entire lives with our parents getting angry, defensive, silent, sarcastic, bitter, or revengeful in the face of their actions. These aggressive behaviors become engrained in our psyches, a second nature. As I explained in chapter 11, on panic buttons, we come to believe that there is no "wiggle room" between our parents' provocation and our reaction. They incite; we get defensive. We snarl. We throw our heads back in a guffaw of disbelief. We tell them they are out of their minds. We walk out of the room in a disgusted huff.

We know that these behaviors are unproductive—nothing ever changes, after all—but we've bought into the illusion that we have no choice, that these are natural reactions our bodies create to protect ourselves.

But what if the opposite were true? What if emotional honesty, judiciously applied, were the most effective way to jump-start change? What if, in the midst of your usual anger and defensiveness, you simply told your parents how they were making you feel? No vitriole, no drama, no accusations. Just a description of your emotions, stripped bare of comment and blame. For example:

- "Dad, when you say that, you make me feel very small and incompetent. I really don't believe you intend to cause that reaction, but you do. I feel like a kid, which is very uncomfortable for me."
- "Mother, you're hurting my feelings when you compare me to my sisters. I believe you love me and want the best for me, but I'm working hard to feel good about myself, and when you bring up how great they are doing, it sets me back really far. It really makes me feel like crying."
- "Folks, you know what? I know I usually clam up when you try to tell me how to invest my money, but this time I really want you to know how I feel: like you don't trust me. I feel like you still hold it against me that I had that drug problem ten years ago. That really hurts me because I've done so much to gain your trust in the years since."

I'm not recommending this for the usual reasons a therapist or religious leader might—that honesty is always, by definition, the best policy, no matter what the outcome. Sure, I believe that honesty is the best way to communicate in many situations, but I'm also a realist. And what we're seeking here is a plan that works. Telling people how you feel is great, but it isn't always effective. Just "letting it all hang out" with your parents without also employing strength, boundaries, and self-control can be counterproductive. Exposing your feelings to your parents all the time in every situation is usually a bad idea because it puts you in a childlike position.

But if used consciously and strategically, honesty can be a valuable part of your parent-management repertoire, especially when your parents are accustomed to seeing you as defensive and unreachable. When they strike out and you respond with your customary defensiveness, they counterpunch as any other familiar combatant would, striking back mindlessly. Remember, they don't care if the interaction is productive; they could probably battle on into eternity. It's you who wants things to be better. So it's up to you to be the one to add a disarming element to the discussion.

So stop dead in the midst of your clever, wounding retort and try honesty, even—dare I say it?—earnestness. I know it's tough to push yourself to be open with your parents after all these years of hiding your true self, but I am not suggesting you open the flood-gates. On the contrary; I am asking you to try a limited experiment. Tap into how their words or actions are making you feel on a deep, unguarded human level—and tell them about it in a quiet voice.

You may not like feeling so vulnerable, but you really aren't risking much. Remember, you're in control; you're choosing to reveal yourself. If their response is negative, it's very easy to back away or try something else.

But I think you may find them quite responsive, or at least shocked into silence. After all, it's probably been a long time since they saw you without your fierce mask on. You've got the element of surprise on your side. Sometimes that can give you an opening to talk to them frankly about the dynamic you're trying to change. It may even move them to reveal a deeper part of themselves, which will help you understand them. They may even offer you some spontaneous emotional support when they realize they've hurt you, that you're in pain instead of in battle.

• Chapter 23 •

Flatten Them with Flattery

When our parents display a swollen sense of superiority, we tend to react—and overreact. Self-involvement, grandiosity, and vanity, all familiar characteristics of difficult parents (and, alas, traits that tend to get worse with age), drive us batty. A parent's self-absorption, something we learned to accommodate as children because we didn't know any better, becomes increasingly obnoxious as we become adults.

This is why you need to get their vanity to work for you.

To suggest such a thing may sound manipulative, but frankly you don't have much choice. That type of behavior points to borderline narcissism (see the bibliography for some helpful books on this subject), which is very hard to change. A wildly inflated sense of self is often hardwired and is among the best-defended psychological frameworks. In plain language, you can't argue a narcissist out of thinking the world revolves around him or her.

So your best bet is to appeal to the Achilles' heel of all vain people: their susceptiblity to flattery. Instead of trying to embarrass them by holding up a cruel mirror to their distorted self-image—a common impulse—you are better off using carefully calibrated positive reinforcement to steer them toward more bearable behavior. The trick is to get them to measure up to their grandiose self-image.

("You think you're perfect, Mom? Well, here's a chance—and a step-by-step plan—for you to prove it.")

This tactic can only work, however, if you overcome your visceral irritation at your parents' self-involvement. You must accept that their behavior is characterological, that is, an inextricable part of their personality. Once you are at peace with that, you can devise a plan to make it work for you.

SILENCING THE SILENT TREATMENT: JORDANA

A stay-at-home mom with two daughters, ages five and seven, Jordana tries hard to please her parents, who are retired and have a contentious marriage. She invites them for overnight visits once a week, makes sure they see their grandkids frequently, buys them thoughtful gifts, and often entertains the entire extended family.

But lately, she has been trying to arrange things so that every get-together is not a huge, exhausting production. On a recent Sunday, for example, she invited just her mom and her mother-in-law over. She figured they'd have a "ladies' brunch" with her two little girls. She suggested that her father go out for lunch with her husband, Jorge, a plan her father seemed to think was terrific. "I thought it would be so nice," Jordana told me, ruefully. "I thought my mom would really enjoy getting away from my father, because all they do is bicker."

Instead, her mother, a stickler for decorum who is very proud of her wealthy upbringing, was deeply offended. She didn't say anything over the phone, but when she got to Jordana's apartment, she was sullen and nearly silent. Even Jordana's mother-in-law noticed. Eventually, Jordana jimmied the truth out of her in the kitchen: she thought Jordana had been terribly rude not inviting her father for brunch. She claimed that Jordana's father had been very upset.

Jordana was confused—her father had sounded delighted when she had told him of the plan—and besides, why did her mother care so much?

Jordana and I talked for a long time about her parents' tense marriage, and Jordana realized she had to accept that her mother felt protective of her father despite the friction between them; she needed him along as a foil and probably always would. But one question remained for Jordana: "Does accepting that mean I have to put up with the silent treatment?"

Pouting was her mother's way of handling any conflct, and the Sarah Bernhardt routine was wearing Jordana down. "Why can't she just talk about what's bothering her? Why does she have to be such a drama queen?"

As we brainstormed, Jordana conceded that the direct approach probably wouldn't work. Instead, I suggested, she could appeal to her mother's vanity and sense of herself as a "regal" individual. Her mother often acts childishly, but in her mind she is as forbearing and benevolent as Saint Francis. Since her mother clearly prides herself on her "graciousness" and aristocratic behavior, why not appeal to her in that vein?

Jordana reported back a week later: "I brought the brunch up on the phone. I could tell she was still miffed about it. I said, 'Mom, I can tell this really upset you. Know how I can tell? You're usually so gracious, even when you are offended. I've always admired how you put other people's comfort ahead of your own. That's what you always taught me to do, and I really value it. That's why I was shocked when you were acting hurt at brunch—you even let on to my mother-in-law, which seemed really out of character for you. No matter what people throw at you, you've always worn a smile and then, later, spoken discreetly about what upset you. I couldn't imagine you doing something that would make another person uncomfortable.'"

Her mother sighed and said, "Well I was very upset, but that's over now."

From that day forward, Jordana made a point of always praising her mother's graciousness, even in the absence of it. When Jordana entertained the family, she made sure she asked her mother to participate in ways that showcased that graciousness: "Mom, would you mind answering the door for the guests instead of letting Jorge do it? I'm stuck in the kitchen cooking, and you're really good at making people feel welcome." During telephone conversations with her mother, Jordana would refer to things that Jorge had done to upset her in front of other people, but she would always follow the anecdote with the news that she had made sure not to give her husband the silent treatment, instead waiting graciously until after the guests had left to discuss the problem with him. "I always remember how you taught me to do that, Mom," she would say. When her daughters pouted in front of her mother, Jordana would say, 'Now girls, Grandmama taught you to never pout. It's not gracious. Always say, 'Excuse me, Mom, but you're upsetting me. May we talk about it in private?' That's the best way to get your point across."

After two months of Jordana's careful, consistent attention to the problem, her mother was modeling that behavior for her grandchildren, abandoning her Sarah Bernhardt routine. What choice did she have? It was more important to her, on a deep ego level, to be seen as a "queen" instead of a "drama queen." And for Jordana, that was real progress.

PART III

FUTURE SHOCK

● ● ● ● ● ● ● ● ● ● ● ● ● ● ●

TROUBLESHOOTING THE HOTSPOTS

As I began researching and writing this book, I started to catalog the most frequent complaints I heard from clients about their parents. Of course, this list isn't comprehensive, but some of the items on it probably ring a bell or two for you. In sharing how clients have used the techniques I discuss earlier in the book, I hope to provide a blueprint for dealing with any sort of problem you might have, whether or not it's on this list.

But do us both a favor: deal with each frustrating, confusing, confounding, irritating, amusing, worrisome interaction one at a time. I know that once you get the "religion," that is, the fever to make change, it's tempting to say to yourself, "OK, now everything is going to be different," but it's much saner and more practical to see change as incremental. You and your parents have been doing this destructive tango for years now, and you can't expect to tackle all the missteps at once.

So you have to make choices. How should you decide what to work on? Use your past experiences in other areas as a guide. Do you generally work best by taking on the most dire problem before the others? Or are you the type to work up a head of steam by first securing an easy victory? Do you consult the *I Ching* on such things, or are you someone who likes to begin with number one on a list? There is no right answer; just stick with a modus operandi that has served you well before. You've got enough pattern-changing on your plate; no need to alter *all* your habits.

Approaching this list one item at a time is not without logistical problems. No doubt while you are concentrating on one behavior, you will encounter a conflict with your parents over another sort of frustrating interaction farther down the list. If you blow up at them regarding that issue or back down when you know you shouldn't, don't beat yourself up. Instead, forgive yourself quickly and refocus on the behavior at hand. Put all other points of conflict in an envelope for later. There will be plenty of time to deal with them, one by one, once you have mastered the change you are working on.

One additional advantage of choosing what you are working on and letting go of the rest is that it will give both you and your parents a breather on some levels. If you can truly let the other annoyances go, you will find you are more focused and, ironically, free of the nonstop irritability that comes from finding a whole score of your parents' behaviors unbearable. As for your parents, they may not be happy that you are reassessing your approach to *any* of their behaviors, but they will be subliminally relieved that at least you are no longer expressing unhappiness with their very existence, which may be your usual pattern.

Most of all, be patient. Changing the way you deal with your parents is a lifelong commitment—for everyone involved.

Chapter 24

They Manipulate Me with Health Crises (Real and Imagined)

There was no way of ignoring it—Mo's seventy-four-year-old mother, Eleanor, was going blind.

For two years, Mo had pretended that it wasn't happening, that Eleanor's macular degeneration wasn't really progressing, that her driving hadn't gotten downright scary, and that she could still read street signs, still negotiate the aisles of the supermarket.

Mo, a thirty-nine-year-old advertising manager at a big corporation, had managed to put the whole thing out of her mind. Her strategy was avoidance, scaling back her calls and visits to her mom. But despite these tactics, she couldn't seem to bury her concern; it played on her mind, sending her into periodic depressions. Once, a year earlier, Mo had tried to talk to her mother about whether it might soon be time for her to give up the car, perhaps move into some sort of assisted living complex, but the conversation had quickly escalated into an argument. Eleanor berated Mo for treating her like a child, so Mo just backed off and cut their contact down to a minimum.

But Eleanor's attitude had become erratic in recent months. She was in denial about the encroaching blindness, hopping into her Volvo and going off to her job as a special education teacher like always—banging up her fenders on pillars and walls, but miraculously avoiding any serious collisions. Yet at the same time she was also obsessed with a vague stomach ailment. Her doctors had assured her there was nothing wrong with her gastrointestinal system, but some nights she peppered Mo with calls at all hours, asking Mo to find her a holistic healer or an osteopath.

"I know you're busy," she would say weakly, "but could you go on the Internet and look up an article on undiagnosed intestinal viruses that ran in *Scientific American*?"

Mo found herself pulling away even more, not answering the phone at night. Instead, she'd numbly listen to her mother's feeble voice on the answering machine . . . and pour herself a stiff drink. She cringed at the obvious manipulation of her mother's imagined stomach ailments and yet felt deeply sad and helpless about her mother's disintegrating health. "I just shake my head until my neck hurts," she told me. "And when I finally fall asleep, I dream that she's on a raft floating away across the ocean and I can't reach her. Or that she's banging on my door and I'm crouched in the closet, praying for her to go away."

Of all the ammunition that parents bring to the front lines of conflict, issues of health have the impact of a bullet through the heart. At the very core of the dynamic between adult children and their parents lie the ultimate elephant-in-the-living-room issues of death and mortality. Yours as well as theirs. Even when you are dealing with friction that seems to have nothing to do with aging (and death), such concerns reverberate in the background.

Even if your parents are essentially healthy now, even if their health complaints are mostly invented just to get your attention, they will eventually get older . . . and sicker. That's why any physical complaint they express to you may cause you to respond with an unconscious dread. And that dread will put your defenses on high alert and affect your responses.

The first step is to be honest with yourself about your emotions toward your parents' decline. You can't possibly figure out a workable strategy to deal with their complaints—or even sort out the phony ones from the real ones—until you have leveled with yourself.

You need to figure out if what you are experiencing is anger, grief, sadness, worry, or—most likely—some combination of these emotions. You need to dive down deep. Is Mo, for example, upset with her mother's obviously psychosomatic stomach ailments because she is worried about the long-term implications of her mother's failing eyesight? Is she worried that when her mother goes blind, it will be she who has to ferry Eleanor around? Is she angry because her brother, Simon, who lives halfway across the country, flies in twice a year like a hero and then disappears? Is she feeling

old herself now that her mother is slipping away? Is she resentful that her mother is simultaneously acting like a supermom and a weak child, leaving Mo with nothing but confusion?

As Mo learned, these problems don't get solved quickly, but the first step is to identify them. Letting them simmer will only keep you from doing what is best for you and your parents. You are much more likely to choose a strategy of avoidance—never good—if you aren't willing to confront your fears of the future. Mo realized she was in denial about her mother's blindness and was channeling that into anger about her mother's bogus stomach complaints because it was easier than dealing with the real problem. Doing research into macular degeneration helped allay some of her fears. In the past, she had simply taken Eleanor's word for everything and avoided confronting the facts. Once she knew more about her mother's disease and its prognosis, Mo felt much less out of control and was less likely to back away from her mother, a strategy that was making her mother feel abandoned and probably contributing to those stomach complaints.

Learn from Mo. As she did, I suggest you take the next parental health crisis—real or imagined—as an opportunity to confront the future. Most of us will eventually have to deal with the decline of at least one of our parents; it is a good idea to start the process now, when they are relatively healthy.

MAKE A PLAN, AND KEEP IT FLEXIBLE

1) Face Your Fears

Sit down in a quiet, darkened room and let your mind wander to the worst-case health scenario with your parents. What are your *real* fears? Are you worried that they are close to dying? Guilty that such a thought doesn't upset you as much as it "should"? Are you concerned that they will become dependent on you? Angry that the responsibility may fall to you because your siblings are not picking up their share? Don't censor yourself. Get it all out in the open.

2) Confront and Educate

The first person you must confront is you; next, your parents. You need to be confident that you can deal with any health crises that will come up. If you aren't acquainted with your parents' finances, try to get them to talk about it *now*. It is always better to tackle such issues *before* it is absolutely necessary. Read up on whatever incipient health conditions they have. Perhaps you might go along on a doctor's visit or find out about their long-term health insurance.

To strike up a conversation on estate planning, you might casually tell your mother that a friend's family is in an uproar because her grandmother died and left her estate in shambles. (Notice I say *grandmother* rather than *mother,* which will make it easier for your mother to accept your message.) Then tell her that this has made you wonder if you should work on *your* will. Ask her if she knows how to make out a good one. Ask her about her experience with such things, if her parents or your father's parents had a will, and whether dealing with it was helpful or hurtful. Ideally, you will work the conversation into a more direct exchange about *her* will, but it's a good idea to "warm her up" first. (You can also modify this technique to ease into a discusion of how she would want to be cared for if she becomes infirm.)

It's smart to start such conversations with the "example" of someone else. If one of your mother's friends is in a nursing home, feel your mother out for her thoughts on nursing homes. If you have read one of the many articles about long-term care insurance, nursing-home care, and elder care in general, you may wish to reference that as well. Just be aware that most parents are very uncomfortable talking about these issues with their children. This is a process that may take a fair amount of time and several conversations, which is why it's good to start early.

When you see a newspaper or television story about a famous person who has an ailment similar to your father's, call him and talk about it "off the cuff," without making reference to his own health issues. (You can often divine your parents' feelings about their health conditions this way, and it's less confrontational.) Then you can segue into a personal aside, "Would you want to be treated with such a medical procedure, Dad, or is that not your kind of thing?" If he says no, delve deeper and ask, "What, then, would you prefer? It's important that I know your desires so that I can be sure you get the kind of treatment and care you want. I know it is hard to talk about this, but it is so important that we both know what you want and I can prepare in the best way possible to make that happen for you."

Janet's mom, Eunice, told her over tea that her doctor had diagnosed her with high blood pressure and put her on medication. Janet used that opening to mention that a friend's mother had recently had a stroke and was not doing very well. Eunice picked up the thread, telling Janet that she didn't want any extraordinary measures taken if that happened to her. But she made it perfectly clear "not to think about pulling the plug before six months. I hear people can recover a lot during the first six months, and I would hate to miss my shot at it."

3) Start Thinking about Your Boundaries

Exactly how much care are you willing to provide your parents? It is impossible to answer this question with certainty until you are confronted with a real health crisis. Nevertheless, it is important to start exploring your own feelings on the subject now. There are no rules for what is an "acceptable" amount of involvement. That threshold is different for everyone and changes as your parents age. I have had clients who assume that their parents will eventually move into their house; others are certain their parents would be no more likely to consider such an arrangement than they themselves would be to offer it. The important thing is that you start examining alternatives that may be available to you, so there are fewer surprises.

Angela always knew that her parents would move in with her when they were unable to live on their own. In fact, she renovated her house to include a suite for them with a private entrance. Then, soon after his twentieth birthday, a drunk driver hit Angela's son, Joey. He was paralyzed and needed to live at home, so that remodeled suite became his. Although she knew that her parents understood, she was worried about how she would care for them when the time came.

Because she felt guilty, she avoided talking about the subject and prayed for her parents' continued good health. But for almost five years, she was visibly nervous whenever either of her parents became ill, even with the slightest cold.

Finally, her parents raised the subject with her. They told her that they were looking into a senior community that was not too far away from her house, one with both an assisted living and a nursing facility on the premises, and they were planning to move into it together while they were still a vibrant, healthy couple. The problem was solved, but Angela had suffered for years in silence.

4) Resist Role Reversal

James Halpern, a family therapist who deals frequently with adult children and their aging parents, cautions us to "maintain the family hierarchy." By that he means that we need to remember that our parents are still our parents, no matter how old they get. This is not just a biblical commandment—"Thou Shalt Honor Thy Father and Mother"—it's a matter of self-preservation.

Unless your parents are incapacitated, treating them like children is damaging to both you and them. Their anger stems from the elemental fear that they are losing control of their lives. Most parents, when asked what they fear most about growing older, would reply, "Becoming a burden to my children. I don't want to become dependent." Your anger comes from deep, underlying— and understandable—resistance to giving up the comfort of having a parent there to protect you and take care of you (even if your parents weren't particularly nurturing). You are also probably terrified that your parents will become a vortex of need, siphoning away your energy and resources. In the end, your resistance to this reversal of roles may turn you into what Halpern refers to as the *anti-mother* (or anti-father, I might add)," angry and withdrawn.

TIPS

- Do not take over any caregiving functions until absolutely necessary, and even then, try to give that responsibility to a third party if possible.
- Be very careful not to speak to your parents as though they are children.
- Do not become obsessed with how your parents are losing their faculties; instead, concentrate on what they still do well. How can your mother help you with decorating decisions? In what ways are you willing to ask your father for career advice? By enlisting your parents' help and involvement, you are sending an important message: that you value them. Admiration is a remarkable tonic.

FEELING THEIR PAIN—EVEN IF IT ISN'T THERE

Sixty-nine-year-old Jill retired recently as an office manager for a mortgage banker and is in good health. When her son, James, comes to the door of Jill's condo, he can hear her bustling around in there with her usual springy step. But as soon as he knocks, the click of her heels slows down to a drag. Now she sounds as if she is Jacob Marley or Livia Soprano, milking the situation for effect.

No answer. He knocks again. No answer. The steam starts to rise from his collar. He knocks once more, loudly this time. "Hello?" she calls out in a Methuselah voice. "Who is it?"

"It's me, Mom."

"Who?"

"Me, Ma. James."

"Who?"

By this point, his palms are sweaty and his fists are clenched. "Mom, *open the door*!"

"Sorry, dear," she says, as she opens the door at last. "It's just so hard for me to hear these days. And who thought it would be you? I haven't heard from you in days!"

That scene seems like the setup for a joke, but I defy you to find an adult with elderly parents who hasn't experienced a variation on this theme. Among the hardest yet most important skills you can develop is to assess the difference between real complaints and ones that are an emotional ploy. You have many options about how to handle both of those situations, but it is very important to distinguish between the two. Granted, as your parents get older and develop real health problems, the line gets blurry, but for your own mental health, you must separate the two states as much as possible.

Mo realized that her strategy of avoidance was among the things fueling her mother's phantom stomach complaints. Very often parents—in the throes of sadness, fear, and depression over aging—are also feeling terribly lonely. Unconsciously (OK, sometimes not so unconsciously), they try to pull their children closer by inflating—or creating—health complaints. Often they are too scared or too proud to admit they simply want more attention. They fear rejection (probably justifiably a lot of the time, and you have a perfect right to find their needs overbearing), so they "play sick." When they do, you wind up feeling manipulated.

This scenario may be even more complicated if your family has a history of not talking openly about such subjects as loneliness. So now your parents' feelings are seeping out along the increasingly permeable membranes of their emotional life.

Sometimes the physical and psychological problems are meshed, compounding your confusion. Lina came to me because her father, a former CIA agent, had grown progressively more depressed in the years since Lina's mother died. Her father was eating horribly, barely going out, and had gained fifty pounds, which put additional stress on his blown-out knees. Yet he insisted that he was "fine." (Note that his behavior had an emotional as well as a physical component.) He felt he was being very manly and stoic about his situation, but of course, he was unconsciously crying out to Lina for help. Yet whenever she offered it, trying to get him on a healthier diet, to enroll him in an exercise program at the Y, or to persuade him to visit a doctor who might prescribe an antidepressant, he waved her away.

Yes, such manipulations are irritating, but what can you do when nothing you try seems to help?

Often I find there is a parallel here with children who act out to get attention. I worked with one mother whose nine-year-old fell out of trees and resorted to all sorts of physical stunts, breaking bones on several occasions. It turned out that he felt that the only time his parents showed him love was when he was injured. And there was probably some truth to that, because they were preoccupied with their younger son, who had recently been diagnosed with a hearing loss.

The "accidents" stopped when his parents gave him more reinforcement and cuddling, spent time with him, and really listened to him. He no longer needed to fall out of trees to be noticed.

I am not suggesting that the cure for your parents' psychosomatic illnesses or hypochondria is to give them unlimited attention. Rather, I am suggesting that you be careful to avoid a common pattern: ignoring the emotional messages your parents are sending until they jack up the complaints to involve physical ailments. Ask yourself, "How does my mother or father benefit from being ill?"

Here are some ways to deal with parents who try to manipulate you with physical complaints. Not all strategies will work with all parents, but most parents will respond to at least one.

- *Listen more actively for the first signs of loneliness or frustration.* Sometimes, inquiring sincerely about your parents' feelings can preempt a litany of physical problems. Use empathic "mirroring" techniques: "You sound sort of lonely, Mom. Maybe I'm imagining it, but that's what I hear in your voice. I know it must be hard living alone." And remember that you don't have to immediately jump in and try to fix things. (When they start speaking about why they are lonely, for example, it may trigger guilt in you, but don't give in. Just practice the guilt exercise discussed in chapter 3.) Really listening sometimes can make you feel sad because it forces you to confront the fact that your parent is in pain, but that's OK. Recognize that you can stand a bit of sadness if it helps your parent consider his or her feelings are being recognized.

- *Reward health.* Whenever your mother is feeling OK, offer a special treat, perhaps an unexpected visit from you and the kids or a spa treatment or a shopping spree. On one of his good days, take your father fishing or out to eat at his favorite restaurant. Let your parents know with your actions how much more pleasant it is for you to be with them when they're feeling good. Make it clear how much better they look when they are active and productive—vanity can be a helpful tool. Praise them for taking care of themselves not merely because it is good for them but because they're a role model for you and your kids.

- *Make limits clear.* If rewards don't work, let parents know that you have mulled it over and come to a decision about just how much you are willing to deal with on the health/sickness front (calling them twice a week before work; going with them to the chiropractor every other Saturday) and that no amount of dramatizing is going to get you to change. Nor will you punish them or make ultimatums ("If you don't stop going on about your bowels, Dad, I'm not going to call you ever again"), which only breeds hostility and sends you places you won't know how to get back from. Instead, rely on consistency and a good mantra. "Mom, I know you're feeling lonely and your lower back pain seems unbearable right now. I wish you were feeling better. I'll call you Wednesday morning, as I always do. And we'll have lunch Saturday, like usual."

- *Employ diversion.* This technique is perfectly acceptable. Many parents simply have a habit of complaining; it's a behavior they're not even conscious of. Just as many of us have learned that sometimes the best way to deal with children's complaints is to wave something colorful in front of their eyes, you can use a grown-up variation of that strategy to divert your parents.

The way to do this is to acknowledge the initial complaint: "Yes, Mom, I know you are concerned about walking from the car to the soccer field, but we will walk slowly and I will be next to you. Just think about how great Andy will feel when he sees you in the bleachers, rooting for him. He is so lucky to have a grandmother who is interested in his game. You are the best."

Now whip out your diversionary tactic. One tactic is to talk about other people's problems. For decades soap operas have helped shut-ins feel as though there was life beyond their living rooms. You can do the same thing, by using the compelling narratives of your pals and coworkers. Don't gossip; instead, explore empathy, and get your parent involved. Is the guy in the cubicle next to you struggling with a midlife crisis? ("Oy, that Porsche Boxter! . . . Have you ever had a friend go through this, Dad?") Is your childhood pal trying to figure out what to do with his life after all these years? ("Mom, what happened to people in your generation who never found themselves?" She may have insights.) In addition to providing a diversion, this is a good way to get them engaged in a philosophical question that can take them outside their narcissistic obsessions with their health.

Another way to divert your parents is to ask them to join you in a volunteer task to help those who are less fortunate than your family. If you are able to get your parents to go along with you to a homeless shelter or a hospital ward for AIDS babies, there is a good chance they will not feel comfortable dwelling on their own trumped-up pain.

- *Saviorize.* Ask your parents to help you with problems, health or otherwise. As I've said before, this is the best, least-used, all-around solution I know of. A parent who feels needed will automatically assume a more adult role that is inconsistent with complaining.

Overall, when it comes to your parents and their health crises—real or imagined—the most important thing to remember is to think before you respond. Assume that your automatic reactions will be tangled up with your emotions, even if you aren't immediately cognizant of them, so don't trust yourself straight off. Take time to consider all the possibilities before you act—or overreact. And make sure that you have at least begun the process of facing the future and have started to plan for it.

You cannot stop your parents from channeling their fears over getting old into manipulative behavior any more than you can stop them from getting old, but you can harness your own fears and stop jumping like a well-trained dog when your parents push your buttons. Just slow everything down. Unless your parents fall gravely ill suddenly, there is actually very little that constitutes a true health crisis, no matter how it is painted. Think of it instead as "life," which, by its definition, includes a winding down.

The real crisis is letting yourself remain in an angry or scared daze in an attempt to avoid looking into the future. Yes, dealing with your parents as they age is among the greatest challenges most of us will ever know, but the sooner you see it as a part of a process and picture yourself coming out the other side intact, standing shoulder to shoulder with the millions of people who have gone through the same experience, the sooner you will see the future as a brighter, less frightening place.

• Chapter 25 •

They Make Themselves a Little Too Much at Home

"My parents come over once a week," Diana told me, her voice heavy with irritation as she leaned back on the couch in my office. She is a forty-year-old divorced lawyer who recently moved back to her hometown for a great job. "And it's always a variation on the same theme. My mother dissolves, and I mean she *weeps*, at the sight of my messy silverware drawer. And while I'm steaming as she sorts the teaspoons from the tablespoons, I notice that my stepfather has installed himself on the couch, shoes off and glass of my best bourbon on the new coffee table—no coaster, of course—snoring away. It all happens within fifteen minutes of them coming into the house. They're like an infestation of killer bees. I don't know how to stop them; they overwhelm me. And I feel terrible afterward—spent and humiliated."

Home is indeed where the heart is. It can also be where your heart is in your mouth when your parents are around.

Home is the most fertile battleground for the people I work with and their parents. Some parents have a great deal of trouble understanding that their grown children's homes are not just extensions of their own abodes or psyches. Sometimes this is a replay of childhood dramas, especially in families where the kids' rooms and inner lives were not off-limits (parents riffling through their children's drawers, bursting into their rooms unannounced, and in general disrespecting privacy), but not always. For some parents, these extremely annoying behaviors don't materialize until the kids grow up and create a home of their own, or until there are grandchildren involved.

The underlying reasons parents transgress physical boundaries in your house are varied, but it is important to realize that it is not always the casual, thoughtless act it appears to be. Unconsciously, your parents may experience your home as a "scary" place. Not in the haunted house sense, of course, but in the threatening, uncharted territory sense. To them, your home represents your autonomy, that they may not approve of the choices you have made, and that you are beyond their control. They may have had parents who had a hard time separating, and this pattern of nitpicking may be deeply ingrained. Putting their mark on your space, claiming it as their own territory or "fixing it," is their way of dealing with their anxiety. It's not appropriate, of course, but as the "adult" in this situation, you must understand that their actions are an expression of underlying conflict. It is *your* job to deal with it effectively.

This sense of displacement can manifest itself in mundane ways, which are nonetheless *very* irritating to you.

FIGHTING THE HOME FIRES

Physical encroachment calls for physical solutions. Animals instinctually know this—their primary motivation is often to defend their own territorial limits through any means necessary—but people sometimes need to learn it. Here are a few simple guidelines:

You Don't Have to Entertain Your Parents in Your Home
Yes, you may have long nursed the dream of having the folks over for a lovely weekly meal, planned it in your head, right down to the

part where your dad puts down his crème brûlée spoon, pushes away from the table, and says, "Honey, you certainly have created a great home here; thank you so much for inviting us to be your guests for the evening," but, alas, wishing won't make it so. Remember, you have given up the idea of the fantasy parent, so if your mother and father are not ready to respect the sanctity of your home as they do the homes of their friends, it may be best to avoid entertaining them. This is not denial; it's wise accommodation. If your home triggers your parents' worst qualities, it's time to create new rituals—on neutral turf.

If you live nearby and you see them often, start planning ways to change your customary habit of inviting them over—or tolerating their "just dropping by." Find good restaurants, pack a picnic for the park, or meet for coffee in a good café. Perhaps it's best if you meet them at your kid's soccer game—bring some of your dad's favorite munchies—or you can pick your mother up after her manicure and go for a drive.

Don't panic if your guilt reaction is triggered when you start to plan these new approaches. In many families, especially ones in which big, home-cooked meals are the center of social activity, there is an implicit message that you aren't a "good child" unless you invite the folks over. Don't buy into the propaganda—relating to and being generous with your parents does not require playing host to them. That one-big-family-around-my-kitchen-table stuff is wonderful—unless it's not. It's better to have a pleasant meal in a restaurant than a contentious one at home. It may take some experimentation to gauge which locales elicit the best behavior from your parents, so be patient. It is worth the trouble; in most cases, you will be pleasantly surprised how a carefully chosen venue can moderate their behavior.

Diana decided to stop having her parents over once a week; instead, she arranged a once-a-month bowling date with her stepfather and made a standing weekly date with her mother, Tess, to meet at the community college where Diana teaches a course. This increased time together put a lid on any complaints her mother might have had over the change. Why did she pick her school? Through trial and error Diana discovered that Tess seemed somehow humbled by the setting and the respectful reaction Diana got from the students. In Diana's home, Tess felt free to rearrange her daughter's life and her silverware drawer; on the campus, she was too busy feeling proud of Diana (and frankly, a little intimidated) to cast herself as the leading expert on how to live and where to put teaspoons.

Mother and daughter created a ritual of going to the espresso joint in the student center and splitting a croissant. The students were amusing to watch, and the vibe was exciting for both of them. They spent a lovely hour together instead of the usual two excruciating hours they used to spend having dinner at Diana's house. The plastic utensils, as Diana noted with amusement, were often jumbled together in the same bin at the espresso bar, but Tess never said a word.

Drop-kick the "Drop-in"

It is nice to be able to drop in on someone unexpectedly. It presupposes intimacy and enables us to say to ourselves, "I am so accepted in this person's life that she is quite comfortable having me around whenever I have the urge. That's how close we are."

And some hosts are so relaxed that they truly do not care who drops in on them. It may be hard for you to believe, but some people are delighted when their parents show up on their doorstep unannounced. However, if you don't feel that way and your parents persist in dropping in unannounced, you should not tolerate it. It is perhaps the most flagrant common abuse of boundaries.

There is no subtle way to stop your parents. You're going to have to lay down the law. But the easiest way to get them to accept it without a major hoo-ha is to allow them to make dates about as frequently as they once dropped in. In other words, if they tended to stop by once a week, make a weekly date with them. (And don't force them to call you all the time; you should take some initiative.)

But while this is the easiest solution, there is no requirement that you must see them as often as they want to see you. They may live nearby and are accustomed to ringing your bell most mornings on their walk around the neighborhood, but you may only wish to see them twice a month for dinner, with plenty of notice. It is up to you. One tip for engineering such a transition: plan something particularly pleasurable for them when you do see them. And make sure you tell them how much you enjoy being with them.

Communicate Your Expectations and Repeat Them Often

You might use some version of the following:

- "Mom, when I am in your house, I respect your things and your design decisions. I expect the same from you."
- "Folks, I know you like the spontaneity of dropping in, but I'm not comfortable with *anyone* doing it, not even you guys. You'll just have to accept that you need to call first."
- "Dad, I am perfectly comfortable with how you treat the furniture at your home, but in my house I use a coaster and I expect everyone to do the same."

THE OUT OF TOWNERS

These days, many parents live out of town and descend on their children's home for long, tense visits (or short, tense visits!). If having your parents stay with you creates a great deal of stress in your life, your marriage, and your family, rest assured that you are in good company: I know very few people for whom these visits are entirely pleasurable. And guess what? Your parents probably aren't enjoying themselves much either.

It's not just them; it's hard having *anyone* stay in your home. There is rarely enough room, and guests inevitably disrupt your routines. And when it's your parents, the situation is exacerbated by special anxiety. Are you keeping house well enough to please your father? Is your mother going to try to cook one of her inedible Thai recipes? Is that noise you heard last night your stepmother not being able to sleep on that futon mattress? Is your father going to monopolize the bathroom all morning?

In some cases, you have no choice but to invite your parents to stay. Neither you nor they may have enough money for a hotel, or you may live too far away from one to make that option work. Those reasons are valid, and later in this chapter I will talk about how to make those necessary visits more bearable.

But in many cases, clients have another reason for weathering such tortuous visits: "If I asked my parents to stay in a hotel, their feelings would be hurt." This sort of response, while understandable, comes from deep in your well of unproductive guilt. It ignores the fact that having your parents at your house causes *everyone* grief—you, your kids, and your parents. They may indeed feel rejected if you ask them to stay in a hotel or a short-term condo rental, but that feeling will usually subside after you get them to do it the first time. By their second visit, as they stretch out in their comfy hotel room after a nice dinner with you, they will notice that your puppy isn't scratching at their door and the crossbar of the sofa bed isn't cutting into their back. As they sit on the balcony of their hotel room, drinking their coffee in anticipation of seeing you and the kids for lunch, they will be happy or at least more relaxed. (*Note to self:* Don't expect Mom and Dad ever to admit openly that they like this new arrangement.)

And you will have your territory back. Another plus: because you will be less uptight, you will be more gracious during the time your parents spend with you.

HOW TO BREAK THE NEWS TO THEM

Every parent is different. You may want to combine all the following approaches and customize them to your parents' response. That is, anticipate their protestations and be ready with your own comeback.

- *Be direct.* "Mom, I love you very much and I'm looking forward to you visiting. I need to talk to you about the visit. Are you willing to hear what I have to say? The thing is, I get really tense when I have overnight guests. The house feels cramped, and as a family we have a hard time losing privacy. You probably have noticed that we're not at our best, and I can tell that makes you uncomfortable too. So I've got a solution: I've been researching condos nearby that you can rent for the week. It's not at all expensive, and this arrangement will turn out to be really wonderful for all of us."
- *Make yourself the problem.* "Mom, I have been really going through a lot of stuff lately, really feeling very hemmed in by the kids and how much of a mess the house is. I know I snapped at you the last time you came to stay, and I really was upset at myself for that. Do you think you and Dad could do me a big favor and stay at this condo complex down the road? It would take a lot of pressure off me." What if your mother interjects that she can help you get your house in order? Having anticipated this response, you tell her that that's a great idea: "Here's how we can make it work beautifully. You can come over every morning from the condo. We'll have breakfast together, and after I leave for work, you can attack a section of the house. That would be so wonderful for me!"
- *Throw the kids into the deal, with a little saviorizing on the side.* "Mom, I thought you might want to have Ashley

and Jake all to yourself, and I would love a few days off. What if we rented you a cottage at the lake for a week and the kids stayed with you for a few days? It's only twenty minutes away, and we'll be able to have dinner with you every night. You have no idea how much they would love it, and I would be really grateful for your help."

IF YOUR HOUSE HAS TO BE THEIR HOUSE FOR NOW

If practicalities preclude you from putting your parents up elsewhere, you'll have to find a way to live more harmoniously during the time they are in your house. Here are some tips.

- *Plan at least one "vacation" for yourself for each two days they stay.* This can be a night out with friends, an hour alone at the gym, or an afternoon drive to the mall, anything that gets you completely away from them. Make sure there is some indulgence involved so you feel as though you really did something nice for yourself.
- *Invite other people over.* Having more than three consecutive meals alone with your parents is likely to send your anxiety level through the roof. Have a dinner party or invite friends to meet all of you at a restaurant. This strategy has additional benefits: casually blending your parents with your pals sets a more adult tone for your relationship with your parents. Don't worry about them embarrassing you; they will likely be on their best behavior with your friends, and believe me, your friends will love it! (Feel free to brief them on any ticklish topics beforehand.) There is perhaps no better way to convey to your parents the message that you want them to rise to the level of mature "friend" than to trust them in a social situation.

- *Try not to share a bathroom with them.* It won't kill your parents to share with your kids; toothpaste stains aren't permanent. And some privacy will increase your sanity quotient. If you're worried that they will get huffy because you're pushing them off on the kids, sheepishly allude to some digestive problems you've been having. Works every time.

- *Make their living quarters as separate and comfortable as possible.* You want your parents to spend time there, which will give you some room. And if they're comfortable, they'll be more relaxed. If the only place you can put them is in an alcove off the living room, buy a nice piece of fabric to make a divider. If they are in the guest room, drag the recliner in there. (There might even be room for that minifridge you keep in the garage.) *Note:* Disregard this advice if their visit is open-ended. No need for them to get *too* comfortable.

- *Establish off-limits zones, with humor and grace.* If, for example, your mom drives you insane by taking over your kitchen, try putting up a funny sign. Nancy Cocola and Arlene Matthews suggest: "No admittance if you hope to eat in this century." Point to it with a smile if she ignores it, or take a red marker and underline the words in her presence. If your parents have a tendency to come into your bedroom unannounced, I suggest a sign that appears to be directed at the kids: "Alert: Mommy and Daddy need a little time alone; please knock."

- *Employ diversion if they get underfoot.* If your parents don't come equipped with their own hobbies, have plenty of projects available that will make them feel needed (and give you the satisfaction of checking off items on your to-do list!). Stick with things they really like to do—a stack of shirts that needs to be mended by your mom, the genius seamstress; a fence that desperately needs to be fixed by your dad, the ultimate do-it-yourselfer.

Many of my clients have found photo albums to be a lifesaver. Gather in a large box all the pictures you've taken of the family lately and ask your parents to put them into the beautiful albums you've bought. (Remember to get enough prints for your parents to have their own copies.)

- *Press the kids into service.* One of my clients makes a point of *not* taking her kids to the park the week before her parents come. That way, they are especially enthusiastic to get out there with Grandma and Grandpa. In most communities there are weeklong classes or workshops that you can sign the kids up for; ask your parents if they're willing to go along to oversee. Overall, don't be afraid to fully turn over some child care tasks to your parents during the time they are there. It will make them feel trusted and needed while also giving you a break. But screen yourself: don't foist off the odious tasks; that will breed resentment. Instead, stick with things they truly enjoy, like helping with homework or reading bedtime stories.

• Chapter 26 •

They Don't Like My Spouse . . .
or That I Don't Have One

It was April, a dreaded month for Harris. April meant Easter, which meant clashes with his family. His wife, Deborah, was Jewish, and his family had never accepted her. Throughout their seven-year marriage, his parents' disapproval had been a low rumbling in the background but hadn't been a major issue because he and Deb lived in California and rarely visited his folks back in Biloxi. But last year, Deb and Harris moved to Mississippi, because he was taking over the family trucking business.

His parents were always polite to Deb, but distant, which was painful for her because her family had been close and she was used to a lot of chatty intimacy with relatives. "She's a real nice girl," they'd say whenever anyone asked, "just a bit different." As for the couple's five-year-old twins, Harris's mother spent much less time with them than she did with her other grandchildren. "Deborah's raising them in her own way," she would say, cryptically.

The major holidays were the worst days of the year. Harris's mother, who taught Sunday school at the local Baptist church, started tiptoeing around Deb as each one approached, occasionally saying something about "our faith." Or she tried too hard, conspicuously avoiding the word *Easter* or *Christmas* or—heaven forbid—*Jesus* in front of Deb. Harris's father said nothing, simply hiding out behind his *Reader's Digest.*

For Deb, April was doubly hard. Not only did she have to deal with Harris's parents, but to her, April meant Passover, and her family was back in California, too far away to join her for the traditional seder meal. It hardly seemed worth it to her to go through all that trouble of making a seder meal just for herself, Harris, and the twins. When Harris first told her about moving back to his hometown, she had fantasized that she would teach his family the Jewish holiday traditions, that she would cook up a storm, and that they would all have a great time. But his parents seemed horrified when Harris suggested it. "You guys talk about the Old Testament all the time in Sunday school," he said. "You talk about the nobility of the Jews. Finally, you've got one in your midst, and you freak out. What's up with that?"

His parents had no good answer. "It just makes us uncomfortable, that's all," his father said.

Harris didn't know what to do. He loved his new job, and he loved his folks. He wanted them to love Deb, who had originally wanted to love them back but lately had been growing hostile toward them.

As Easter and Passover approached, Deb wept as she made the matzo balls for her chicken soup; Harris's parents left a message on his private number telling him that they prayed for him and his children. "I just don't know what I'm supposed to do," he told me, phoning in long distance. "Do I have to choose between my wife and my parents?"

So here you are, an adult, finally, having left the nest and created an independent life. Perhaps you've gotten married or are considering tying the knot. Maybe you are living with someone. Or you're going it alone, either because you want to or because you just haven't found the right person to be your partner. You may have struggled with those choices, asking yourself, "Is this the right person for me?" or "Is this marriage worth saving?" "Am I better off on my own?" or "Will I ever find someone to love?" You may still be asking yourself these questions.

And despite how far we have come from a society in which parents chose our mates, they are still part of the equation. They may no longer control the process, but they wield great power nonetheless. Tapes of their voices play in our heads; their judgments linger in the air; their approval of our spouses—or our choice not to have one—still looms over us. Their opinions can complicate an already complicated process. When our parents disapprove of our decisions, it strikes a deep chord, often paralyzing us. I have counseled countless men and women who, under all sorts of strain, have shown courage, wisdom, and great strength of character, but who crumble like an autumn leaf in the face of their parents' disapproval of their choice of spouse.

This can be an extraordinarily difficult problem, freighted with history—not just your personal history but the history of generations. Your choices in marriage ignite your parents' sense of their mortality; will the family line be carried on in the way they've always assumed it would? Will those multigenerational family snapshots look the way they had imagined? Does Christmas morning, with the dreamed-of perfect kids smiling as they open their presents, bring the happiness that they believe is rightfully theirs?

You too have these concerns, even if you're not conscious of it. When you marry someone your parents think is "wrong," you are bucking your lifelong programming. Even if you do so blithely, you may find that later you are stung by underlying recriminations. When your parents react negatively to your choice of spouse, it casts a long shadow on your life, and theirs. It can also hurt your spouse and any children you might have. That's why it is paramount that you confront these conflicts.

If you are single (straight or gay), coming to terms with your parents' disappointment will be a crucial step in dealing with aging, friendship, the creation of a community, and loneliness.

Some of the parental hotspots I've discussed in this book can indeed be dealt with by letting nasty comments and insensitivity roll off your back, making a joke, or using diversionary tactics. Such lighthearted fixes won't work in this case. How can you stop your parents and spouse from "going at it"? Is it possible to achieve some lasting peace with your parents when your choices—or maybe it's just fate—mean that some of their dreams will never be realized?

IF YOUR PARENTS AND SPOUSE ARE AT WAR

You may think, "Hey, this isn't my fight," but you are wrong. You are the pivot point of conflict. In fact, you're the only reason this problem exists. Your spouse thought he or she was marrying you, not your wacky family; your parents probably didn't have much say in your selection of a mate. But even more important: you are the one whose decisiveness and boundary-setting will have the most impact. You are the one who is most likely to change the situation.

This responsibility may not please you. It's easier to throw your hands up or simply deny there is a problem and tell your spouse he or she is "just being oversensitive." But not only are such responses horribly hurtful to your spouse and almost always poisonous to your marriage; they are, ironically, destructive to your relationship with your parents and your own sense of autonomy.

Your first step in dealing with this situation is to examine the criticisms of your spouse with an objective eye, searching for your parents' true motives. How you deal with these criticisms—and you *must* deal with them—will be determined by your painstaking examination of their complaints.

If the Motives Behind Your Parents' Criticism Are Suspect
Bear in mind that smart parents who have a healthy relationship with their grown kids generally keep their mouths shut, even when they see things they don't like. So if your parents are vocal in their

criticisms in a way that is less than delicate and caring, there is a good chance that their motives for speaking up are not as pure as they claim.

They may be jealous that you have found intimacy with your spouse, something that's lacking in *their* marriage. They may be angry that you and your spouse have decided to create an autonomous unit, which—by definition—excludes them. They may, like Harris's parents, see your spouse's differences as a threat. Or they may be unable to accept that you are no longer exclusively theirs. Underlying these emotions are feelings of abandonment, loss, betrayal, and incomplete separation. To deal with them, some parents reflexively do what they can to drive their child's spouse away.

It can be painful to see your parents act that way, especially when they may ramp up their affection for you as they escalate complaints about your spouse. You likely have a complex relationship with them and may have your own issues with separation. Or you may be in such denial that you have blocked out what's going on.

To ascertain the purity of your parents' motives, ask yourself the following questions:

- Do your parents make their criticisms in an obvious, indiscreet manner? Are they rude to your spouse, or do they discuss your spouse with friends, neighbors, or relatives?
- Do your parents criticize your spouse bitterly to you in private and then act as though everything is hunky-dory when your spouse is present?
- Conversely, does your spouse complain that they are mean to her in private but sweet as pie when you show up?
- Do your parents blame your spouse for things that are clearly beyond his control, such as your children's' health problems?
- Do your parents nurse grudges against your spouse for minor or even inadvertent offenses?

- Have your parents consistently found fault with your past relationships?
- Do your parents consider themselves moral arbiters with a monopoly on the truth?
- Do your parents think that race, religion, and social class are more important than an individual's qualities?

Answering yes to any of these questions is a dead giveaway that your parents' motives are "impure."

It is not important that you confront them with this knowledge. Instead, make it clear to your spouse and your parents that your primary responsibility is toward the person you married, that if your parents put you in the absurd position of choosing between them and your spouse, you will choose your spouse.

When Harris realized that there was no way to justify his parents' lack of respect for Deborah's religion and culture and that his attempts to ameliorate the situation were only making it worse, he sold his motorcycle and used the money to fly Deb's entire family to Biloxi for Passover. Not only did they have a huge seder, but the next day, Easter, he escorted all nine of them to his parents' church for the morning service. His parents were shocked into silence when the clan walked into the room, but their friends welcomed Deb and her family. The next day, some parishioners asked them over for lunch and peppered them with questions about the Passover seder.

Unfortunately, there was no miraculous transformation in the behavior or attitude of Harris's parents. That didn't stop Deb and Harris, though. With the whole problem finally out in the open, they embarked on a program of direct confrontation and strategic humor aimed at desensitizing and enlightening his parents. Deb started an Internet support group about interfaith marriage. She actively made friends in the community and was invited to lecture about Jewish traditions in the Sunday school—not by her mother-in-law but by the pastor. Their marriage thrived.

If you cannot make a stand like this, you may damage your marriage irreparably. Consciously or not, your parents are trying to separate you emotionally from the person you married. And if you have been paralyzed by the situation, they have succeeded. By presenting them with an indivisible, united front, you make it clear that their efforts are for naught, that no matter how divisive they are, you will not be driven apart. (Chapter 14, "Getting Your Spouse in Your House," may be helpful to you in this regard.) As I have noted throughout this book, the key to managing your parents is consistency. If you are able to bond on this issue with your spouse, consistently showing that you will not be manipulated or played off each other, you will eventually beat back your parents' complaints. By doing so, you increase the possibility that they will tire of putting up a wall of discomfort or hostility.

Your parents may never embrace your spouse, but eventually, they will probably ease up once they see that their disapproval is not chipping away at your commitment, and that it is pointless to hold on to the hope that they will win you back. Meanwhile, you and your spouse will emerge from this struggle with an even tighter bond, which is what's *really* important here. Don't believe me? Ask your spouse which means most: getting your folks to accept him or her—or having you make a stand that shows you are unequivocally in his or her corner.

If Your Parents' Criticism Is Valid

While many parents criticize their children's spouses because of their own insecurities, be aware that this is not always the case. You must be open to the possibility that your parents may have a point in believing that your spouse isn't good for you. Before you assume that your parents are merely trying to make your life a hell on earth by cooking up complaints, ask yourself two questions:

1. Is my parents' main criticism that my spouse doesn't respect me? This is a huge red flag. Listen carefully to the way in which your parents offer criticism of your spouse. The tip-off is if they

offer few if any complaints about the way your spouse treats them, focusing instead on how your spouse treats you or your kids. Do they worry that your spouse is controlling, abusive, or unfaithful? Another tip-off is that your parents have tried to give your spouse the benefit of the doubt and don't seem to be milking the situation for self-aggrandizing drama. If you're still on the fence, bounce this question off a close friend or two . . . but brace yourself for an opinion you might not want to hear.

2. If my parent's complaints are mainly about how my spouse behaves toward them, does my spouse contribute to the problem? To answer this question, examine your spouse's overall behavior, not just the way he or she interacts with your parents. People tend to play out their insecurities and fears on many fronts, not just with the in-laws. If your parents complain that your spouse is jealous of the time you spend with them, is he easily made jealous in other contexts? Is she intimidated by other people in your life or overly sensitive to criticism in general? In short, does your parents' criticism ring true in the other parts of your spouse's life? Again, this is a good time to compare your perceptions with those of a close friend—or a sibling. Choose someone you trust, someone you know will be fair, and, again, be ready to hear whatever he or she says. If you are hesitant to do this, consider your own motives: Are you afraid of what your friend or sibling will tell you?

If you find that there is some element of truth to your parents' criticism, you must first deal with your own feelings about what you have discovered before you can make changes. Realizing, for example, that your spouse is mistreating you or your kids can be devastating. Facing the fact that your spouse is acting out his or her own deep problems in these clashes with your parents can also shake you by making you take a hard look at who your spouse is and what is in store for you in the future. I strongly recommend some professional help with this task, for you will be making decisions that will affect the rest of your life and possibly the lives of your children as well.

After you have come to grips with the situation, the next step is to deal with your parents. The key here is to adequately acknowledge the problem and their feelings so that you can get them to back off. Convey to them that although they have a point, their criticisms are not helpful. You must make it clear to them that it is now *your* responsibility to do something about the situation. You might tell them—without going into detail—that you intend to broach the subject with your spouse and would appreciate it if they would put a lid on their behavior to make that discussion less volatile.

You must take charge. Like it or not, you are the point person in your spouse's antagonistic relationship with your parents. The sooner you take the dispute out of their hands, the greater the chance is that it will be resolved or at least diffused.

Once you have dealt with your parents, you will indeed have to deal with your spouse. Do not underestimate how difficult this process can be. I strongly recommend that you enlist the help of a therapist. Working with a caring professional you trust can make all the difference.

IF YOU DON'T HAVE A SPOUSE AND YOUR PARENTS CAN'T ACCEPT THAT

Nearly 15 percent of Americans over the age of forty have never been married. Some of them will eventually take the plunge, but most won't. This is a huge change from the 1960s, when 96 percent of people over thirty-five had tied the knot, most of them when they were in their midtwenties. The reasons for this swelling of the ranks of the never-married are varied; fewer gay people bend to pressure to pretend they're straight; women have gained economic freedom and no longer feel as compelled to find a husband-provider; a significant number of people simply decide that they don't want a partner for life.

Chances are that your parents, who were raised to believe that life wasn't worth living unless you got married and had kids, are having a tough time with your singleness. If you are also unhappy about not having found a mate, their pressure is no doubt making things worse; if you aren't interested in finding one, it has probably made your relationship with them very difficult. They may bug you constantly, tell you why it's your fault that you're not married and give you pointers on how to change your marital status, fix you up compulsively, or drop a trail of demoralizing, guilt-inducing hints. They may genuinely worry about you or use expressions of concern to cloak their anxieties. Or they may simply grow awkwardly silent at the mere mention of marriage, theatrically swallowing the lump in their throats when they run into that friend of yours from high school who now has three kids, a dog, and a suburban McMansion.

Whatever their routine, it probably drives you up the wall. And most likely you've adopted a standardized set of postures to defend yourself, an elaborate kabuki of protest: you roll your eyes, threaten to hang up the phone if they continue carping, hold your hand up in front of their face like a traffic cop, beg them to quit bringing up the subject, shake your head until it feels like it's going to drop off, repeat the word *stop* until it echoes in your head without meaning. But admit it; nothing works. It may be time to try something new—or at least an improved version of an old approach.

Disarm Them with Honesty

You may think you're being honest by going through the motions described in the preceding paragraph, but such approaches tend to harden into a "routine." Instead, sit down with your parents after a pleasant dinner—one where this subject *wasn't* a source of conflict—and tell them that you need to discuss something important. Leave behind old baggage; don't get that irritated *been-there* look on your face.

If your mother has an annoying habit of trying to fix you up, you might say: "Mom, remember last week when we had that fight about that friend of Aunt Emily's you wanted to fix me up with? Well, I was pretty upset afterward, and I want to talk about it. I know you're just trying to be helpful, and I appreciate the underlying impulse. Please understand that you are making things worse. I may not show it, but I'm really unhappy about my situation. When you do those things, I feel as though you are saying that I'm not worthy of your love unless I'm married. It's very important to me to know that you love me no matter what. So please give me a commitment that you are not going to mention a fix-up again."

You may have to have this talk with your mother two or three times. Every single time she mentions a fix-up, no matter how casually, open the discussion again. Begin by bringing up the agreement you reached in the previous chat, in a calm tone: "Mom, remember how you committed to not fixing me up?"

Show Them You're Not Alone

Take your parents to a singles' support group, or a night out with your other single friends, or let them look over your shoulder as you chat on an online message board about being single. This excellent suggestion came from one of my clients who, in response to her parents' nonstop talk about her married siblings and their wonderful children, took them to a singles' support group where the evening's topic was "dealing with parents." Although she had been telling them for four years that she was not alone in her situation and begging that they be more sensitive to the fact that she wasn't single by choice, it wasn't until they heard others talking about how pressure from their parents compounded the challenges of not having a mate that the message kicked in.

Offer Empathy

Like it or not, many parents have a tough time coming to grips with the fact that you aren't ever going to be June Cleaver or Cliff Huxtable, the happy parent with the stable marital relationship and plenty of room in your heart and home for Grandma and Grandpa.

They didn't bargain for a son like Jerry Seinfeld (the picky single character on the show, not the husband and dad he has become in real life) or a daughter like Carrie Bradshaw of *Sex in the City*. If you're gay, there's a very good chance they didn't figure things would turn out this way at all.

I know their attitude probably irritates you profoundly and you are thinking, "Tough luck," but try a little tenderness, at least as a changeup. Expressing a little understanding of their dashed hopes may be enough to keep them in check.

Dad: Every time I see Tony with his grandkids, I feel like crap. I can't believe you're thirty-eight and you're still acting like a kid. When I was your age, I had a wife and three teenage kids.

You: I know you're upset that I'm not married.

Dad: Do you think you're going to be young forever? How many women do you have to have to know what's going to make you happy?

You: It must be very frustrating to see all your friends with grandkids. I'm sorry I haven't been able to provide you with that joy.

Dad: If you're so sorry, why don't you do something about it?

You: I'm not willing to have children just to please you, but that doesn't mean I don't understand that it's very difficult for you or that I can't imagine what you're going through. My life is very satisfying to me right now, which I know seems weird to you because you made the choice to get married right out of college. I'm sure that if I had been born in your era, I would have done the same thing. Things are different now, which makes me really glad and happy that I have options, but I'm sure the whole thing is really confusing for you.

For at least three months, try this approach every time your parents bring up the subject of your singleness. Always be patient and understanding; never lose your temper or even show irritation. Just listen—remembering the importance of body language—and offer soothing empathy. Right or wrong, they are genuinely upset and confounded by the fact that you are, in their eyes, "defying nature."

I cannot stress how important it is to heed the conflicts that arise when your parents cannot adjust to your spouse or to the fact that you don't have one. No matter what happens—whether your parents and your spouse learn to live with each other or you decide to see less of your parents or you wind up dissolving the marriage—it is better to do something, anything, rather than stay in a daze of denial. This is especially true if you want to save your marriage and avoid simmering resentments that will plague you and your spouse for many years. In this case, not to decide is to decide by default—rarely with good result.

If you are single and never get married, you too will eventually have to come to terms with the path your life has taken, to create a meaningful life beyond traditional expectations. Making peace with your parents is a crucial step in that process.

• Chapter 27 •

They Are Not There
in the Way I Need Them to Be

Judith was struggling—on almost every front. At thirty-six, she longed to be a poet but had had limited success getting her work published. The company she had worked for for three years, an Internet retailer, had recently gone into bankruptcy without giving her severance pay. Her apartment building in Silicon Valley was being sold, and it looked as though she would be evicted. Her credit cards were maxed out. As for guys, well, she hadn't had a decent date in fourteen months, which, she admitted, might be a function of the depression all this bad luck had put her in.

But the thing that hurt her most was that her parents, who had the resources to help her, didn't seem concerned. In their early sixties, they lived in a bucolic New England town, in a house that was paid for. They traveled the world, did a lot of gardening, and had a close network of friends. Whenever she called them with her bad news, they were vaguely sympathetic but never offered anything more. "They never lift a finger—or a checkbook—to help," she said bitterly, as she hunched over in a chair in my office one afternoon.

She was devastated that they didn't make a big noise when she told them she couldn't afford to come home for Christmas. "Oh, dear," her mother had said. "Well, maybe you'll be able to make a trip back east in the spring." "That was it," Judith said to me. "No,

'We'll send you a ticket,' or even an 'Is there anything we can do?'" The only effort her father had made was to ask if she was in therapy. "Gee, thanks, Dad," she almost said. "And how am I supposed to pay for *that*?"

Their "crimes" seemed so obvious to her. Like the big wedding they had given her older sister, Hillary, a few years ago that must have cost $30,000. Why should she be discriminated against just because she wasn't married? When her brother shattered his leg in a skiing accident in Lake Tahoe, just a month after his fiancée had dumped him, her dad flew out there to offer him emotional support and help him get settled into his apartment in L.A.

Why didn't her situation merit that kind of support or even that kind of cheerleading? She had won a national poetry award in college, after all; why couldn't her parents be like other parents of artists, who understand that their offspring probably won't make much money and may need a hand or at least some encouraging words? Isn't that what parents are supposed to give you, no matter what? Aren't you always supposed to feel that they are in your corner, that there is a safety net if you need it? Isn't that what being a family means?

We've talked a lot so far in this book about what you may feel that you "owe" your parents. But we haven't talked much about the opposite: what you think your parents "owe" you. If you are irritated with your parents because they fall short of your expectations on this score, you are wasting valuable time. Living with agitation or bitterness of this sort is very painful and does more than almost any other sort of child-parent dynamic to chip away at your self-image and strength.

The short answer to the question of what your parents owe you is this: nothing. I know that seems harsh, but there it is. No matter how unfair and painful your childhood was, no matter how much you took care of your parents or now do so, or how much you need a break, once you reach legal age, your parents are free to ignore your needs entirely. You, of course, don't have to be happy about this—you can reject them entirely or limit contact with them—but you do have to accept that they have a right to give you as much (or as little) as they choose.

You may read the last paragraph and say, "But what about what's right, what's moral? Shouldn't my parents *always* be sensitive to my needs?" In an ideal world, yes. But this is not an ideal world. Your parents may be self-involved or narcissistic. They may have grown up in families where children's needs weren't important once the children reached adulthood. Or they may simply be tired of putting your needs first. They may even think that holding up that safety net is holding you back. Most important, they may have a completely different reading of the situation. I will guarantee you that Judith's parents do not see themselves as selfish. On this issue, parents and grown children are often on completely different wavelengths.

Take the concept of *respect,* for example, which many of my clients say is a top need of theirs. Forty-year-old Marie sees her mother's constant disapproval as disrespect. "I'm not perfect, but I have a decent record of making good choices, at work, in my personal life, so I don't know why she insists on undermining me," she told me. "The result is that I don't even want to tell her anything. And I'm always feeling angry and as though I'm censoring myself." Her mother, Amanda, a sixty-three-year-old, had a slightly different take. "I think respect means being able to be honest. I think I would be disrespecting Marie if I kept quiet when I think she's making foolish moves."

Another hole people fall into is the "giving-and-taking" pit. They are convinced that they give selflessly, but are angry over their parents' lack of reciprocation or even appreciation. What they don't know is that their parents rarely see themselves in the same light. Ilene, a twenty-eight-year-old, spends at least two hours a week on the phone with her divorced father, Glen, who complains endlessly about his girlfriend. He never asks Ilene about her life. "He is totally self-absorbed," said Ilene. "I feel as though he just sucks me dry." When I talked to Glen, I asked him if he felt he and his daughter had a good relationship. "The thing I'm most proud of in my life is that we have a real relationship of equals," he said. "I think that's because I ask her for so little."

These are just a couple of examples of how far apart most parents and grown children are on this point. Asked the question "Do you feel you are responsive to your children's needs?" most parents I talk with believe one of three things about themselves:

1. They are completely responsive to their kids' needs.

2. They don't have any responsibility for their children's needs now that their kids are grown.

3. They have spent plenty of their lives being responsive, and now it's *their* turn to be taken care of.

The point I am making is that you and your parents will probably never agree on what they "owe" you. So don't waste your time ruminating on this subject. The likelihood that any method you might choose to get them to see that they are selfishly, heartlessly ignoring your "needs"—from crying and pleading to a tense, intense powwow with them—will probably just make things worse. As we've discussed in other chapters of this book, trying to get your parents to see that you are right is a bad use of your time and energy. In this case particularly, such an approach is likely to wind up making them even *less* responsive to your needs.

So what can you do? Well, that depends on how realistic your expectations are. If you have taken a long, hard look at who your parents are, and if you are not expecting them to change overnight into paragons of empathy, generosity, and responsiveness, there are some steps you can take to raise their awareness of your needs.

- *Put aside your hurt feelings.* There are lots of reasons why you feel your needs are not being met, but if you carry that "injury" with you, you will sabotage the future. Dwell on what you can change about tomorrow, not yesterday.

- *Identify small things they can do to acknowledge—if not meet—your needs.* The more specific your request, the better. Stay away from vague exhortations like "I want you to try to understand me better," or "I want you to "be more patient with me." Instead focus on simple, doable tasks: Call you once a week instead of always waiting for you to call. Let you finish telling them about your investment ideas before chiming in with their opinion. Stop complaining about your spouse in public places. When you make requests of this sort, you stand a better chance of getting them met.

- *Sit them down and calmly, quietly ask for what you need.* People often stew about how their needs are not being met without being explicit about those needs. They want their parents to be sensitive to them, but they don't want to have to actually ask outright for something. Alas, in this situation particularly, if you don't ask, you don't get.

  Warning: Body language and tone of voice count. So does vocabulary. Position yourself in an open, approachable way. Keep your voice warm and conciliatory. Avoid sweeping opening statements like "You never think about my needs" or accusations like "You're so self-involved." Focus instead on making it easy for your parents to meet your needs. Saviorizing is always good in these circumstances. "Mom, I know that since Dad's death last year you've been uncomfortable when I bring up his name, but I really need to be able to talk about him sometimes, especially with you. I agreed not to talk about him at length because I know it gets to you, but I would really appreciate it if you would give me a little time on this subject. I know it's hard, but it would really be helpful for me."

- *Take responsibility for perpetuating the problem.* If you have made it hard for your parents to fulfill your needs, or even know what those needs are, acknowledge that.

Here's how Judith eventually approached her parents. "Folks, I know I haven't been easy to deal with lately, that I've been moody and depressed, but I would really appreciate it if you could lend me a little moral support. It's clear that you aren't comfortable giving me financial support, and I realize that I may have been putting subtle pressure on you to do so, which may be driving you away. After giving the matter some serious thought, I realize that what's really important to me is knowing you are in my corner, that you believe I can pull myself out of this funk."

- *Don't couch your request as a quid pro quo.* It may seem fair and logical to use your generosity toward your parents as a benchmark for how you wish to be treated ("Mom, I don't understand why I spend three hours a month taking care of your bills and paperwork and yet you can't find time in your social schedule to take care of the kids for an evening once a month"), but it usually backfires. Taking that approach devalues the act of giving, suggesting that you are giving only to get back. (Generosity and caring must be their own reward.) Instead, have the courage to ask them outright for what you want, independent of what you give them.
- *Prepare a backup request.* If your parents balk at your narrowly focused request, suggest a compromise. If you're reasonable—and stay calm—there's a good chance they will eventually agree to meet you somewhere in the middle.

You: I know it's Christmas, Dad, but I'd really appreciate it if you wouldn't put out that huge punch bowl of eggnog this year. As you know, I've been in AA for the past couple of months, and it's really tough watching everyone get sloshed but me. You know how much I love eggnog.

Dad: Look, I'm not going to change this family's traditions just because you have a problem with alcohol. There's no reason the rest of us have to suffer. Eventually, you're going to go into the world, and people there are going to be drinking.

You: I see your point. I'm just hoping that we could compromise for this first year. How about if we make the eggnog without booze and put a bottle of bourbon on the side? Or we do one "spiked" bowl and one "virgin" bowl? I'd really appreciate it.

Dad: I'm not too happy about it, but if it makes it easier for you, I'll do it.

You: I know you're not too happy about it, so I especially appreciate it.

Be sure to thank your parents when they acknowledge your needs, even if they make only the smallest gesture. Remember, they don't owe you anything. Asking for their support is inherently different from other parent-management techniques designed to assert your rights and protect your territory from intrusion. In this case, you are asking them for something that is, hard though this is to swallow, theirs to give.

Facing the fact that your parents have no obligation to be there for you whenever you think you need them is among the most painful parts of truly attaining adulthood, no matter how old you are. It's the ultimate showdown at the Separation Corral. But once you are able to accept this reality completely, an enormous weight will lift from your shoulders. Accepting that you are not being deprived of something that is rightfully yours is liberating. And it is among the quickest fixes you can make; the moment you release your parents from this unpaid "debt," you will notice that your relationship with them will immediately improve. They will sense that you are no longer dragging around your disappointed expectations, and you will be ready to accept whatever gestures of caring and kindness your new attitude may elicit.

An Emancipation Proclamation

1. My parents do not "owe" me help, no matter how great a kid I was and still am.

2. If my parents are self-centered or oblivious to my needs, that is their own cross to bear, not mine.

3. Any help I give them I do so out of free will, without thought of or expectation of reciprocation.

4. My parents will never make up for the bad things they did to me, and I will not expect them to.

5. My parents do not owe me the same treatment they give my siblings.

6. I will no longer try to get my parents to admit that they are not sensitive to my needs; instead I will experiment with ways to encourage their responsiveness.

7. I will go elsewhere, including my inner resources, to get my needs met.

• Chapter 28 •

They Want Too Much of My Time

Lenore and Jake, both twenty-nine, had been married only a year when his parents moved from the suburbs into the city, near the hip neighborhood where the young couple lived. His parents had both retired recently and were a bit bored. Their marriage had been rather lifeless for years, so they focused too much of their attention on Lenore and James.

They would call every day just to say hi and push for a date—dinner, a movie, coffee—at least twice a week, sometimes more. Lenore didn't want to upset her in-laws, and Jake avoided conflict at all costs, but both felt put-upon. "It's had a really bad impact on our marriage," Lenore confessed to me. "I dread hearing the phone ring. When I walk to the grocery, I'm afraid I'll run into them. I know they're having adjustment problems and I don't want to hurt their feelings, but they're driving me insane and really ruining this nice, early part of our marriage."

Jake looked at the carpet sheepishly as Lenore spoke. "I've been hoping they'd adjust," he said finally, "but they haven't. I don't know how to talk to them about it. I know them; if I say anything, they'll get huffy and be hurt. Then they'll punish us by not calling for a month."

• • •

Many of the people I work with who have frequent contact with their parents are shocked when I tell them that the amount of time they devote to these interactions is, in fact, optional. If you are seeing much more of your parents than you want to, you need to reassess your boundaries. Or perhaps it's time for you to go where no child in your family has gone before.

This behavior pattern may be long-standing and therefore hard to change, but it can be done. I believe strongly that it is worth the effort. If your parents' demands are making you crazy, I'll bet the time you spend with them isn't pleasant for you or them. It is better to interact with your parents less frequently but more pleasantly than to give them all the time they want but be miserable the whole time.

Unfortunately, few parents understand this human algebra instinctive. Most seem to want as much time as possible with their kids, even if that time is wasted in tense anger. So it's up to you to change the situation. Here's what you need to do:

1. *Level with yourself about why it feels that you're spending too much time with them.* Until you know why you are so uncomfortable, you won't know how to come up with new parameters. Is the problem that your parents are demanding or annoying and you stew silently with anger? Or that you don't have enough time with your spouse or family? Do you feel infantalized by their attention? Do you worry that you're using their attention to distract you from the fact that you don't have much of a personal life?

2. *Target a more comfortable level of interaction.* Twice a month instead of once a week? One call each Sunday evening instead of three calls at your office every day? Yes to Christmas but no to Thanksgiving? Would it be better to visit in the summer instead of midwinter so you could go fishing with your father, which always relaxes both of you? Should you set aside the morning commute to the office to make a short but loving call to your mother on the cell

phone instead of dreading her myriad interruptions throughout the day?

3. *Make friends with guilt.* When you decide to scale back your time with your parents, you will almost certainly have an attack of conscience. Nothing is more precious to your parents than your presence, and yes, you are restricting that. But take my word for it: your qualms will pass. Just wait 'em out.

4. *Acknowledge that your parents are likely to feel rejected and act dejected when you set new time boundaries.* Don't let that deter you. Instead, review their personal narratives and their needs, and anticipate their reactions—without caving in. Role-play how you will stand strong in the face of their disappointment.

5. *Commit to getting more from less.* Your overall goal is a more satisfying relationship with your parents, so remember that you aren't cutting the time you spend with them simply to have fewer miserable dates. You are trying to make the time you spend together more pleasurable for both them and you.

6. *Find ways to make the new schedule attractive to them.* "Dad, I just bought myself a recliner for the express purpose of relaxing in it during our new Sunday night sports recap. I've got the phone nearby."

HOW TO DROP THE BOMB

There are two basic approaches. One is the passive path: not telling them. Those who opt for this strategy simply decide, for example, that they will no longer take their parents' daily calls or show up every Friday night for dinner. When the phone rings, they let the machine answer, using caller ID to screen.

Passive is fine—provided your parents aren't the type who'd react by ratcheting up their demands or fomenting a confrontation. As noted earlier, the important thing is *not* to get your parents to see that you are right, but to change your behavior. In this case, the goal is to have *better* interactions with your parents rather than just fewer of them. If you can improve the quality of your time with them by cutting down the amount of time you spend with them—even if you have not explained to them why you are doing it—you will have achieved that goal.

The second approach, which I prefer, is direct communication. Telling your parents in a gentle yet firm way that you need more room—and dealing with their disappointment—is a giant step on the road to growing up.

Among the tools you might want to marshal for this task are:

- Understanding their past (see chapter 5)
- Keeping your eye on the prize (see chapter 12)
- Getting your spouse in the house (see chapter 14)
- Role-Playing (see chapter 15)
- Speaking their language (see chapter 19)
- Diversion (see chapter 20)
- Saviorizing (see chapter 21)
- Flattery (see chapter 23)

Whether you decide to take the passive route or come right out and tell your parents, don't fail to act. If you just grin and bear it, you will eventually get so irritated that your feelings will seep out and poison every moment with them. You may act rashly, cutting off all contact, a stand you will likely be unable to maintain. Then you will reluctantly return to the same unsustainable schedule, feeling guilty and still full of rage. This is just the treadmill dynamic that you must bust out of.

Lenore and Jake came up with a fantastic plan to gently wean his parents from their time-gobbling ways. They combined skillful diversion with saviorizing and worked brilliantly as a team.

With Christmas approaching, they gave his parents a series of theater workshop tickets. They chose this cultural institution because they knew it had an active membership, thinking this would be a place where his parents might regularly see other subscribers who could become friends.

Soon after, they called his parents for a dinner date. (That was a switcheroo. A pattern had been set: that Lenore and Jake never called his parents.) Toward the end of the dinner date, over coffee, Jake told his parents how much he and Lenore enjoyed having them so close, and how much they loved them. But, he said, he and Lenore needed their help. (This was a well-planned speech that Lenore and Jake had role-played several times.) He said they had been struggling to create a "special unit" for themselves, which they had decided was very important in building a solid marriage. He told his parents that their careers had made it hard to carve out an identity as a couple. Many of their friends' marriages had run aground because they had never created that early intimacy, he told them. He and Lenore said they wanted to start having children within a couple of years and therefore needed a lot of time alone together to create a solid base before the babies arrived.

Jake then launched directly into the conflict: seeing so much of his parents, even though it was a pleasure, was cutting into their time alone. Surely they could understand the importance of creating an identity as a couple before the kids were born, right?

Both his parents nodded, though they stayed silent.

Lenore then piped up: "It's going to be hard for us not to have you around so much, but we really feel we have to do this for ourselves and we really appreciate your sensitivity and support. We hope you won't feel slighted. It has nothing to do with how much we love you."

Jake told them he and Lenore wanted to make a regular Tuesday night date with them. "That way we can really plan for it."

His parents were quiet. Lenore and Jake knew what was on their minds: the mistakes they had made in their own marriage. Lenore and Jake knew his parents had always put the kids first, for better or worse, and Jake was smart enough to use that to his advantage. He made his parents partners in helping their son have a better marriage than theirs. *That,* his parents could do. That made them feel needed, which in turn defused their pain over not being able to see Lenore and Jake so much.

Lenore and Jake carefully selected the activity for the first Tuesday night date with his parents: a special members-only tour of the museum's new exhibit. His parents agreed to attend, but on the tour they gave Lenore and Jake the silent treatment. Having anticipated that reaction, Lenore and Jake let his parents deal privately with their mixed emotions, instead of asking them if they were OK. The younger couple made a point of ending the night on a grateful and happy note, giving Jake's parents particularly ardent hugs.

Lenore and Jake stuck to their guns, and after a few Tuesday outings, his parents loosened up. There were still some incidents, however. A couple of months into the deal, his mother called with really hot theater tickets for a Thursday. "I told her we would be willing to switch that particular Tuesday for Thursday," Lenore recalled. "She was clearly disappointed that she couldn't lure us into seeing them twice that week, but I held my ground. When his father tried the same thing a month later—a Diana Krall concert on a Friday—we just said we couldn't make it. We didn't have plans, but we felt it was important not to let things slip back into old patterns. It hurt not seeing that show, but we knew it was best to be consistent. Now we have a nice Tuesday routine. They are used to it, and we don't spend all our time and energy thinking of ways to avoid them. Or feeling guilty."

• Chapter 29 •

They Are Offended When I Don't Share Personal Details of My Life

"I don't need an alarm clock," said Heidi, a thirty-four-year-old chiropractor who is single and has an active dating life. "I have my mother. Every morning at eight-oh-five she calls in a cheery voice, asking me how I am, what I did the night before. She wants to know if I saw *Sixty Minutes* or read that 'awful' editorial in the paper. She tells me about a 'simply gorgeous' sweater that she couldn't resist buying for me. Did that great guy I had a date with the week before call yet? How did the conversation go—exactly? Do I mind that she sent copies of the local newspaper article that mentioned my name to every person I've ever known?

"It gets kind of creepy how much she wants to know about me, so I try changing the subject. But when I ask her about herself, she says, 'Oh, nothing's new' and directs the conversation back to me. I know she hates her job and doesn't have many friends, and I try to be sensitive, but God, it's like she wants to suck the blood out of my veins, like she wants to graft herself onto my life. Sometimes she calls me ten times a day. When I tell her I'm going out on a date, she calls me on my cell phone at nine-thirty in the evening, knowing I'll most likely be out at dinner with the guy. She wants me to excuse myself and go to the ladies' room to talk to her.

"The weirdest part about it is that I care what she thinks. If she tells me she gets a bad feeling about a guy, I start to wonder about him too. If she is very enthusiastic, I get totally hung up on the guy, thinking he's mister perfect, when he's not. I try to shut her out, but she gets terribly offended and we wind up in a fight that I eventually have to patch up. The whole thing makes me anxious and sad, even angry sometimes, but then I just wind up feeling guilty. I worry that her life is empty, and what kind of pill am I, denying her what seems to be her only pleasure—being involved in my life."

When I'm counseling new parents, who often have a great deal of anxiety about how to be the best parent possible, they seem vexed by one particular question: What's the single most important thing to give a child throughout that child's life? Unconditional love? The tools for self-discipline? A sense of social responsibility?

I tell them that the answer is simpler: your primary job as a parent is to prepare your children to leave you behind. Parenthood is—or should be—an exercise in planned obsolescence; if you have been a good parent, the best thing you can hope for is that your child will be eager to get out in the world and live a strong, deliberate, independent life. Your children don't belong to you, I always tell clients, they are on loan. That's why parenthood is the most unselfish of pursuits; doing a good job automatically means you lose it.

This is a very tough pill for some people to swallow, which is what is likely happening if your parents are overinvolved in your life at this late stage in the game. Let's face it, parents like this often started out with a less-than-altruistic reason for having kids in the first place. Perhaps they craved companionship and something meaningful to take up their days. Or they wanted to create a life that would have a better shot at the world than they were given. Maybe they were unhappy in their marriage and wanted a new focus. Or perhaps they wanted to prove that they could be the wonderful parents they never had.

At any rate, they probably threw themselves into the task, and the one thing they never planned on was letting go. *Separation* wasn't in their vocabulary and still isn't. They figured that they would have their kids around—in whatever way they imagined— forever. After all, that's what most of their mothers got a generation ago. Back then, grown children across the board felt strong societal pressure to maintain ties to their parents—financial, social, and emotional. Sure, that meant the parents (read: mothers) had to take on some child-care duties in return, but it was rarely full-time because your mother herself probably wasn't working outside the home.

These days, parents like yours are in a bind, especially mothers. They're squeezed between generations. They don't want to act as an unpaid full-time baby sitter (which you might actually need if you have young kids and a job); nor do they want to be shunted aside. In addition, they may have mixed feelings about you having a job: envy that they never had a career and the independence that comes with it, as well as fascination with the glamour of it all. Whatever the case, they are probably experiencing an avalanche of painful, confusing emotions surrounding the process of separation.

You may also have more ambivalence about this issue than you are aware of. Parents who are overly involved in the lives of their adult children generally were always this way, and you may have been confused for much of your life about how much information about yourself is enough to give them. The parents who now fixate on the intimate details of their children's lives are often the same ones who went through their kids' drawers or felt free to barge in on their children at any time of the day. They are often the sort who created a parent-child relationship without boundaries, and you may have enjoyed this to some degree, especially if your parents were comforting and supportive. If you didn't reject their intrusions when you were a kid, you probably still have mixed feelings yourself about what is appropriate.

The first thing you must do is confront those feelings. You can't begin to draw more appropriate boundaries until you are honest with yourself about breaches you may welcome or even invite.

- Does having your parent hang on news of your every activity make you feel loved or cherished on some level?
- Do you sometimes enjoy sharing extremely intimate details with him or her?
- Do you let your judgment be affected by your parent's opinions?
- Do you ever let your parent have access to your personal belongings? (Does your mother do your laundry, always weigh in on your clothing purchases, buy major items for your home, tidy the place up when she's visiting?)

Heidi, for example, had given her mother, Adelaide, her cell phone number, even though Adelaide had shown herself incapable of using it only in emergencies, as Heidi had requested. In preparing to change her relationship with Adelaide, she had to confront her own actions. Why had she given her mother the number when it was clear Adelaide had no intention of reigning in her need to connect constantly with Heidi? Heidi came to realize that on some level Adelaide's hunger for the details of her life was pleasurable; it made her feel desirable and loved—unlike the way her dating life had lately been making her feel. Some of the times when her mother had called her while Heidi was out on dates, she actually did go to the ladies' room and whisper to her mother about how it was going. Heidi's own history played a part in her mixed feelings about her mother's ministrations; an only child, Heidi had at times thrived on such involvement. It made her feel less lonely.

Once she realized her ambivalence, Heidi was ready to move on to the next step: taking a close look at Adelaide's history. Doing so would enable her to understand what her mother was missing, what motivated her to want to lose herself in her daughter's life. Adelaide had come from a large family—six kids—that had lived together in three rooms. They were incredibly close and shared virtually every detail of their lives. There were no doors to speak of and no off-limits corners. Heidi's grandmother had moved into Adelaide's house as soon as Adelaide got married, and she took care of Heidi almost full-time until Heidi went to school. "My mom and her mom used to fight all the time, but they still were all over each other, in each other's business twenty-four/seven."

Heidi's father, Frank, had left by the time she was seven. Paradoxically, he had been a very private man who had kept plenty of secrets, including a drug habit. Adelaide's mother's intrusiveness wasn't responsible for driving him away, but it had created a great deal of tension, and Heidi had vivid memories of their arguments.

Adelaide had always poured a great deal of energy into Heidi, buying mother-daughter outfits and supervising her homework and social life rigorously. By the time Heidi reached high school, she was acting out, being wild as a way of asserting her independence. "That was the period when I actively bucked her," she said. "But the more I acted out, the more intensely she threw herself into my life. It was a very bad time."

In recent years, Heidi had turned into the sort of person Adelaide had always wanted her to be. Her chiropractic practice was thriving, and she had a great condo overlooking the city. Heidi acknowledged that in the early years of her career, she took great pleasure in making her mom proud. She tolerated Adelaide's overinvolvement because it came without the criticism she had withstood for so long. But in the past two years, as Adelaide was nearing retirement, she had dived even deeper into Heidi's life. Her intensity and unquenchable thirst for details had begun to wear more heavily on Heidi.

To change the pattern, Heidi had to work on three things: ascertaining where to draw boundary lines, perfecting a mantra to shore up those lines, and tolerating the guilt inherent in making some of the areas of her life off-limits.

Heidi decided that her top priority was to get her mother out of her personal life, so she concentrated on that. She simply didn't want to discuss men with Adelaide.

To set the stage for new boundaries, Heidi took a concrete, physical step: getting a new cell phone without giving her mother the number. She asked Adelaide to rely in the future on e-mail, rather than cell-phone calls, in an emergency. With a wireless hookup, Heidi was able to check her messages many times during the day, but she found that much less intrusive than phone calls. And she knew Adelaide wouldn't get the same satisfaction out of contacting her by computer that she did from calling, and therefore was less likely to abuse the privilege.

Admittedly, this new arrangement was a largely symbolic gesture, as there were many ways Adelaide could continue to inundate her with contact. So Heidi sat her mother down for a talk. "Mom, I love you very much, and I feel very lucky that you are proud of me and want to be involved in my life. Most aspects of it I gladly share with you. That doesn't mean that I'm comfortable sharing all of it, however. I know this is hard for you to accept, but in the future I'm not going to answer your questions about dating. That is my private life, and I choose not to share it. If I tell you I'm going out on a date, you should feel free to ask me how it went, but if I answer 'fine' and change the subject, the subject is going to stay changed."

Heidi had already settled on both public and private mantras to help strengthen her resolve.

- Private mantra: I don't need to confide in my mother to feel strong or loved.
- Public mantra: Mom, I'm not going to answer questions about men. Is there anything else you'd like to talk about?

Heidi also made a big effort to expand the repertoire of activities she engaged in with her mother. That gave them more to talk about. It also leveled the playing field; instead of talking only about Heidi's very full life, the new activities gave them a way to focus on her mother's life. She coaxed Adelaide into taking bridge lessons with her and took her cross-country skiing. She made sure to consciously file away the memories, funny moments, and stories about the friends they made; recalling those new moments was the best diversion for her mother.

Adelaide didn't take to the new regime very well at first. She tried every means at her disposal to get to Heidi, from pouting to total silence. For a week or two, she left messages on Heidi's machine about how she was having fainting spells, wrote Heidi long letters about how Heidi would one day regret shutting her out. For a solid week she didn't answer Heidi's phone calls. But Heidi held fast, practicing her guilt exercises to desensitize herself.

What made the difference for Heidi was her persistence in staying honest with herself. She was vigilant about screening herself for resistance, forgiving herself for a momentary desire to go back to the way things were, and pressing on. At her bedside and in her office she kept a photocopy of a journal entry she made after one particular dustup with her mother. "Why do I answer her when she asks me those questions?" it read. "I always wind up feeling like a little kid afterward; I always regret the words the minute they're out of my mouth. I don't need validation from her to do the right thing, to know how I feel about a guy. I won't disappear if she doesn't keep track of me every moment."

• Chapter 30 •

They Put Me in the Middle of Their Marriage (or Divorce) Problems

"I can't believe you said that to the parking valet."

"What the heck are you talking about?"

"You told him to be careful with the BMW."

"So?"

"You're so condescending. You treated him like he was an idiot, like he was going to crash it into a wall or something."

"No I didn't. I was just saying, 'Please be careful with the car, it's new.'"

"And you had to mention three times it was a BMW, to make sure he knows you're a bigshot with an expensive car!"

"What are you talking about? Every time I turn around, you've got something else to complain about. Don't talk to the valet like that, don't tip the waiter so much, don't wear that shirt. It never stops with you, does it?"

"Well, maybe that's because you're completely oblivious to anyone else's needs but your own. You walk around like you own the place, and I'm just trailing along behind you like the hired help. You ignore everything I say."

"Well maybe I'd pay attention to you more if you did anything but nag-nag-nag!"

Stop it! Jeremy thought, ready to scream. *Just stop this crap once and for all. If you hate each other so much, why don't you just split up?* He tried to block out the sound of his parents behind him in the backseat, but his head was swimming so fiercely that he could hardly see the road.

His wife, Pam, sitting in the passenger seat, was silent, but Jeremy knew what she was thinking. After ten years, he knew she was sick of the way his parents fought, and none too happy about how Jeremy insisted on spending so much time with them anyway.

This is really great, Jeremy thought. *My wife thinks I'm a jerk, my parents are tearing each other apart bit by bit, and we're headed for a rainy weekend together in the country. How do I get myself into these jams?*

If you've spent much of your life trapped between your parents as they battle (or freeze each other out), you are probably very tired of it by now. Even if their conflicts are relatively new or have grown vicious only lately (growing older can, sadly, turn a serviceable marriage into a miserable one), you are probably, like Jeremy, ready to scream, "So strangle each other for all I care—just don't make me listen to ONE MORE ARGUMENT!"

But you don't scream at them, do you? Instead you block your ears or try, in vain, to broker a peace. Or you grit your teeth until your gums bleed. You go to their house every year for Thanksgiving, even though the entire day is fraught with tension; you take them out for dinner, even though you dread the evening for weeks. Your father complains bitterly about your mother when you two are together on the golf course; your mother cries on your shoulder about his infidelities as you help her do the dishes.

You might think life would be better for everyone if they just split up, but even that might not do the trick. Your mother tries to pry information out of you about your father's new girlfriend; your father has a few too many martinis and tells you things about your mother's libido that you really don't want to hear.

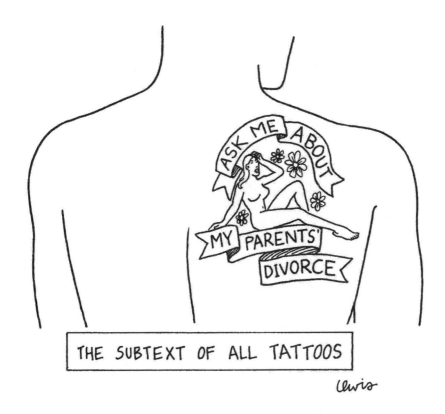

ASK ME ABOUT
MY PARENTS' DIVORCE

THE SUBTEXT OF ALL TATTOOS

Lewis

So why do you put up with it? Why don't you erase all trace of your parents from your Palm Pilot or move to an island in the South Seas? Why do you—a mature adult wrestling with your own demons and dreams—allow yourself to be used as a human shield in a war that is not yours and never will be?

There are a lot of reasons. You probably feel deeply tied to one or both of them, or feel sorry for one or both of them. Perhaps you still cling to the fantasy of a harmonious family. If your children adore your parents, you may have decided that that is reason enough to tolerate the constant bickering. Or maybe, beneath your cringing, you like the "action." Maybe refereeing the fights gives you a raison d'être, a purpose. No matter what the circumstance, you probably think you are only doing what's right.

Unfortunately, you are doing the opposite. Getting out of the middle of your parents' bad marriage—or bad divorce—dynamic will improve your relationship with them. Even if you think you are getting some emotional dividends from playing umpire (or perhaps just a glimmer of satisfaction for keeping them from killing each other), being a pawn in their destructive game is dehumanizing—for you and for them.

IF YOUR PARENTS ARE STILL MARRIED

News Flash: there is no law that says you must see your parents together. Loving them as individuals has nothing to do with loving them as a couple (you can easily love each of them but *hate* them as a couple), and you have every right to see them separately. Yes, I know that despite their horrible chemistry, your folks still insist on going everywhere together. They have their own strange reasons for wanting to be joined at the hip, but you do not have to accept this. Telling them you intend to see them separately may engender some theatrics at first, but they are no doubt well aware, at least on some level, of how awful they are to be with as a couple. If you inform them of your intentions skillfully, they will eventually accept your decision.

You: Folks, I'm calling to tell you that I've made a decision. After our last dinner together, I've decided that for the foreseeable future I'd like to see each of you individually. You have every right to fight as much as you want, but I am no longer going to be a witness to it. I love you both very much, and I want to enjoy your company—separately.

Your mother: That's ridiculous; we don't fight that much. And it's your father's fault. If he wouldn't be so negative all the time, we could have a nice time.

You: Dad?

Your father: Obviously, I'm not permitted to have any say here . . .

Your mother: Well, I'm not going to embarrass myself by going out alone. We'll be civilized the next time we see you. I just won't talk at all. You'll see, we won't argue in front of you.

You: This is not up for discussion. I won't force either of you to see me, but that is the only way I am willing to see you. Think about it. One advantage is that we can do things we would never do as a threesome. Dad, I thought we could go to a ball game. And Mom, I was hoping you would go with me to the flea market downtown to pick out stuff for my new apartment. You know how Dad hates that sort of thing. I'll call you each next week to make dates.

Breaking the Sounding-Board Barrier

Getting your parents one-on-one is a good thing, but you must make it clear to each of them that you do not intend to listen to criticism of the other. You may think that you are doing your parents a favor when you let them rant to you, that you are letting them blow off steam or helping them "think things out," but there is no way I can put this too strongly: *you are wrong.*

Why? To begin with, you are simply widening their drama, like ripples on a pond. The fights are bad enough; don't extend their shelf life by listening to your parents relive them—with extensive commentary.

Second, by listening, you become a player in their sick dynamic—a puppet, really—even if you don't take sides. They will likely try to use you to send messages to their partner, or ferret out information from you. This is precisely the sort of thing that will derail your efforts to create a mature relationship with each of them.

Lastly, you are inviting competition between them for your affection and approval. No matter how neutral you try to be, you will not be able to stop them from trying to win you over to their "side." This, again, is dehumanizing to you and is another way of perpetuating their destructive dynamic.

Resist Taking Sides

As legendary journalist Edward R. Murrow once said in discussing Senator Joseph McCarthy's witch hunt for Communists in the 1950s, "Some stories don't have two sides." Perhaps your mother has had serial affairs and lies constantly to your beleaguered "nice-guy" dad. Or your father browbeats your mother mercilessly over the smallest things. In short, it seems obvious to you who is in the right, and it's hard not to take sides, especially when you see a parent getting hurt.

That's a natural impulse, but one you must resist. You have to make sure you are not judgmental. These situations are almost always more complicated than they appear from the outside. Remember too that your parents are adults, even if they don't act that way. Even the most put-upon person bears some personal responsibility for staying in a miserable relationship.

As for trying to persuade a parent to leave the marriage, my advice is *stay out of it*—unless there is blatant abuse. Your parents must make their own decisions. A generation or two ago, your mother, who was likely untrained for work outside the home, might have needed your help when leaving your father, who was probably the breadwinner. But these days most women are aware of their options, are acquainted with plenty of other women who have escaped bad marriages, and have made a conscious decision to stay. Remember: as miserable as they seem, they are adults who bear the responsibility for their choices.

Learn to Leave

When your parents start to fight in your presence, I suggest you take a time-out. That means getting up and walking away. Do this whenever they clash, even if it means leaving your table in a restaurant or stopping the car and sitting on the curb. Don't be melodramatic—don't yell or throw your napkin down in disgust—simply rise and leave quietly. Return after five minutes, and if they are still battling, leave again. If they have stopped, take your seat and carry on as though it never happened. Be upbeat and light-hearted. They will get the message. Eventually.

Caveat: you *must* be consistent. You cannot moan and sigh or get angry about their bickering one time and then take a time-out the next. Nor can you take the time-out graciously most of the time but occasionally toss in a snarky comment as you walk away. You must always do exactly the same thing: spot the signs that a fight is coming, rise quietly, and leave. Always come back after the same amount of time. Always resume your seat with a smile and plunge back into the conversation. This is a form of behavioral conditioning, so it will work only if you do it in a even-tempered, controlled manner that your parents can come to count on.

IF YOUR PARENTS ARE NO LONGER TOGETHER

It's hard for many people to move on. There's no use cursing your bad luck in having parents who have not handled their divorce well. You aren't alone; nearly half of the people I deal with have divorced parents, and half of those parents *still* have fractious relationships. Sometimes it's money issues, other times it's lingering jealousy or resentment; some parents are simply still in love with a spouse who dumped them. In all these cases, it's tough on the children, even when they are adults. But there are some things you can do to extricate yourself from their never-ending tension.

Value Each Parent as a "Newborn"

If your parent is stuck in the drama of a divorce, emphasize your willingness to see him or her as a newly formed individual, free of the tangled web of the past. This is the time to aggressively pursue a new one-on-one relationship. If you have a family, don't settle for getting each parent together with your kids; that's great, but be aware that being a "third wheel" at family get-togethers can exacerbate their feelings of isolation. Instead, ramp up the buddy activities—go fly-fishing three times a year instead of just once. Or initiate new ones, things your parent couldn't do with you while married, for whatever reason. Snowboarding. A book group. Pottery class. Last-minute trips to Las Vegas. A weekend at a spa. And remember, no talk of the ex-spouse. It's a new day.

Don't Carry Tales

When a parent is struggling with divorce, it's important that you not contribute to the problem by relaying information about the ex. I know it seems unnatural—why shouldn't you be able to answer questions about your father or mother or mention something they are doing?—but such data are poison to a person in the death throes of a relationship. New information keeps memories and obsessions alive. Plus, such exchanges damage your independent ties to each of your parents; it reduces you to the role of messenger for the parent seeking information, and it violates the privacy of the person who is being asked about.

No Scorekeeping

The favorite game of the acrimoniously divorced is tit for tat. But don't play along. Do *not* allow your parents to manipulate you by requiring that you spend the same amount of time with each of them. "Dad, just because I spent Christmas with Mom and her boyfriend does not mean I'm going to hang out with you on New Year's. That's a game I'm not gonna play. I know you're in a bad way lately, but I don't want us to get into that pattern. I spend time with you because I love you, not because I spent X amount of time with Mom. I'm not going to measure our lives out like that."

The same thing goes for gifts. Sure it's fun to let your parents try to buy your affection (ah, the cashmere sweaters, the sailing lessons, the fancy meals out . . .), but it is a fool's game. Not only does it once again make you merely a trophy, but it exacerbates the juvenile dynamic they've got going.

Try this on for size: explicitly tell the parent who is showering you with goodies that you have no intention of showing those gifts to the ex. And tell that parent you would love him or her just as much if the gifts to you were nothing but time and affection. See what happens.

Institute a Strict "No-Dishing" Policy

Many parents who are married complain about their spouse to their kids, but such carping pales in comparison to the sort of thing that goes on postdivorce, especially after the kids are grown. Once couples are divorced, the floodgates of unhappiness and recrimination often open, letting a tidal wave of vitriol flow downhill . . . to you. Do not under any circumstances stay in the path of this outpouring. It is detrimental to all concerned.

Usually, it takes direct and decisive intervention to break this pattern. Don't wait until your parent is in midrage to bring up the subject; that will likely lead to anger, embarrassment, and silence. Instead bring it up during a calm moment when the good feelings are flowing. You might say: "Mom, I need to talk you about something. Lately whenever we're together, you start ragging on Dad, and it upsets me. I know you're still angry, and I understand why. I know you feel you need to talk about it, but I am not the right person for that. You need to find someone else to talk to. What I'm interested in is you, and our relationship. I want us to concentrate on us. I'm not going to discuss Dad with you anymore."

If that doesn't work, you'll have to go to the next level. "Mom, I told you that I get uncomfortable when you start in on Dad, so I've decided that the best thing for me when you start doing it is to leave the table. I'll come back in a few minutes, after I've walked around a little to let us both calm down. I'm not mad and I understand how upset you still are, but it's not good for me to hear it. So this is the way I've decided to deal with it from this point on."

. . .

When it comes to your parents' marital problems, the rule of thumb is: don't overestimate your ability to help. You are not going to solve their problems—you never have and never will. They may tell you they need you to smooth the way or just "be there" to listen, but that is merely a thinly veiled attempt to rope you into their domestic drama. It's time for you to realize that you will not bring them together or even stop them from slowly killing each other. Instead, concentrate on helping them establish independent personae—new identities you can relate to as an adult.

Removing yourself from your parents' battles will also pay off in your own relationship. Adults with a long history of mediating their parents' conflicts often have trouble negotiating the shoals of their own personal lives. They tend to have deep ambivalence toward intimacy and trust, or avoid conflict so zealously that they can't deal with even the day-to-day tensions of marriage or partnership. These patterns are deeply engrained and take a lot of time, energy, and self-awareness to change, but you will be amazed at how much easier it will be to make progress once you pull yourself out of the fray with your parents.

• Chapter 31 •

They Manage to Slip an Insult into Every Conversation

I can't believe how well everything is going, Polly thought, as she walked with her father and her two young sons through Disney World. The kids, ages five and eight, were giddy with delight, and her dad, not one for wild emoting, seemed to be getting a real kick out of watching them. The weather was wonderful, and even the lines weren't making her father tense. He actually was smiling, showing teeth even, as he joked with eight-year-old Matt about Goofy being, well, a touch light in the head. *Maybe he's really changed,* she thought. *Without even trying, could we have somehow turned a corner in our relationship?*

"Everyone ready for lunch?" she asked, glancing at her watch. Before they had a chance to answer, though, she remembered that she had promised to phone her boss, the president of the children's advocacy group she volunteered for back home. She had told her boss she would call before 1:30 P.M., and it was already 1:45 P.M. "Gosh, sorry, I've just got to take five minutes and call the office."

The kids groaned theatrically. Her father, however, was notably silent. She whipped the phone out of her pocket and, stepping a few feet away, started to dial. Then she heard it, the thing she had been expecting—and dreading. "Some job, where you don't get paid and

255

you run errands for someone," her father murmured under his breath, just loud enough for her to hear.

Polly grew stiff, the sound of the ringing phone echoing in her ear. When her boss picked up, she could barely concentrate on what the woman was saying about the one-hundred-dollar-a-plate fund-raiser coming up. *Why does he have to do it every time?* she thought. *Why does he have to get that nasty shot in there just when I think we're really getting along so well? Why does he have to diminish whatever I'm doing?* Suddenly, the fund-raiser, which she had slaved to make a success, seemed so petty, so unimportant. She tried to remember her husband's words: don't let him get to you. But instead she flashed on her sister Terry, a lawyer, who tried huge criminal cases that her father, himself a criminal attorney, followed like a groupie. *He thinks I'm a failure,* she thought. *He thinks I'm nothing but a housewife. Nothing will ever change between us.*

They come at the moment we least expect them, lobbed into a pleasant conversation like a Molotov cocktail, throwing everything in sight into a harsh, dim light and ruining even the nicest memories. If wounding a loved one with a zinger were an Olympic sport, your parents would probably have a slew of gold medals by now.

Why do they do it? There are as many reasons as there are types of insults. They may be trying to control you or keep you dependent on their approval. Or they may believe it's their "duty" to be "honest," albeit in a sneaky, side-of-the-mouth way. They may have grown up with just the sort of undermining parent they have become, always keeping their child off balance with wisecracks and sarcastic asides. They may just be rigid, demanding people—or passive-aggressive types who don't have the personal skills to bring up sensitive issues directly.

How can you stop it? There is no single answer, I'm afraid, no magic comeback that will silence them or turn them into the supportive, kindly folk you long for. That doesn't mean there is no way to deal better with their assault and no way to diminish its effects; on the contrary, there are many approaches you can try. Parents who can't resist a "shot" are best dealt with through an organized program of trial and error.

One thing that's for sure: what you've been doing up to now hasn't been working. Losing your temper, freezing up, pouting, turning scarlet, or downing a fifth of bourbon has not resulted in your parent stopping his or her flamethrowing. Nor has this strategy helped protect you. The key here is to experiment to see what will work. Although there is no guarantee that you can stop your parent if he or she is determined to undermine you, you can certainly discover better ways to deal with the insults. And if you find an approach that is more comfortable for you—and, most important, you are able to use that technique in a consistent fashion—you may

"You couldn't put on a tie?"

be able to take the wind out of your parent's sails. If you are no longer exhibiting a response that is satisfying, your parent may cease making the effort to mess with you.

To record the effect of all the approaches you try, you will need to use a notebook. Decide on a format to keep track. I like this one: make five vertical columns; label the first column "technique," the next column "shot," the third column "response," and the fourth column "outcome." The last column is for "effectiveness rating."

Choose three or more responses or techniques from the seven discussed in the following paragraphs. You will have to try each one for a minimum of a month (or more, if you interact infrequently with your parent).

1. *Ignore him.* Yes, I know this sounds like a cliché, ironically one that your parents may have used on you when you were a little kid hounded by bullies. ("Now, just ignore those bad kids, and they'll stop bothering you.") But I doubt you understand the dynamics of true oblivion. To ignore your parent's nasty comments, you'll have to work on controlled breathing, relaxing your facial muscles to the point of blankness, and what I call "internal humming," which entails replaying over and over in your head the chorus from that all-too-catchy song you've been trying to forget. You will have to master the art of pretending your parent is speaking Swahili, which you don't understand, imagining your parent as a cartoon with a bubble over his head containing the words *blah, blah, blah, blah,* or picturing him as a braying animal in a zoo. In other words, you'll be working to develop an inner dialogue that automatically drowns him out.

2. *Ask questions.* In wounding you with a nasty aside, your parent is trying to stick an arrow in your side, but in general, he is not trying to stop you in your tracks. He doesn't want the attention to be thrust back on him; he just wants to bother you a little, to cause you to falter slightly, to get under your skin. To invert this equation, play social scientist and ask him questions to figure out why he bothers. The key here is to remove yourself emotionally from the

moment. Pretend he is the father of a friend and you are helping that friend get to the bottom of her father's psyche.

Caveat: keep your voice very calm. Stick with the tone you might use on a tour at the natural history museum when you are asking a guide why the white-tailed marsupial eats turnips exclusively. "Dad, I hear your denigrating comment, and it makes me wonder exactly what response would be satisfying to you. Do you want me to get upset? Would it be better if I turned away in embarrassment? I'm really very confused about the whole thing. Please tell me precisely what you're trying to convey. Then I can work up a response that would be gratifying for you so we can move on." Don't forget, your tone is crucial here. Don't use even a hint of sarcasm or nastiness. Be genuinely curious. Turn the attention patiently back on him. But don't get cute or stoop to his level. Remember you are a scientist, and this is research.

3. *Ambush him with honesty.* Instead of slinking away, growing angrily silent, or blowing steam out your nostrils, tell him the truth: that you are hurt. Don't blame him; be a bit vulnerable. Start by giving him the benefit of the doubt, which will disarm him further. "Dad, I am assuming you aren't trying to hurt my feelings because I know you love me, but you've managed to do so nonetheless. Your comments make me feel incompetent, as though I've disappointed you. Instead of enjoying the moment and believing we are having a good time, I wind up not wanting to spend time with you at all. I can't imagine why you would want to hurt me like that. Can you explain it to me?"

4. *Surprise him with empathy.* A parent who purposefully undermines his child with hurtful, indirect criticism is a parent in trouble. He may be afraid of your independence or threatened by your success. He may see you as an extension of himself or worry that you will turn out as badly as he has. He may be stuck in the mire of believing the world will judge him by how his kids turn out. These are all painful states, the refuge of unhappy souls. So take pity on him and try a little kindness. "Dad, I know you are upset

that a daughter of yours is not working at a paying job and has instead decided to do nonprofit work. I know you're having a hard time understanding how that's OK with my husband and it's giving me a lot of pleasure. This must be very difficult for you to think that I am reflecting badly on you; otherwise I'm sure you wouldn't bother trying to hurt me with nasty comments. I don't like to see you putting yourself in this position, which I'm sure is painful for you. Is there anything I can do to help you better understand my choices?

5. *Make jokes.* By now you probably have a pretty good idea of the sort of comments your parent is likely to make. You know what sets him off and what aspects of your life are apt to elicit a snarky dig. So why not have some good material prepared? Nothing renders nastiness more absurd than humor. If you can truly make skillful light of the issues, you will diffuse a great deal of tension. The best way to do this is to prepare heavily; trying to be funny spontaneously when you are still stinging from a parent's comment is too tough for most of us. But having a routine ready can be a great remedy to having your buttons pushed. The Internet is a great resource for jokes: you can go to any of the dozens of joke sites and plug in a subject. Many "blogs" also recycle material from David Letterman and Jay Leno. "Now that you mention it, Dad, have you heard the one about the unemployed actor who rents a dog suit for an audition?"

6. *Lay down the law.* "Dad, I love you, and usually I like being with you. But I am no longer going to tolerate your side-of-the-mouth criticisms. If you wish to discuss these issues with me in a direct, adult fashion, I will be glad to do so, but the next time you choose to take a potshot at me, I am going to quietly stop whatever it is I'm doing and walk out. If we are eating, I am going to lay down my share of the check; if I am driving you somewhere, I am doing to drop you at the nearest bus stop. I will do this even if I have the kids with me or there are other people around. I am not joking; just try me."

Naturally, this technique requires that you follow through to the letter. You must keep your voice very, very calm when you are explaining what will happen. Letting your parent get a rise out of you defeats the purpose. And you cannot—not even once—let a comment slip by. This is a very high-risk strategy, but if you are able to maintain your commitment to it, you will find it is *very* effective.

7. *Give him a second chance.* Sometimes we all let an ill-advised comment slip out and immediately wish we could take it back. Why not give your parent a chance to do so? "Dad, I heard that comment you just made under your breath, and I have a feeling it's not what you meant to say. I don't believe you meant to demean me like that. Is there something you'd like to say directly to me? I'm open to a brief discussion if you'd like. We'll just put down our defenses and talk about it, OK?"

In your notebook, write down the technique you are trying, the actual comment your parent made, the response you gave, and the outcome of the interaction. Finally, give yourself an effectiveness rating from one to five. Remember that you must try each technique consistently for at least a month to gauge its effectiveness. (If you find a winner early on, just stick with it!)

Dealing with a parent who offers criticism in a backhanded manner like this is very trying, but take heart: there is likely a way you can interrupt this pattern—provided you can break your own habits of capitulation. Of all the repetitive "dances" that take place between parents and their grown children, this is the most mind-numbingly common. Many people spend their entire lives reenacting this two-step over and over. The slights are small when taken one at a time, but over the years, they act like a diamond ball-peen hammer, wearing you down bit by bit.

Once you break the pattern, however, you will be surprised at how much more optimistically you approach every interaction with your parents. If you are not subconsciously dreading the moment when they will send a blow dart into your side, you will be more able to let your defenses down and regard them as individuals. They too will be liberated; they don't know it, but making nasty comments is like drinking slow-acting poison mixed into a fruity cocktail. It tastes good at first to let a nasty comment slip out, but over time it corrodes your insides. Once you break them of the habit by changing your approach to their utterances, they will be happier as well.

• Chapter 32 •

They Expect Constant Admiration and Attention

A few months after Jenna's father died, she called her mother, Kay, and suggested they go together on a garden tour of Savannah's mansions. As they boarded the bus in their town fifty miles away, Jenna recognized Lydia, a woman she knew slightly from the public library, where she worked. On the way to the city, they chatted and swapped gossip. Jenna was aware that her mother, usually a gabber, had gone quiet, even though she lived in the same town and knew all the characters they were discussing. She sat, face-front, wearing a tight little smile.

When they got to Savannah, Lydia said she was meeting a friend, so Jenna gave her a peck on the cheek and waved good-bye. "Gosh that was a treat running into her, right, Mum? She's really very cool, isn't she?" But Kay was silent.

And she remained silent all day. Although the gardens were breathtaking, she walked through them like an automaton. Jenna made a few attempts to get her to interact, but Kay just put on a fake smile and kept walking. "Are you sure you don't want to tell me what's bothering you?" Jenna asked. "Nothing is bothering me," came the curt reply.

Jenna's head began to swim. She was sorry she had asked her mother on the date, sorry she was trudging through these darned gardens. She began to feel terribly guilty, though she wasn't sure why.

On the bus on the way back, she read a magazine, barely concentrating; what else was there to do? When she dropped her mother at her door, Kay announced to her, in a sanctimonious tone, that she wasn't angry; she was hurt.

"Hurt?" Jenna asked. "What about?"

"Well," said Kay, in a wounded tone, "you spent all that time talking to that woman on the bus and acting as though I wasn't there. And you didn't really make an effort to find out what was wrong. To top it off, you read a magazine all the way home. This was supposed be our day together. Why shouldn't I be hurt?"

Children are often said to be a bottomless pit of need; they crave attention, recognition, reassurance, and admiration. But don't underestimate your parents' need for such things, especially if, like Kay, their behavior borders on the narcissistic. I've avoided diagnostic lingo for the most part in this book because I think it often obscures plain truths and I don't find labels very helpful, but in this case it's probably useful to be able to recognize if your parents have some symptoms of mild narcissistic personality disorder. They may not have a full-blown case of this syndrome (though that's not impossible), but even in small doses, it's very frustrating. By now you probably can recognize the symptoms: a grandiose sense of self-importance, the belief that she is "special," the need for excessive admiration, a sense of entitlement, the quickness to take offense, the lack of empathy.

Alas, narcissism is one of the least mutable of personality traits. It is virtually impervious to reason, and it's often defended by a wall so high that no one gets in. For narcissists, the most important thing in life is to get their needs met. Now. Period.

Many people who have grown up with a narcissistic parent have developed one of three approaches to such behavior:

1. They feed the beast, giving the requisite attention, admiration, et cetera.
2. They ignore and retreat.
3. They protest and terrorize.

As a child, you are very vulnerable to parents like this. Because you're programmed to try to please them, when they demand unreasonable amounts of attention, you try to give it. Sometimes you grow angry and disgusted and reject the manipulation. Of all the functional psychological impairments, narcissism is often thought to place the greatest burden on children.

But as an adult, you are free to decide precisely what you are willing to give. (Gosh, it's a relief to be grown up!), not that the attention-seeking behavior of your parent is any less obnoxious or draining, but now you have a few more options. Unlike a child, you have the wherewithal to realize that you can only please a narcissistic person temporarily, if at all. That's the way personalities like this work; by definition they are never satisfied. I know that sounds discouraging, but it's actually a very powerful piece of information. Once you know that with people like Kay the best you can hope for is to keep their need for attention in check for a brief time, you are freed from taxing, quixotic attempts to make everything better. With parents who need all eyes on them and a constant fix of admiration, you scale down expectations that they will ever change, focusing instead on protecting yourself against their demands.

Like many people who are mildly narcissistic, Kay had found a buffer; for her, it had been Jenna's father, Boris. He had fed Kay's tireless ego gladly. An easygoing guy, he had been happy to act as a courtier. He marveled at her clothing and style—she did have a great flair for dressing, even Jenna had to admit—and let her drag him to art museums all over the world. Kay could be quite charming, Jenna told me, and had sung opera semiprofessionally; when they threw parties, he would play piano and she would perform, stunning the audience of their friends into quiet admiration. It was clear Boris was quite enraptured by her, and while her need for kudos was never quite satiated, his constant flow of compliments kept it somewhat under control.

Jenna, on the other hand, had long ago rejected Kay's preening. When she was a child, she had refused to compliment her mother, adopting a posture of outright defiance; when her mother swept down the staircase in a new dress, Jenna would tell her she looked ugly. Her mother had never stopped trying to get her admiration, which sometimes resulted in a battle during Jenna's childhood, but her father was such a soothing, mitigating presence that the household had been generally peaceful.

In the past few years, Jenna had come to enjoy her mother more, appreciating especially Kay's taste in art and music. Kay had mellowed a bit, she had become good company, but she still needed plenty of attention and Jenna left that to her father.

But now that her father was no longer around, what was she going to do? she asked me. "I feel bad for her, but I don't want to just pick up where he left off. I want to have a relationship with her, but I can see that if I don't set the tone now, we're going to keep having conflicts like the one we had on the garden tour."

I understood why she was hesitant to step into her father's role. She did not have her father's personality or his patience. Most of all, she did not have romantic love to blind her. Obviously, she and her mother would have to find some other way to interact.

With people whose narcissism is all-encompassing and powerful, there is little you can do. But Kay, like most parents, was not in that category. She had flashes of sincere interest in culture and other people. She could spend an hour in a museum or appreciate architecture or listen to Vivaldi's music with a rapturous smile. She loved meeting artists and asking them about their work, and she devoured biographies of geniuses like Picasso and Vermeer. Those instincts were dominated by a gobbling drive to be the center of attention, it's true, but Jenna decided to relate to those higher impulses as much as she could. Otherwise she wouldn't be able to have a relationship with Kay at all.

But Jenna realized she would have to satisfy at least some of Kay's need to be admired in order to gain access to Kay's better qualities. This was tough for Jenna, who had always distinctly refused to give Kay her due. "I don't really have any speed setting except 'Defy' when she fishes for compliments," she said. "I automatically say the opposite of what she wants to hear."

Calibrating how much admiration to give and when to limit it is a delicate game when you're dealing with narcissistic tendencies. Here are seven guidelines to keep in mind.

1. *Know where the "gold" is buried.* In other words, have a firm grasp on what quality in your parent you are trying to bring out. Focus on that positive "nugget," instead of working only to squelch the unpleasant self-involvement.

In Jenna's case, she was trying to relate to Kay through culture and art, a passion they shared.

2. *Accept that you will have to pay some homage.* I know it can be excruciating, but it's important to check yourself for unproductive defiance. In order to mine the positive values, you will have to satisfy the "beast" a little.

Jenna realized that she would have to break her habit of never giving Kay any credit for her beauty and fantastic grooming. She developed a series of compliments—"Nice threads, Ma," "Woo-woo," and "You sure look sharp"—that didn't make her gag but gave Kay enough satisfaction that she could be diverted by other subjects.

3. *Use "guided reinforcement."* That means directing many of your compliments toward the areas you want to emphasize. People with mild narcissism want admiration across the board, but they often have sensors that enable them to zero in on where the attention lies. They will gravitate to whatever area in which you regularly offer ego gratification.

Jenna wanted to emphasize Kay's cultural interests, so she organized a trip to Memphis to see a Matisse exhibit because she knew Kay was a fan of the artist. Over lunch the week before, she asked Kay to fill her in on Matisse's life and recommend some books. In fact, Jenna knew more about Matisse than she let on, but she let Kay pontificate. Kay was very amusing in her telling of the story, and besides, this kept the spotlight on her while giving Jenna a bit of fun.

4. *Saviorize.* Remember that riding in to save the day is a real winner with parents who are narcissistic. Granted, you will have to go heavy on how you are grateful to them for their help, which may be a turnoff for you, but keep in mind that you are getting your needs met. Being right isn't what's important; making progress is.

Jenna, for example, needed clothes for a job interview. She didn't like shopping and didn't care much for clothes, but Kay adored both. So she asked Kay to pick out a few things for her and bring them home. Before, Jenna would have balked at giving Kay the satisfaction, but she realized, why fight it?

5. *Preempt problems.* If you know your parent is a brooder, like Kay, make sure you confront trouble spots early. And get used to the fact that no matter how much you try to anticipate such trouble spots, your parents will spend a great deal of their lives conveying to you how offended they are. This will annoy you deeply, but it won't kill you. Like guilt, it is something to which you will have to desensitize yourself.

"If I could do over that day on the garden tour," Jenna told me, "I would have turned to my mother at the beginning of the bus ride and said, 'I'm going to spend a little time talking with this friend, but I'm aware that I'm on a date with you. I'd like you to participate in this conversation, but if you don't want to, that's OK too. I'll soon turn my attention to you, OK?' And I would wait until she said 'OK' in response. Then, even if she acted out, I would have been better prepared for it."

6. *Know when you've had enough.* Paying a tad of homage is one thing; violating reasonable limits is another. Be prepared for the moment when you will have to draw the line; even people whose

narcissistic tendencies are relatively mild want that mile when you give them an inch. Accept that that is their nature. Don't blame or rage; just know your limits. People with this sort of personality throw off all sorts of signs that they are going to push until you refuse to cooperate, so don't act surprised when you see it coming. Be prepared to retreat, gracefully and quietly. Be firm but kind.

Jenna could say to her mother: "I appreciate that you shopped for me; in fact I appreciate it enormously. You have fabulous taste. No one is better. I hear that you want me to model all the clothes for you, but I'm not going to do that because that fashion show thing makes me uncomfortable. I'm going home to try everything on in private, and I'll call you as soon as I decide what to keep. We're not going to discuss it any more. You're really great, and I'm lucky to have you as a mom."

7. *Learn to live with the fact that nothing is ever enough.* Add this truth to the list of things, like death and taxes, that are inevitable. No matter how much you give a person who has an inclination toward narcissism, that individual will always want more. You will have to make some kind of peace with this truth. Yearning for that sun-kissed moment when your parent says simply, "You have done enough, my child," is counterproductive. Saying good-bye to the fantasy will lift a weight from your shoulders.

Jenna adopted this private mantra: "Nothing is ever going to be enough, and that's good enough for me."

When you're dealing with a parent whose hunger for appreciation, admiration, and attention (the three As) is high, you must not expect miracles. *Containment* is the watchword here. This is not an area for experimentation; it's an area for clear limits—and limited expectations. But if you can overcome the common tendencies either to fawn over this sort of parent or to defiantly ignore his or her needs, you may be able to cut a middle path. Keep your eyes on the prize: the best-quality contact possible with the least amount of obsequiousness.

• Chapter 33 •

They Embarrass Me

"Waiter," Jan's mother, Pat, called to the young man who had served them and was now headed for the kitchen. "Waiter!" Pat repeated, in a screechy voice that made half the restaurant turn and look. "Waiter! The sea bass is hardly cooked!"

For Jan, it was as if someone had flipped a familiar switch in her head, and now there was no stopping her whole body from catching on fire. Her face flushed, her stomach jumped, sweat rolled down her back in a long rivulet. She looked longingly at the floor, wishing she could liquefy entirely and slip unnoticed between the cracks in the terra-cotta tile.

"The service here is a joke," Pat said, turning back to Jan, theatrically fussing with the linen napkin on her lap. "There's no way I'm going to give that guy a tip."

"Please, Mother," Jan whispered. "Not here."

"These fancy restaurants think they can intimidate you, but I don't buy into that," Pat said. "If I'm paying these prices, I expect service."

It had been six months since Jan had seen Pat, but it was always the same: they met for lunch at a place that Pat picked out, somewhere that Jan could never afford, and nothing was good enough. Pat complained about the food, tortured the waiter in a high-handed manner, demanded obscure condiments, spoke in a loud stage whisper, and often undertipped ceremoniously.

"It's two hours in hell," said Jan, a divorced documentary producer, as she sat on the edge of a chair in my office clutching her knees. "I am so mortified, I could just curl up in a ball and disappear."

Many of my clients fear being in public with their parents because their parents inevitably do something that embarrasses them. In fact, Jan's restaurant experience is more common than you might think. (I recently conducted my own informal survey on this subject by asking over two dozen waiters how often they were treated rudely by a parent to the obvious embarrassment of his or her grown child at the table. I was not surprised by the response: virtually all said this happened at least twice each shift.)

Being embarrassed by your parents' behavior is, for most of us, the ultimate hot button. You might be able to deal with their other problems, the ones that surface when you're on the phone with them or in private, but when you're in public and they start doing their thing, your internal warning siren starts "woop-woop-wooping" in your ear. Within moments, it's deafening, and that tingly sensation flows through your body, rendering your limbs useless. Watching the way innocent bystanders react to your parents' foibles, with pity or disdain, is an excruciating experience.

What can you do to make your parents stop? Well, I'll bet that losing your temper hasn't worked that well. Neither has going to insane lengths, for example, taking them only to five-star restaurants—they still find stuff to complain about, right? As for saying nothing and hoping the problem won't happen again, well, that's just wishful thinking.

There are several techniques to inhibit or modify your parents' most embarrassing tendencies, but before you choose one to try, you must screen yourself to make sure you aren't contributing to the problem. Ask yourself this tough question: Am I embarrassed by who my parent *is,* or by what my parent *does*? This is a very important distinction. Are you ashamed of your parent's very essence—his or her ethnicity, lack of education, way of dressing, accent, or demeanor? Do you wonder what your life might have been like if you'd had "dream parents"? The fact is that sometimes we wish our parents were simply different people. We wish they had had a more refined upbringing or used proper grammar. We cringe at the sight of their polyester pantsuits or white patent leather shoes. We're not merely embarrassed by them but ashamed. And this shame makes their actions downright unbearable. It's pathetic enough to see your father in that garish tie, with that big gut straining the buttons of his jacket. But watching him try to use his Russian charm to muscle his way past the receptionist in your office is downright humiliating.

You are probably hesitant to admit that you're embarrassed and ashamed by your parents if it's true; it sounds so superficial and, well, wrong. But for many of my clients—and my friends—it is true. Trust me here: admitting it makes it much easier to face. There is nothing sinful about acknowledging that you wish your parents were more genteel or socially acceptable, less flashy, more intellectual, less reactionary, and more sophisticated. It's an age-old dilemma in our upwardly mobile society; chances are at least one of your parents was ashamed of a parent at one time too.

The question is: How can you work toward accepting your parents while minimizing the behavior that embarrasses you?

You have to work on the first part first. Your parents probably are more comfortable with their identities than you are. They may very well see themselves as a big improvement over their parents, so they are flummoxed by your embarrassment.

Remember that they want from you exactly what you want from them: to be taken for what they are. If you are able to do this better, you will have a clearer head in trying to inhibit their worst social acting out. You will be able to differentiate who they are from what they do.

Ask yourself:

- Are they basically good people, regardless of their tacky manners and dress?
- Are they doing their best?
- Are they just as embarrassing when they are around others?
- Have they overcome obstacles (gone further in school than others in their family, built a business from nothing, escaped a confining childhood to become a success)?
- Do they accept my choice not to be like them? Are they proud of me?
- Are they struggling to act nonchalant or socially acceptable in some public place when in fact the situation makes them uncomfortable?
- Is my underlying disapproval of them making them even more uncomfortable and therefore contributing to their embarrassing behavior?

The best way to accept your parents is to remember that they are not an extension of you. Try for a moment to stop thinking of them as your parents. They are just people, albeit people with bad manners or questionable taste or a lack of understanding of social nuance. It's crucial to create a mantra for yourself that reinforces the separation between you and them. They are totally separate human beings whose manners and demeanor do not reflect on you—unless you allow them to. One of my clients found the following mantra helpful: "The more my mother does embarrassing things, the more I realize how amazing it is that I've gone as far as I have."

Once you've truly faced the fact that you may be somewhat ashamed of who your parents are—and taken steps to accept them—you can concentrate on some behavioral modification techniques to make them bearable. Employing these techniques is a very good way to convert embarrassment—the ultimate passive emotion—into action.

- *Tell them how you feel and suggest alternatives to their behavior.* Don't wait until you are in the very situation that tends to cause you embarrassment. (Don't take them out to eat as a pretext for this discussion, for example, if they're at their worst in a restaurant.) Instead, take them aside for a specially planned talk during a neutral or pleasant moment. If your mother routinely embarrasses you in front of her friends, you might say: "Mom, perhaps you're unaware of this, but whenever we run into one of your friends on the street, you immediately launch into a diatribe about how great I'm doing. The person you are talking to gets very uncomfortable, and so do I. I know you are very proud of me, but please don't bring me into the conversation. If you want to talk about me when I'm not there, that's fine. But it's not fine while I'm standing next to you. The next time someone asks you how you are, please tell her how *you* are. That's what she's asking. If she asks me about me, I'll answer her. Better yet, I'll say, 'I'm fine, Mrs. Jones. How are you?'"
- *If your parents embarrass you inadvertently, find gentle ways to educate them.* Often people are too embarrassed *for* their parents to help change accidentally embarrassing behavior. They worry either that they will hurt their parents' feelings or that by dealing directly with the situation, they will make it more "real." So they ignore it and suffer in silence. Instead try some loving, nonjudgmental language to subtly help changes take root.

  One of my clients had a father who ate too fast and often wound up with food on the front of his shirt. He tended to be overly sensitive to criticism and knew that his daughter was a bit ashamed of his working-class background, so she had to be careful not to offend him. One night at a restaurant she used a saviorizing technique to slow him down. Before their food was brought to the table, she told him she was on a new "mission." "My friends all tell me I'm a buzz saw," she said. "So my new thing is to eat really, really slowly. I put down my fork after every bite. Would you mind participating? You're a fast eater too, Pop. I just know you'll be a naughty influence. Let's see if we can do this together, OK? We'll make a game of it."

- *Set boundaries.* Chances are, the ways in which your parents embarrass you are pretty predictable. So take them aside and tell them gently but firmly that that behavior is no longer acceptable. For example: "Mother, I have asked you repeatedly not to show up unannounced in my dental office waiting room and show my baby pictures around. If you continue to do so, I'm going to leave my patient in the chair and gently escort you to the elevator. I'm not angry, and I'm not going to yell. I'm just going to escort you out. This is how I'm going to handle the situation from now on."

  Follow-through is crucial. But believe me, if you consistently are able to do what you say, their behavior will cease. Try this in a restaurant: "Folks, if you two insist on having an argument again in public while I am at the table, I am going to calmly put my napkin down, leave my share of the bill, split the restaurant, and drive home. I'm not going to try to get you to stop fighting or to get angry at you. I'm simply going to leave. No discussion."

- *Make sure you're not making things worse.* Sometimes parents and their adult children are simply a terrible fit. Their behavior may bring out the worst in you. While dining out with your father, do you fuss over the wine list pretentiously? Well, don't be surprised if he insists that the bottle has "turned" when the bottle comes, or asks the waiter if the restaurant carries Pabst Blue Ribbon. Do you insist on taking him to the symphony when he'd rather see a Yankees game scheduled for the same night? Then don't be shocked when he asks loudly where "the can" is in the midst of a Schubert adagio. And remember: like any human being, your parents can sense when you are ashamed of them. And generally, that doesn't bring out their best behavior. Is it any wonder?

- *Try a change in venue.* If your parents tend to act out in a particular setting, don't go there. I know it's often convenient to take your folks out to a restaurant, for instance, but that seems to be the number one place for parents to melt down. (The server-patron relationship seems to bring out the worst in people, especially as they age.) So why not try a "geographic cure"? Invite them over for takeout or a home-cooked meal.

  Or at least scale down your choice in restaurants; why take them to a white-tablecloth place if they'll berate the waiter? If they insist on going to a highbrow haunt, be firm—and direct: "Dad, I'm not comfortable going to that place because you are rude to the waiters, as we've talked about before. If you're going to be rude to the waiters, let's have you do it in a place where the waiters can be rude back. I have a list of more casual places here."

- *Bond with the people they are embarrassing you in front of.* You may feel horribly humiliated in the moment and worry that the bystanders are looking at you with contempt and pity, but the truth is that they are probably thinking to themselves, "I just hate it when *my* parents do that." Waiters feel your pain, believe me. It can really make you feel better to create a bond with those people subjected to your parents' bad behavior. That will stop them from feeling sorry for you, which is part of the reason you are so embarrassed. If you knew they didn't pity you, you could scoff off the incident better yourself. You might take the waiter aside when you enter a restaurant and say, "Look my mother is an enormous pain, so I'm sorry in advance if she acts badly." (Never underestimate the power of a ten-dollar bill slipped into a waiter's hand.) Or exchange exasperated can-you-believe-this-guy glances with the store clerk your dad is giving a hard time to. Such tactics will help you disperse some of your closely held embarrassment by proving to yourself that your parent is not an extension of you, that you have the situation under control.

It's definitely possible to limit the extent to which you are embarrassed by your parents. In fact, it's one the behaviors that's most amenable to change—if you are willing to take the necessary steps. Just remember, you are not a passive actor in this drama; your level of embarrassment may be directly connected to how settled you are with your parents' identities. Don't confuse what your parents do with who they are.

You don't have a responsibility to tolerate repeated inappropriate behavior that comes from a lack of impulse control, sensitivity, or empathy on their part, and taking action to minimize that will immediately allay some of your embarrassment. But you do have a responsibility to accept their cultural and personality differences. That sort of embarrassment will only evaporate when you see yourself as a wholly independent person.

Chapter 34

They Use Money
to Manipulate Me

Of all the icy blasts that blow on love,
a request for money is the most chilling.
—Gustave Flaubert, *Madame Bovary*

"I'd kill him," said Luanne, "but that would knock me out of his will, right?" I told her it was a good sign that she was still able to joke about the situation—that meant she hadn't given up entirely. Her husband, Kurt, though, sat stone-faced.

Luanne was talking about her father, a prominent lawyer, who used his money to manipulate them. Kurt was struggling in his advertising career, and Luanne's father was making the most of that. "He's loaded, and he dangles her inheritance in front of us all the time," Kurt finally sputtered. "Whenever he thinks we aren't giving him enough time with the grandchildren or that we haven't been sufficiently reverential, he drops little hints about changing his will. I try not to react, but I feel so angry and humiliated that I can't sleep."

Adding to their tension was the fact that Kurt and Luanne were living way beyond their means, in a big house they had gutted and rebuilt to make everything perfect for their five-year-old twins. Luanne chimed in: "I feel like strangling my father, but I don' t want to get him mad at us because we'll probably need his help to send the twins to college. I feel like I have to choke down my words."

What neither of them said until I coaxed it out of them was that they regularly took money from her father, always let him pick up the tab at their frequent dinners together (he always chose the restaurant, naturally), and allowed him to take the twins on weekly toy shopping sprees. "We feel guilty depriving our kids of things just because I've made some mistakes in my career," said Kurt. "We feel it's our responsibility to them to swallow our resentment of her dad's manipulations."

Luanne confessed that "Dad's" behavior was also hurting their marriage, spurring arguments about Kurt's job. "I try be supportive of Kurt in his career, and I know he's doing his best. But I guess I'm sort of angry that he's put me in the position where I have to take money from my father. And of course, my father makes sure that he lobs in plenty of cutting remarks about how Kurt isn't really up to snuff as a provider. I find myself internalizing that message and taking it out on Kurt. It's really a mess."

Isn't it strange how money, which is supposed to buy freedom, so often winds up purchasing little more than slavery? Luanne and Kurt are far from alone in agonizing over how to broker financial peace with a parent. Some years ago, a *Redbook* magazine survey of 450 American couples, ages twenty-nine to fifty, and their parents asked them to rate the topics that caused the most friction between them. Money was at the top of the list for more than 30 percent of the couples *and* their parents. Most of the remaining 70 percent put money either second or third, below lifestyle and ambition— both of which are directly linked to money matters.

While it's true that the issue of passing money from one genera- tion to the next is an age-old problem, you're right if you sense that the process has never been more contentious than it is today. That's because the economic relationship between parents and grown children has shifted radically in the past couple of decades.

It used to be that most parents in the United States came from the working class. They were thrifty folk who muscled their way up the economic ladder, scrimping and saving so that their kids could go to college. As they aged, those with less money moved in with their kids, and others lived modestly on their pensions and/or Social Security checks. When they died, in their late sixties or early seventies, they left their grown kids a small inheritance, if anything. The average middle-class bequest in 1953 was $3,300—about $24,000 in today's dollars. Split between three children, that was maybe enough to pay for a nice family vacation for a family of five or a semester of college tuition for each of the three children.

The current generation of aging parents is a whole new breed. Due to booming financial markets and a strong economy in the 1980s and 1990s, many now own valuable real estate and healthy stock portfolios. They are living longer and stronger as well, and working way past the traditional age of retirement. Today, the average bequest of a home-owning parent is more than $200,000. And 10 percent of the estates are worth more than $500,000. Given the low birth rates in the United States for the past few decades, that amount is rarely split between more than two children. The difference between a $24,000 inheritance and one of $200,000 (or more) makes this a high-stakes game.

There are obvious advantages to having wealthy parents. The economy likely hasn't been as kind to us as it was to our parents. Whereas they bought their homes for peanuts, now the cost of entering the real estate market can be prohibitive. Keeping the kids in popular brand-name clothes isn't cheap either. College can cost $40,000 a year. So there are Mom and Dad, sitting on that nest egg, offering money to ease our way.

But money, we have all learned, doesn't come cheap. It always has strings attached. Money is not just an entry in your checkbook ledger; it's associated with love, power, fear, rejection, security, status, guilt, greed, freedom, and indulgence. Many financial transactions—getting a home mortgage, confronting credit card debt, buying a car, balancing the monthly budget—are fraught with emotional baggage, but the passing of money from parent to adult child is probably the most "loaded" transaction of all.

Sometimes, things work out beautifully. Your parents cheerfully write you a check for $100,000 to start that risky new business venture or send you $15,000 folded inside a note with a smiley face on it because they think it would be lovely for you to see Florence in the spring. Perhaps they *insist* on supporting you while you pursue an acting career, or beg you to send the kid's tuiton bill to them every month.

But probably not. It's more likely that money—the kind they have and you need—has caused you pain and frustration. Perhaps, like Kurt and Luanne, you have taken big gifts from a parent and discovered it's a Faustian bargain that isn't worth the emotional turmoil. Or you're taking money as a sort of payoff for the lousy childhood you think they gave you. They owe it to you, you tell yourself, even though somehow the payoff never manages to make the pain go away.

Perhaps you have had the opposite experience: you're angry that your parents *never* help you out, although they have plenty of cash. Maybe they gave plenty to your sister, who married a dermatologist and has a baby, and made it clear that forever-single you, with your penchant for jazz musician boyfriends, are out of luck. Or, in an all-too-common scenario, you may have taken money from your parents assuming it was gift, and now you realize—yikes!—that they expect you to pay them back. Another pattern I see all the time is that parents give their child an outright gift, but with a hidden "rider": they have the final say in how you spend it. They expect to be consulted on how you landscape the backyard or raise the kids.

Whatever the particulars, when it comes to parents and money, the sad punch line is almost always the same: no amount of cash can make an unhealthy relationship better. And most often it makes things much worse.

Like it or not, confronting money issues with your parents can be the most important step you can take toward making peace with them. Money may not be the deepest manifestation of how you are destructively entwined with your parents, but it is certainly the most obvious one. To put it baldly: if you are in conflict with your parents over money, your chances of establishing a healthy adult relationship with them are pretty much zero.

Breaking the money chains will not be easy. First, you may have to be more honest with yourself about your complicity in this conflict. One of the other things that has changed in our society in recent years is that grown children aren't as hungry for financial independence as they were in the past. Many of my patients in their late twenties and early thirties think it's OK to be partially or even entirely supported by their parents. They rationalize that the economy is weak and that they just "need a little help." Even some of my older patients allow their parents to subsidize them, using the same sort of excuses even though the fundamental problem is that they have a lifestyle they simply can't afford.

Some therapists believe that you can take money or big gifts from your parents on a regular basis and still attain happiness and independence. I disagree. My take is brutally straightforward: financial independence is a crucial component of a healthy relationship with your parents and a fundamental step toward building a strong sense of your own identity.

Except for those rare circumstances in which parents and their grown children are in perfect harmony about "sharing" resources, I have found that taking significant sums of money (or even lavish gifts) from parents usually creates much worse stress than it alleviates. The reasons are obvious. Taking money reprises childhood ties—Mommy and Daddy are powerful and benevolent, as long as you follow *their* rules, of course. You don't have to be responsible or live within your means, because they will pick up the slack. You don't have to plan for retirement because they will leave you plenty of money. You don't have to delay gratification to save for *your* kids' tuition because they'll foot the bill.

And if they use money to control you, that makes it that much easier to stay angry at them, which, as we discussed in chapter 4,

"The 'Gift' That Keeps on Taking—and Taking: A Word about Anger," you may desire unconsciously. Adding to that anger may be your suspicion that your parents don't respect you. But can you blame them? By remaining dependent, you are feeding into their underestimation of you, their belief that you are incapable of taking care of yourself.

Taking money usually means giving in to regression. You can, like Luanne and Kurt, suffer in silence and tear your marriage apart. Or, like some of my other clients, you can scream and yell and take the money anyway. Both strategies lead to unhappiness.

These are not just issues of money; they are issues of maturity. Becoming completely independent is the first step toward positioning yourself in a dynamic, adult relationship with your parents. How can you work on making your mother less intrusive in your life when she is covering your kids' private school tuition? How can you cut off your parents' cutting comments about what a failure

"They say we can go there for Thanksgiving or they can cut us out of the will. Our choice."

you are compared to your brother the lawyer when you bank their little check every month?

Don't panic; I am not saying you should never accept a gift or a loan from your parents. It's OK if you have a medical emergency, for example, or unexpectedly lose a job you've held for a long time, or need a small loan to tide you over until you get a financial settlement. Or if your parents sell their house and want to share their windfall—and beat inheritance taxes—by giving you a onetime gift of a few thousand dollars. Birthday and wedding gifts—within reason—are untouchable. It can be a joy for parents to give money occasionally, and you should feel OK taking it—provided that you do not need that money to exist day-to-day and have searched your heart and are certain that the gift or loan is not fraught with emotional peril.

When considering whether to accept a significant monetary gift from your parents, ask yourself:

- Does it come with strings attached?
- Will I be resentful when those strings are pulled?
- Will I be too dependent on this money, unwilling or unable to live on my own income?
- Do I feel I deserve this money to make up for childhood wounds?
- Do I resent my parents for not being more generous?
- Will I put up with unacceptable behavior from my parents because they are giving me money?
- Am I less independent than I would like to be?
- Do I lie to my friends about how much money my parents give me?
- Will taking this money make me feel like a failure in any way?

If you answer yes to *any* of these questions, you need to tear up that deposit slip and map out a plan for gaining financial freedom from your parents. The same goes if your anger for your parents stems from *not* getting money from them. There's a very good chance that you have serious money woes with your parents even if you are not getting a dime from them.

Confronting money entanglements with your parents is especially hard because this is one sore spot that involves real stuff— material pleasures, financial lifelines. You can ponder the more theoretical issues of separation and guilt, but remember that you are not powerless. You can do this. What you may have to give up is worth less than what you will get. Keep in mind that the illusion of power you get from "free" money is just that, an illusion. Freedom does not come from money; it comes from being able to take care of yourself.

FIVE STEPS TOWARD FINANCIAL DÉTENTE WITH YOUR PARENTS

1. Pick up the Restaurant Check Half the Time

Parents and grown children often perpetuate childhood patterns and behaviors without realizing it. This doesn't just happen when parents are much richer than their adult children; many of my patients let their parents who are retired and on a fixed income pay for expensive dinners every time they go out together. They have plenty of excuses—their parents insist; it makes them feel good; they can't afford to pay for the fancy places their parents like—but however you slice it, it's still bologna. Such behavior is infantalizing. If you want to have a healthy relationship with your parents, they need to accept that you are an adult, and you need to act like one. And don't tell me that your parents make an embarrassing check-grabbing scene whenever you reach for your wallet. If you really want to pay, you will find a way. Slip the maître d' your credit card before you even sit down. No matter how you do it, make it clear to your parents that from now on, you will be picking up the tab every other time you all are out together.

If you truly can't afford to do that, you have two choices: you can tell them that you'd prefer to go to less expensive restaurants, regardless of who's paying, or you can decide that it's OK to let them take you to swanky places, but when it's your turn, you'll take them to a place you can afford. Also, there's nothing wrong with saving up to take them out to an expensive restaurant once or twice a year. Remember: this isn't a game of "Can You Top This?"; it's supposed to be a show of love and respect.

Going Dutch? There are advantages and disadvantages. On the pro side of the ledger, going Dutch may make it easier for your parents to get used to the idea that they are no longer picking up every tab. The downside is that you both lose the thrill of "taking care" of the other, being the "big spender." Paying the entire bill can help you get on a more even footing with your parents, help you create an equal, mature relationship with them.

The key here is flexibility and creativity. Make whatever arrangement is most comfortable for you, as long as it involves you paying your share.

2. Pay Your Own Way through Life

If you are out of school, you should be on your own. That means living on your own and supporting yourself. Granted, plenty of adults in their twenties (and even thirties) move back with their parents when times are tough, but I think it's almost always a bad move. It undermines your independence, puts an undue burden on your parents' own relationship (or precludes them from adjusting to the fact that they now have to live their own lives), and sends you hurtling back into childhood patterns.

But moving back home is merely the most extreme form of financial dependence. There are others, like expecting your parents to pay for graduate school. I wholly support experimentation, risk-taking, and artistic dedication, but I think you should pay for it. Where's the risk if Mommy and Daddy are holding that big safety net? If that means taking a job waiting tables to pay for trips to exotic places or just to pay the bills while you write poetry, so be it. Believe me, your poetry will be better when you take financial responsibility for your life.

Try this on as a mantra: *I am an adult, and I can take care of myself. Whatever choices I make, I will pay for. And I will send my parents a card from a beach in Bali when I succeed.*

3. Live within Your Means

"Your means" means what you *earn*. That does not include the $1,000 your parents send you every month to make ends meet. If you believe that having a five-bedroom Tudor home is worth the lack of self-respect eating at your stomach lining because Mommy is subsidizing the mortgage, you are dead wrong. Once you start taking money from your parents to pay for basic necessities like house or car payments, it is very hard to extricate yourself. And in most cases, parents who are significantly subsidizing their adult children's lifestyle tend to become increasingly bold in giving advice, a situation that makes a mature parent–adult child relationship essentially impossible.

One casualty can be your marriage; husbands, especially, can wind up feeling inadequate. We like to think that such sexist distinctions have disappeared, but that's not true. It's one thing to adjust to your wife making more money than you; that's a character-building dose of postfeminism. It's another thing to adjust to your parents (or hers) taking up the slack because you can't support your family. For most men, that's humiliating. In the end, the modest colonial that your paycheck covers will feel much more like *your* home than the Georgian mansionette your father-in-law holds the mortgage on.

Besides, no matter what they say to your face, your parents may secretly wish you would stop taking their money. Sure, they seem to be benefiting from having some leverage in your relationship— leverage that is making you uncomfortable. But after hearing plenty of parents in my office complaining about this arrangement, I'll wager that your folks fret about your dependence on them. Or at least they have as many mixed feelings about the arrangement as you have.

4. Don't Use Your Children as an Excuse to Accept Money

"Hey," you say, "I would never take money from my parents for *myself,* but don't I have a responsibility to swallow my pride for my kids? Don't my kids deserve that trip to Paris and that wonderful private school? Is it so bad if I take money for them? Isn't that actually noble?"

To which I say, "Nice try." What your kids need most are parents with self-respect. Believe it or not, your kids will not be scarred for life if they don't get that battery-powered scale-model Lamborghini or those summers at sailing camp or even the complete Pokemon set. And they sure won't miss those hushed late-night arguments you and your spouse have about how to stop your parents from using their money to manipulate you.

There are, of course, exceptions. If you are really struggling financially—and are living within your means—you can have your parents help you help your kids. For example, they could give you a small subsidy to cover some of the fees for summer camp or music lessons. But you should never let them pay the entire bill, and you must be very clear about the terms. For example, your kids really don't need to know that Grandma and Grandpa are footing part of the bill. It will splinter your authority—authority you will need when you tell them you're going to stop paying for those drum lessons unless they practice. If your parents won't agree to that provision, be wary. People who truly want to help their grandchildren don't demand gratitude from the kids.

College can be a heavy burden for even the most frugal parents, so think carefully about how your parents can help. Consider having them contribute to a dedicated, untouchable long-term fund that can be used only for educational purposes. Note that I used *contribute,* not *fully fund.* There is a big difference. It is important for you not to abrogate your responsibility to cover most of the costs for your children's education. Doing so is all part of living within your means.

5. Don't Confuse a Gift with a Loan

If you do take money from your parents, make sure you know—and they know—whether it is a loan or a gift. Talking about money is almost always awkward, so being clear about this distinction is crucial to avoid pain later.

Parents who give gifts tend to want some say in how the money is spent. If your parents call the money a gift, do yourself a favor and find out what their expectations are up front; ask them if they expect to have any input on how you spend it. Listen *carefully* to their answer. Don't be accusatory; instead, create a nonjudgmental environment in which you can discuss the terms of the gift. It's their money, after all, and you want to make it clear that you appreciate it. They can try to influence how you spend it; it's up to you to accept or decline their terms. Don't intimidate them into *saying* they will be hands-off when you know it is unlikely they will be able to follow through with that. You must have the strength to walk away if you don't like the terms.

The key is to eliminate surprises. If you can get your parents to level with you and admit that they expect to have some say in how you spend the money, it's up to you to decide whether those terms are acceptable. You know my feeling—don't do it—but at least you will be prepared for the tussle that will undoubtedly ensue down the road.

If you take money under those circumstances, do yourself and everyone around you a favor—don't complain. Ever. You made your decision; now live with it. Part of becoming an adult is taking responsibility for your actions. You may feel like screaming when your parents lean on you to pay off your credit cards with the money they gave you, or offer advice on which contractor to hire, or suggest you drop that girlfriend who seems to be interested only in the new Porsche you bought, but you had better learn to smile as you fume.

A loan is an entirely different animal. By definition, it *must* be paid back. Unfortunately, some people—both parents and adult children—use the word *loan* imprecisely because they are uncomfortable giving or getting big gifts. Parents say they are "lending" their kid some money; their children say they got a "loan" from their parents, but neither party actually draws up even the flimsiest financial documents, and the terms for repayment are vague.

Sometimes this works out just fine; the money is paid back expeditiously, and everyone is happy. Sometimes adult children even return the sum with interest, despite the fact that it was never discussed. One of my patients, who works hard to have an adult relationship with her parents, offered them this choice when she repaid the $15,000 they had lent her to pay for veterinary school: she would give them 7 percent interest or take them on a luxurious trip to Montreal. (They chose the trip, and everybody had a great time.)

Too often, vagueness breeds misunderstanding. A loosely defined loan is ripe for manipulation on both sides. Parents may act as though the loan is forgivable but then, when the child steps out of line, drop hints about needing to be repaid. And a little common sense is called for here: if your parents have made you an informal loan that you make no move to repay, don't expect them to be all smiles when you announce that you're taking your girlfriend to Jamaica.

Everyone will be better off if you stick to the dictionary definition of *loan* and come up with terms before any money changes hands. Although it may seem cold or businesslike, a formal or semiformal agreement that specifies the length of the loan, the terms of repayment, and the penalty for late payment will be better for both parties. You don't need a lawyer to draw up such an agreement, but it should be typed and signed. Your parents may protest, saying that it's not necessary, but do it anyway. They will be secretly pleased. And you will know exactly how to plan your budget to repay them.

Consider this bonus: if you are working on other nonfinancial issues with them—say, trying to get them to accept that you are going to marry someone they don't approve of—each payment you make gives you an opportunity to reestablish your boundaries.

Kurt and Luanne eventually found a way to manage her father. After much soul-searching and a couple of years of therapy, they moved into a smaller house, one that's an hour farther from her father's residence. They didn't tell him they were moving until the day they closed on the house, but they did send him a warm note that day, expressing thanks for all the help he had given them over the years. With the profit they made from the sale of their house, they set up a college fund for the twins.

Right after the move, they took her father out to lunch—they chose the restaurant and prepaid the check—and told him that they would no longer take any money from him. Having role-played the conversation a half-dozen times, they told him that he could buy the kids birthday and Christmas presents and, if he so desired, contribute directly (and irrevocably) to their college fund. They explained that these "terms" were for everyone's benefit, and they hoped he would continue to want to see them all, but that the conditions were nonnegotiable.

Her father pouted for a few weeks, didn't take their calls for two months, and sent them a changed copy of his will, which left all his money to charity, but they stood their ground. Slowly he began to see them again—under their rules. When he died in 2001, he left all his money to the twins in a trust, making it clear that he was cutting Kurt and Luanne out because they hadn't treated him with the gratitude he deserved.

"It wasn't a perfect solution, of course," said Kurt. "We didn't like the idea that the kids would inherit so much money when they turned twenty-one because we didn't want it to sap their ambition. One of the things that the experience with him taught us was that money can be really destructive. But hey, we never expected him to turn into a saint, and we hope we've given the twins good enough values so that they can handle it.

"The most interesting thing was how we felt when the will was read. If he had left the money to charity, as we thought all along he was going to, it would have been OK. We went through so much grief with him that we really were over it by that point. It was extremely liberating."

• Chapter 35 •

They Think I Am a Bad Parent

"Maybe I *am* a loser," Adriana said in our first session. "After all, I still live with my father in the house I grew up in. Isn't that the definition of a loser?"

At forty-one, with two young sons and a ruined marriage, Adriana had moved back home the year before. It was really the only arrangement that made sense. She didn't make much money as a court reporter, and her father, Max, had Hodgkin's disease and needed someone to look after his basic household tasks. He couldn't afford a home-care aide. Adriana's mother had died a couple of years earlier, after a long, symbiotic marriage, and Adriana, a wonderful cook who enjoyed housekeeping, was happy to take over.

But there was plenty of tension. Max was a crotchety perfectionist, and the comings and goings of the kids, ages seven and ten, drove him crazy. They dropped their coats and backpacks on the floor, ate while playing games on the computer, and rarely put their dirty dishes in the sink. "He yells at them constantly," said Adriana. "And when he's finished yelling at them, he yells at me, ranting about how I should be a better mother, that I should have taught them to be neater and more respectful.

"When I want to have a treat with my sons, say, chips and dip, he says I am teaching them bad eating habits and do I want them to

293

grow up looking like me? He says this right in front of them. He thinks I am too lenient, and he never acknowledges how much they help me around the house: vacuuming, folding the laundry, taking the dog out. He rails about how we don't eat dinner together like a family. I always feel as though he's compiling a list of what I am doing wrong and how badly they are turning out."

Adriana's customary response to Max's perpetual state of out-rage was, by her own admission, "almost as destructive as my dad's anger." Unable to figure out productive ways to change the pattern, she was instead belligerent with him and did petty, nasty things to get back at him. "The one thing he cares most about is having his tea right after dinner, before the dishes are done. So even though it irks him, I don't get him tea until after I've cleaned up. Night after night I do this. I know I'm being childish, that it just makes him angrier. He'll sometimes roar, 'Why can't I get a friggin' cup of tea in this house?'"

It didn't take long to get Adriana to realize that she had a lot of anger toward her father and that it had deep roots she needed to explore—with an eye toward formulating a game plan for change. "I know I'm a disappointment to him," she said. "He doesn't think I've reached my potential. That I married a bum, which isn't far from the truth. He gets upset that I'm not in better shape, not taking care of myself."

Adriana felt pretty bad about those things too, but seeing her failures reflected in her father's eyes made everything worse. "Why does he need to rub it in?" she asked me, her eyes filling with tears. "As soon as he starts in on me for being a bad mother, I can't see straight. I'm ashamed, and I'm pissed. And I can't get past that, so I just don't do anything."

There is perhaps no greater wound your parents can inflict than to suggest that *you* are a bad parent. The pain ricochets through the generations, piercing your memory and personal history like a bul-let. It doesn't even matter that your parents weren't such great shakes in the nurturing department themselves; hearing such a sentiment from the people who raised you packs a punch. And should you find yourself in financial straits or perhaps stranded as a single parent, their criticisms cut even deeper because they are likely tinged by your guilt over not doing enough for your kids.

Asserting yourself in the face of such criticisms is one of the most important steps you can take in becoming a full-fledged adult. Being able to say with confidence that you are doing the best by your children, regardless of what your parents think, is a significant avowal of freedom. But doing so requires a great deal of soul-searching and preparation. Take plenty of time with each of the following steps.

1. BE BRUTALLY HONEST WITH YOURSELF

Before you can formulate a plan to cope with your parents' criticism, you must be 100 percent sure there is no truth to what they are saying. Just because they are intrusive or even nasty doesn't mean they are wrong. And don't worry; even if there is some truth to what they are saying, that doesn't mean you have to endure their insults. You can deal with your problems *and* modify the way your parents harp on them. But you must frankly, objectively consider the substance of their gripes. This is terribly important because the well-being of your children is at stake.

If there is some truth to the criticisms, you must not allow your resentment of the "messenger" stop you from hearing the message. You must act decisively to change what you know is detrimental for your kids. This has nothing to do with your parents; it is a matter of your own self-respect and your children's future.

Ask yourself:

- Have I ever suspected that the criticism my parent is voicing might have some truth? Even if the situation isn't as bad as my parent insists, is there *any* truth to it?

- Am I not doing anything about this situation even though I know I should because I don't want to give my parent the satisfaction of being right?

- Am I in denial about this problem because I want to protect my kids from my parents' disapproval, even though I know they would be better off in the long run if I dealt with it strongly?

- Am I ignoring this problem because it reminds me of being criticized by my parents for the same thing when I was a child?

- Am I ignoring my parents because *they* weren't good parents? Do I believe that they have "no right" to criticize my parenting, considering how lousy they were in that role?

- How would I react to this criticism if it were delivered with gentleness and love and concern instead of the negative way my parents present it? How would I react if I heard the same thing from a trusted friend?

- Do I have the courage to go to that trusted friend and ask if there is any truth to my parents' criticism? If not, why not?

2. PUT THE WHEELS OF CHANGE IN MOTION

If you decide your parents have a point—even if it is only a small one—you must take action. Not because it will shut your parents up but because it is the right thing to do. Taking action in this situation also has a side benefit: you will be in a much stronger position to address your other issues with your parents after you have truly addressed whatever kernel of truth there is in their complaints.

3. CONSULT YOUR PARENTS' HISTORY FOR CLUES TO THEIR BEHAVIOR

Regardless of whether your parents have a point, their way of making it probably rubs you wrong, and with good reason. If they are crude or hurtful, they may be flashing back either to their own childhood or to your childhood. Sometimes that is so upsetting that they are unable to sugarcoat their criticism.

The underlying reasons for their criticism are varied. Perhaps they come from an entirely different culture and therefore find your parenting style abhorrent. Maybe seeing you with your children throws them back to the fears they had when they were young parents—concerns about their competency, perhaps—and they are now projecting those fears onto you. Or could it be that seeing you with your children makes them yearn for the time when they were in your position, at the beginning of their lives? Or maybe they simply remember all too well your horrible adolescent years and now, as they watch you struggle with your teenage kids, think they can at last see what has to be done.

There are dozens of other scenarios, so don't automatically assume their criticisms are made solely out of ill will. Remember, your parents are as complicated as you are, and as full of anxiety and confusion. Mull over the narrative you created for them in chapter 5. You may find some answers there, or at least some clues about what you should ask them when you finally sit down with them and talk about this issue (see step 5).

4. CONCEPTUALIZE BOUNDARIES

When it comes to your kids, it's not good to let backhanded insults from your parents ride, or to counter with petty hostilities, as Adriana did with Max's tea. Nor is it wise to hiss insults back at them. Ditto on screaming, pouting, shoving your children into the argument, or blaming your spouse.

Such chaotic behavior isn't good for your state of mind or your attempts to achieve grown-up separation from your folks, but more important, it isn't good for your children. Even if your parents' insults are subtle and you do your best to bury your feelings about them while your children are around, those kids, clever creatures that they are, will figure it out. That will undermine your relationship with them—as well as their relationship with their grandparents. Worse, you may wind up defending your kids when their actions are not defensible or not make changes that need to be made just to "stick it to your folks." That is a very destructive strategy indeed.

If your parents take issue with how you handle your kids in a way that is unacceptable to you, you must be willing to stop reacting to their criticisms with your old, ineffective repertoire of behaviors. Now is the time to start exploring new behaviors, tailoring them to your temperament and what you determine will be effective with your parents.

First, you will have to decide how much input on how you raise your kids you are willing to let your parents have. (Will you allow them to interject a minor critical comment that undermines your authority? How about a major one?) There is no "right" answer; everyone has a different threshold. To find yours, you must first level with yourself about how much you can "take" gracefully; anything beyond that will have to be dealt with.

Once you have decided where your cutoff point is, you will have to decide precisely how you will deal with your parents when they cross that line. The paragraphs that follow will give you some ideas. But first, keep in mind that *consistency is king*. You will have to settle on a course of action that you can reproduce over and over, which can become second nature. That is the best way to produce change—and to protect yourself. Another important point: *don't rule out any of the following behaviors, at least not yet*. In my experience, parents can be very surprising on this issue. The generational cycle is fraught with internal conflict. Your parents have a lot going on inside with regard to you and your kids, and you may not be seeing all those elements clearly yet. This may be the time to consult your Second Opinion or a sibling on what strategy might be effective. The key is to do what works. Don't be afraid to experiment. You can:

- Immediately stop whatever is going on each time your parents make an unacceptable criticism and firmly make it clear to them that such behavior cannot and will not continue This may mean getting the entire family to pause, perhaps even pulling the car over, and telling them calmly but firmly that you are not willing to let them continue to act that way.
- Wait until each criticism has run its course, then discreetly take your parent aside and tell him or her that this behavior is unacceptable. Use techniques from chapter 17, "Making Your Body Say What You Mean"; chapter 18, "Toning Down Your Tone of Voice"; and chapter 19, "Reaching for the Words That Reach Them."
- Reconnoiter with your spouse and confront the issue as a team, using the techniques discussed in chapter 14, "Getting Your Spouse in Your House."
- Disarm them with honesty. See chapter 22.
- Laugh or poke gentle fun at them for getting "so worked up over nothing." This is a very effective technique, if you can pull it off. You don't have to *feel* like laughing; you just have to be able to genuinely affect an I'm-not-taking-this-seriously facade after every criticism for at least several months (no undercover bitterness allowed, however). Be aware, though, that consistency is crucial with this strategy; it will backfire if you fly off the handle over one comment and then attempt to act casual in the wake of the next *one*.

Having both a private mantra and a humorous response at the ready will help you with this approach. An example of a private mantra: "I have the right to my feelings about how my parents criticize me, but they have no right to know about them. My humor is my shield." Some lighthearted comebacks: "Oh, Ma, you are getting to be such a worrywart in your old age! Where is the jitterbuggin' fool I used to know?" "How about this, Dad? I promise not to call you when these wild and crazy kids have to be bailed out from jail." "Don't worry, folks. I've hired a private detective to tail your grandson. The kid can't make a move without my man knowing where he is."

5. REQUEST A SIT-DOWN WITH YOUR PARENTS TO DISCUSS A PLAN FOR CHANGE

Even though you may be afraid to hear what your parents have to say, you must push yourself to talk to them face-to-face. Make sure to do your homework; no doubt you already know basically what they will say, and you should have completed steps 1 and 2. That means you have leveled with yourself and know how much of their criticism is valid and how you will address those issues. Be ready to share this with your parents in a way that keeps them informed but preserves your privacy. You should also know what new boundaries you'd like to draw with your parents regarding their behavior.

Your approach in this meeting will be dictated by how you have decided to enforce those boundaries. If, for example, you have decided to "stop the action" each time they make an intrusive comment, you might want to start with something like this: "Mom, I don't like the way our dynamic has developed about the kids, so I want to take some time now to talk about it calmly. I can see you don't approve of what I'm doing, and I'm willing to talk to you about it and get your input, but I'm not willing to let you continue to make those snarky comments. These are my children, and I'm the final authority. That's nonnegotiable. But I do want to understand better your thoughts on these issues. I really believe we can put our heads together to try to come up with a strategy that will make the atmosphere more pleasant for all of us."

Lay out a plan for the discussion. Allow ten minutes for them to tell you what is upsetting them. (You must let them ventilate, listening patiently, even if you know what they are going to say.) Use a clock to make sure they don't go off on an endless tangent. Then give yourself ten minutes to respond. (You're probably going to run over, but that's OK—it's your clock.) In your response, include:

- *A recap of the points they made, to show that you heard them.* ("So what you're saying is that I am too lenient with the kids, that I don't have high enough standards.") Use mirroring techniques to make them feel understood.
- *Sincere questions about their past, to clarify where they are coming from.* "How did your parents deal with dinner table rudeness?" "You're obviously very upset by my kids' attitude toward school, and I'm guessing that there's some connection to the fact that you didn't have the chance for a good education. Am I right?" "I don't remember you being so sensitive to noise when we were kids. Has something changed now that it's your grandkids?" These questions, which you should try to prepare in advance, can open the lines for honest, attitude-free communication.
- *A brief, undramatic description of how their criticisms make you feel.* Don't dwell on your anger or be accusatory. Use calm language to express deeper emotions. Do their criticisms make you feel incompetent? Unloved? Lonely? ("I know you are trying to help me with your criticisms and now I understand better where you're coming from, but perhaps you aren't aware of how your comments make me feel.")
- *Some information about how you intend to change the way you deal with your kids (if applicable).* You don't have to give them an in-depth explanation. In fact, it's best to be circumspect. For example: "Folks, I've been doing some thinking about the points you've raised, and while I don't think the situation is as dire as you do, there are some changes I want to make. The specifics will remain

between the kids and me, but I want you to know that I appreciate that you care enough about us to be concerned, and that the points you bring up are being addressed."

- *Your plan to deal with future criticisms.* If your discussion has been productive, even a little, make sure you acknowledge that ("I think we've made progress here in coming to understand each other"), but then move on to how you intend to handle any inappropriate criticism that may seep out in the future: "Dad, now that I've told you that I am addressing many of the issues you are concerned about, I'm going to talk about how I intend to handle further criticisms on these issues. I am no longer going to pretend to ignore your side-of-the-mouth cracks. When you make one, I'm going to stop the entire family and make it clear to you that those comments are not acceptable. I know that'll be unpleasant for all of us, but that's the way I'm going to handle it."

- *A realistic mission statement about how you hope your relationship will change for the better.* Here's a good example: "Mom, I would like to get some acknowledgment from you that you understand the pressures I am under as a mother, and I'd like to be able to discuss the kids with you in a productive, problem-solving manner instead of being put on the defensive. I will be working on some of the issues you brought up in this discussion, and I would like to be able to talk with you about the progress we are making—provided we can do it in a civil, supportive way that helps me in my goal of being a better mother. That's the kind of mother-daughter relationship I think would benefit both of us."

- *An expression of thanks for discussing the subject with you.* This step is crucial . . . even if they *haven't* been cooperative. Remember, you are an adult, even in the face of their childishness. And mature adults are gracious, even under fire.

Adriana learned a great deal on that summer evening when she took Max his cup of tea (before she did the dishes, this time) and sat down beside him to talk.

After Max ranted and rambled for ten minutes about her children's misbehavior—nothing she didn't already know, she listened quietly and attentively, using all the "body language" tips—she deftly segued into questions about his upbringing. "I asked him if his house had been as orderly as he expected ours to be," she said. "So he started talking about how his father had been a stickler for 'everything in its place,' and how everything ran like clockwork. When I asked him what the best thing about that was, he said he liked the predictability of it, that it made him feel secure even though the Depression was in progress.

"Then I asked him what the worst thing about it was. He was surprisingly open. He said that his father didn't allow the kids to talk at the dinner table; if they talked, even said the littlest thing, he punished them."

Wisely, Adriana made sure her questions were nonjudgmental. That made Max feel comfortable. It had been a long time since anyone had asked him to reflect on his life, to recall his parents and his childhood. He wasn't the type to admit it, but it was obviously pleasurable for him to look back. He was even able to show a small sliver of emotion about how his father's demands had weighed on him. Overall, he admired his father's discipline, and had emulated it as a father himself, but Adriana was able to get him to think about how tough it was to measure up sometimes. "He even let slip that his father had slapped him across the face one night when he dared not only to speak but to criticize President Hoover at the dinner table. I saw in his face the turmoil he still felt over that. I don't think he'd ever told that story before."

Listening to Max helped Adriana see that her father was truly mystified by how she was raising her children. He simply had no way of relating to her loose style. It was scary—literally—for him to watch. It seemed chaotic and dangerous.

As for her own childhood, Adriana realized that she had always been frightened of her father and felt he was constantly judging her. That had made her hypersensitive to his criticisms as an adult. But hearing him talk about his upbringing helped her understand that he had simply practiced the only parenting style he had been exposed to, even though he still felt conflicted about it. In other words, his intolerance of her parenting style was reflexive, not personal. She also realized that her style of parenting had been shaped by *his;* she was easy on her kids—perhaps even too easy at times—partly in reaction to how hard he had been on her.

Her anger at Max had made it difficult for her to see the dynamic from his perspective. As her father talked, she realized that he was in a lot of pain. His strength was waning, even though he was relatively young, which obviously bothered him. It was OK to be taken care of by his wife—hey, that was the way things were in the 1950s and early 1960s—but being dependent on his daughter was humiliating. It meant that he had lost control of his once-orderly house—the last vestige of control he felt he had over his life. The noise his grandchildren made was a painful reminder of that.

After she'd had a chance to process all this, Adriana took a deep breath and started talking about how his criticisms made her feel. Max got a little worked up at that point, saying he "was only pointing out the problems to help her." But she stayed calm, knowing that despite his defensiveness, he didn't want her to feel incompetent. "I know you mean to help, but it's not helping," she told him.

Then she moved on to the toughest subject: whether her father's criticisms had any merit. She had done plenty of thinking about it, she told him. She had decided that the sons were basically fine, healthy, normal kids; that their grades were solid, and their social life was robust. But there were some things that needed attention.

No, she didn't think it was OK for them to eat at the computer, and yes, they were watching too much television. Yes, there was too much junk food in the house. So she had decided to make some new rules. She was not willing to discuss them in depth with her father, except to say that she had decided there should be a family dinner, nice linens and all, once a week. Unlike Max's father, however, she would allow the kids to talk at the dinner table. And they could be excused after twenty minutes, which was the limit of their attention span. Also, she had decided to create a study room for them in the basement, so Max could have the upstairs den as a refuge from their mess.

"Their behavior is not likely to ever come up to your standards, which you will have to learn to deal with," she told him. "But there will be some positive changes in the next few weeks and months. And I would greatly appreciate your recognition of those changes. Your criticism is not helpful, but your support is extremely important to me."

As for her father's nastiness and offhand vicious remarks, Adriana told him she would in the future take him aside after each remark and reinforce her point that his criticism was neither valuable nor appropriate. "I'm not going to get angry or be unpleasant, but I am going to call you on these things," she said. "As you said earlier in this discussion, being organized and disciplined is important. So that's how I'm going to handle this. My goal is to make our relationship better, Dad. I'd love to be able to tap into your wisdom without feeling that I'm asking for criticism. I hope that you will show my kids that you love them for who they are, and that you notice and appreciate the improvements they make. Most of all, I want us all to feel as though we have a place here."

Conclusion:
A Word about When to Give Up

That word is *never*. Even if, after you finish reading this book, you think to yourself, "I just can't do this; I'm not strong enough; it's easier just to let things ride," don't write your parents off—or write yourself off, for that matter. Often lessons are cumulative; we have to hear "the word" a few times (sometime a whole lot of times!) before it gets through. You may one day glance up at the spine of this book on your shelf and realize that you're finally ready to start working on your relationship with your parents. (Depending on the individual, it takes days, months, or even years to take up this battle.) When your desire for a saner, more satisfying relationship with your parents becomes stronger than your fear and resistance, you will know what you have to do.

The human spirit is wonderfully and maddeningly unpredictable in the way it deals with change. Sometimes it takes a very long time for the brain to grasp that change is a good thing. Our culture is geared toward quick fixes and instant gratification, but frankly, there is often a delayed benefit when you are dealing with real, substantial alterations in behavior patterns. Some of the people I have counseled over the years call long after they have left treatment to say that—finally!—they got the message and implemented changes that have made them happier. They sometimes say they regret the wasted years, but I stop them cold, because you cannot use an egg

306

timer on seismic changes like these. Whatever process you needed to go through to arrive at this point was necessary. That goes for you, as you are trying to take steps to change the way you deal with your parents, and for them, in how they react to the changes in you.

This is why you shouldn't give up, even if you have tried the strategies in this book but found your parents immovable, unshakable. The temptation is to believe that they are beyond help, beyond reason, to sink back into your defensive, defeatist stance. But remember, your parents, too, are living beings in flux. What they cannot allow themselves to hear or feel now, they may be able accept in the coming years. If you convince yourself that they will never change (which is far different from accepting them for who they are), you are likely to miss cues they may give you that they are opening up, albeit gradually.

But even if they never "get" you or understand that the relationship you are striving for is one that will make all of your lives richer, the important thing is that *you* have changed. Permanently. If you take this book to heart, it won't matter that they are not yet ready to respond; you will have become a different person and therefore changed the dynamic with them forever.

Another frustrating thing about change is that it often happens so gradually we barely notice it. That tends to be forgotten in the midst of all the one-day makeover television shows, but that's the way life actually works. You don't get a team of stylists rushing into your home and giving you a new identity overnight; every day is a brick in the wall of what you're building. Sometimes you fall back a bit, but if you stay with it, you will make progress.

More important than rating that progress—put out of your mind those ubiquitous before-and-after photos—is striving to maintain the sense that you are in control of your own life, that you are moving forward at whatever pace, that you are off the treadmill. Even if you have not yet achieved the relationship you would like with your parents—or never do—if you are determined not to relinquish yourself to anger, guilt, or silence and are committed to leaving this book and its precepts open in your mind, you will have triumphed.

BIBLIOGRAPHY

UNDERSTANDING CHILDHOOD AND PAST TRAUMA

Bloomfield, Harold, with Leonard Felder. *Making Peace with Your Parents.* New York: Random House, 1983.

Cocola, Nancy Wasserman, and Arlene Modica Matthews. *How to Manage Your Mother: Skills and Strategies to Improve Mother-Daughter Relationships.* New York: Simon & Schuster, 1992.

Fischer, Lucy Rose. *Linked Lives: Adult Daughters and Their Mothers.* New York: Harper & Row, 1986.

Halpern, Howard M. *Cutting Loose: An Adult Guide to Coming to Terms with Your Parents.* New York: Fireside, 1990.

Jampolsky, Gerald G., Patrick Hopkins, and William N. Thetford. *Good-bye to Guilt: Releasing Fear through Forgiveness.* New York: Bantam, 1985.

Kuttner, Robert, and Sharland Trotter. *Family Re-Union: Reconnecting Parents and Children in Adulthood.* New York: The Free Press, 2002.

Lerner, Harriet. *The Dance of Anger: A Woman's Guide to Changing the Patterns of Intimate Relationships.* New York: Quill, 1997.

Secunda, Victoria. *When You and Your Mother Can't Be Friends: Resolving the Most Complicated Relationship of Your Life.* New York: Delacorte, 1990.

Seligman, Martin. *What You Can Change and What You Can't: The Complete Guide to Successful Self-Improvement.* New York: Ballantine, 1995.

———. *Authentic Happiness: Using the New Positive Psychology to Realize Your Potential for Lasting Fulfillment.* New York: The Free Press, 2002.

HELP IN DEALING WITH SELF-INVOLVED OR NARCISSISTIC PARENTS

Brown, Nina W. *Children of the Self-Absorbed: A Grownup's Guide to Getting Over Narcissistic Parents.* Oakland, Calif.: New Harbinger Publications, 2001.

Hotchkiss, Sandy, and James Masterson. *Why Is It Always about You?: Saving Yourself from the Narcissists in Your Life.* New York: The Free Press, 2002.

Lowen, Alexander. *Narcissism: Denial of the True Self.* New York: Touchstone Books, 1997.

Neuharth, Dan. *If You Had Controlling Parents: How to Make Peace with Your Past and Take Your Place in the World.* New York: Cliff Street Books/HarperCollins, 1999.

CHILD-REARING GUIDES AS INSPIRATION FOR DEALING WITH PARENTS

Bluestein, Jane. *Parents, Teens, and Boundaries: How to Draw the Line.* Deerfield Beach, Fla.: Health Communications, 1993.

Bradley, Michael J., and Carroll O'Connor. *Yes, Your Teen Is Crazy: Loving Your Kid without Losing Your Mind.* Gig Harbor, Wash.: Harbor Press, 2003.

Nelson, Jane. *Positive Discipline.* New York: Ballantine, 1996.

RELAXATION AND MEDITATION TECHNIQUES

Bayda, Ezra, et al. *Being Zen: Bringing Meditation to Life.* Boston: Shambhala, 2002.

Buksbazen, John Daishin. *Zen Meditation in Plain English.* Somerville, Mass.: Wisdom Books, 2002.

Khalsa, Dharma Singh. *Meditation as Medicine: Activate the Power of Your Natural Healing Force.* New York: Atria, 2002.

Nhat Hanh, Thich. *Miracle of Mindfulness: A Manual of Meditation.* Boston, Mass.: Beacon Press, 1996.

ACKNOWLEDGMENTS

This book would never have come into being without the invaluable contributions of Nancy Hass, editor, writer, and friend. Her brilliance, insight, sense of humor, and creativity are unmatched. Bob Roe's extraordinary editing talents helped to keep the prose flowing. My literary agent, Chris Calhoun, a wonderful, available guide, always made time to explore ideas with me. Deb Brody, my responsive editor at Holt, saw the promise in this book from the beginning, and the entire Holt family has given me their support throughout.

I'd like to acknowledge, as well, the many people I have met through my practice, seminars, and teaching, who have shared with me their stories that have sensitized me to the nuances of what really goes on between parents and their adult children.

I am a parent as well as a child, and I continue to learn from our sons, Jono and Josh Rosen, and our new daughters, Tracy and Yael Rosen. I cherish their presence and involvement in my life and look forward to all of us continuing to grow into our respective adulthoods together.

My dear sister and constant inspiration, Daryl Roth, and her husband, Steven, honor me with their devotion to our mother and to their children, Amanda and Michael Salzhauer and Jordan Roth, every day.

My friends have also shared their lives and their years of experience with me. I marvel at the ways all of our parent-child connections have transformed and continue to transform over the years. Special appreciation and love to Laurie and Roy Witkin, Janet Weathers, Nancy Miller, Ruth Herzel, Rona and Lee Javitch, Eileen Blank, Suzy Rose, Hope Cantor, Lois Mound, Gary Stolzoff and Suzi Alexander, Maggie Kneip, Linda and Harvey Meranus, Barbara Lane, Annie Gilbar, Norma Feshbach, and Kate Perri, who came into my life at just the right time. Brooke Stewart, Bob Danuszar, and Barbara Ramalho help to keep me in balance.

My husband, Rob Rosen, is the love of my life. His steadiness, humor, kindness, and dedication to our family make it easier for me to be a parent—and child. He continues to support me as I define and refine myself as an adult daughter and as a mother to our adult children.

INDEX

ABOUT THE AUTHOR

DALE ATKINS is a licensed psychologist and media commentator who appears frequently on the *Today Show*. The author of five books, she has contributed to such national magazines as *Ladies' Home Journal, Cosmopolitan,* and *Parents.* She lives in Connecticut and practices in New York City.